DAD

UNTOLD STORIES OF FATHERHOOD, LOVE, MENTAL HEALTH AND MASCULINITY

FROM MUSIC.FOOTBALL.FATHERHOOD.

Curated by Elliott Rae

First published in 2021 by MusicFootballFatherhood

ISBN (Hardback): 978-1-5272-9024-2

ISBN (eBook): 978-1-5272-9025-9

Typeset using Atomik ePublisher from Easypress Technologies

www.musicfootballfatherhood.com

MUSIC. FOOTBALL. FATHERHOOD.

#WeAreDad

By MusicFootballFatherhood

DAD is a collection of stories by MusicFootballFatherhood (MFF). MFF is the UK's most exciting parenting and lifestyle platform for men. Called the 'Dad's version of Mumsnet' by the BBC, MFF is a space for dads who want more open conversations around fatherhood. Founded by Elliott Rae, MFF aims to increase positive representation of diverse fatherhood while providing a space and community for dads to share the ups and downs of parenting.

Our blog has content and resources for dads at every stage of their parenting journey. We have honest, frank and funny conversations on our #DaddyDebates podcast and host regular online and in-person events for our community.

As champions of equal parenting, we work with organisations and staff networks, through our #EngagingDads workshops and talks, to help them support working fathers and work towards gender equality.

www.musicfootballfatherhood.com

@MFFonline_

@MFFonline

In loving memory of Joseph Nkomo.
Our Intellectual. Our Warrior.
Our Trailblazer. Our Dad.
Forever in our hearts.

1950-2021

For all fathers:
no matter who you are,
or where you are –
this is for you.

Contents

Introduction:
Elliott Rae

I needed a space to reflect after becoming a father. It was a difficult time, as you'll read in my story. As a new dad coming to terms with my new role, I started writing. This is how MusicFootballFatherhood.com (MFF), the parenting and lifestyle platform for men, was born. Looking back, it was my own version of therapy, or self-help if you like. It was a place where I could make observations, where I could reflect on my new perspectives and feelings. I was overwhelmed with the positive response and was surprised to learn that many other dads also yearned for more open conversations around fatherhood, to share the ups and downs of parenting. And that is what MFF, and this book, are dedicated to doing.

I realised that the role of the father has changed massively over the last decade and more needs to be done to support the dads around us. We are at the forefront of a global movement to change the narrative around fatherhood and allow for a deeper, more honest conversation amongst families, colleagues and friends.

In putting together this book I had conversations I have never had before with people I have known on a personal level for many years – even friends I have known for over a decade. I was surprised when I realised that I had never gone to this depth with them before, humbled and a little regretful that I had never previously had these conversations. I feel proud that these moments of intimacy and vulnerability are here to be shared with you.

The dads in this book are ready to share their stories in the hope that other men might find echoes of themselves in their experiences. Their experiences of fatherhood are not exclusive to them, but their voices seek to join an emerging crowd of people who are willing to start a conversation in this space. I cried reading their stories. I laughed reading their stories. But most of all, I was relieved. Relieved that so many men were proud to be part of the movement to help us be more open about our fatherhood experiences. As men we are taught, from a young age, not to speak about the things we find tough and not to show certain emotions. Add to that the pressure to live up to expectations of what a 'real man' is - to be strong, both physically and mentally, be the breadwinner and have your sh** together at all times. But if we are not able to talk about the pressures that life and fatherhood can bring, it can very easily become too much to handle. It's time to break the cycle.

What I hope you will find in this book is a raw, brave and deeply moving compilation of stories from men who have bared their souls and committed their emotions to paper – challenging the preconceptions of fatherhood and what it means to be a man. This book touches on themes of loss, grief, trauma, identity, race, culture, relationships and acceptance. The aim is that the stories shared will further the conversations you have around fatherhood, masculinity, mental health and gender equality. We are proud to partner with some amazing organisations who are doing important work in these areas. You will find out more about them at the end of the book; please do explore for professional help and community support.

I am also proud that we have a diverse range of contributors who represent all aspects of race, class, age, and sexuality. This is true diversity, which can only be achieved through genuine relationships and inclusion. Each dad has written in their raw and authentic voice. This was extremely important. I wanted to make sure that the under-represented voices of ordinary people like you and I, whose stories often go unheard, are now listened to and part of the mainstream conversation. These are ordinary men, being extraordinary by sharing their story with the world. Our contributors have come together, from different walks of life, because they believe in the shared purpose, vision and movement. The men in this book represent modern Britain. And they represent you.

The coronavirus pandemic and lockdown has had a profound impact on the way we live and work. There has been some positive progress on the collective role of dads in the UK, with fathers taking on more caring responsibilities than ever before. In 2015, the ONS found that men were spending 39% of the time that women spent on childcare, compared to 64% during the first lockdown in 2020. However, women still do the large majority of childcare and have paid the price in the pandemic with mothers being more likely than fathers to be furloughed and at a higher risk of job losses. As a collective we need to do more to challenge gendered parenting roles. We need to make sure our workplaces are inclusive, both mothers and fathers are considered when policies are developed and that both parents have the option to live and work in a way that best suits their families. We need to move away from the concept that caring is for women and being the main breadwinner is for men – those outdated stereotypes are damaging for everyone: men, women and children. We need to make equal parenting the norm by challenging the messaging around fathers in the media and demanding better from our workplaces and Government. It is an important time for defining how the role of the dad will look for many years to come and we should all participate in a national conversation to move forward and see change. I am proud to bring together so many men who are challenging those stereotypes and I hope their stories will inspire and support your own conversations.

We now know that 12.5% of men in the UK are suffering from mental health conditions like depression and anxiety, and that suicide is the biggest killer of men under the age of forty-five. New fathers are particularly vulnerable as financial pressures and relationship breakdowns can be triggers of new or pre-existing mental health conditions. Of course, this will have devastating effects on families and – by extension – on society as a whole. I believe that we can make a difference by encouraging better dialogue between colleagues, friends, and especially within families; between husbands and wives, brothers and sisters, dads and children. And this is where this book comes in. I hope DAD will help you to share concerns, increase your understanding of the challenges we all face, build stronger relationships and recognise that you are not alone in whatever you are experiencing and feeling.

Our call to action is for more open conversations, like the ones you are about to read.

Each chapter will take you on a journey – I want you to feel immersed in that dad's world. Every dad has bared his soul and they are talking to you. Only you. This is a personal and extremely intimate conversation. So listen, and respond. Respond by having your own conversations with the dads you know, whether that be your brother, husband, uncle, son, friend or work colleague. And share your story with us through our #WeAreDad campaign.

Underlying each of these stories is a persistent and driving force of defiance, humility and strength to be the best fathers we can be for our families. So laugh with us, cry with us and remember that the dad who wrote one of the stories you are about to read may be sitting next to you on the train, or in front of you on the school run.

That dad may even be you.

Chapter 1:

The Birth of Generation Covid: How the Pandemic Affected Our Pregnancy and Labour

James Cooke

And just like that, I'm a father of two. Both boys. Mummy's most definitely outnumbered. However, both parents are overjoyed ... and tired. It's incredible just how quickly you can forget exactly what it's like having a newborn. You carry this cloudy recollection of how the world was viewed through a bleary-eyed mist during the first six months of your child's life, but it's not until you're back in the thick of it that you're truly reminded of what the day-to-day in the trenches is really like.

There are three years between the boys. Just about enough time to forget the baby stage. It's also just about enough time for the world to be turned completely on its head. We've all been forced to live in a brave new world – toddlers, babies and all – as we raise what history will likely dub the 'Covid Generation'.

Two kids. That's the limit we've set ourselves. I grew up the eldest of four children with two younger brothers and a long gap before my sister arrived. Nothing can be more mortifying for a thirteen-year-old boy than discovering that his parents are having another baby! As for my wife, Stacey, she would gain a pair of stepsiblings just before her teenage years, in addition to the brother and sister she already had. Like me, she was also the eldest.

'Growing up with so many siblings must have been a lot of fun,' people often say. There was certainly no shortage of banter and there was never a quiet moment, which ultimately breeds strong personalities.

From what friends and family tell me, I grew into a bit of a 'character' – likely gained through a combination of competing with my brothers and watching way too much pro wrestling. I also learned, particularly during my teenage years, to enjoy a little quiet time to myself, hiding away to read a book, play video games, or attempt some writing. These two halves of my personality gave me the confidence and skill to successfully start a career as a writer in my mid-twenties – just over a year after getting married and more than a year before we had our first son.

As the older siblings in our respective households, Stacey and I recognised how chaotic raising a bigger family can be. We agreed early on that, if we could, we would have two kids. That way, they would always have each other to play and grow with, while things didn't become too much for Mum and Dad. Two kids seem like a good balance. When they're both kicking up a fuss, as parents, we can divide and conquer.

When our first son (we call him Beans, because he's full of them!) was born, the year was 2017 and the scariest things in the news were the early Brexit negotiations and, across the Atlantic, the first days of Donald Trump's presidency. It was simpler times back then, or so it always seems in hindsight.

The birth of Beans wasn't without its complications. From speaking to other parents since, it seems births rarely ever are. Stacey's waters broke, which I learned isn't the normal start of labour, despite what countless movies and sitcoms have taught us for dramatic effect. I remember it clearly because it happened two and half weeks ahead of schedule and it was two o'clock on a Monday morning. When informed, my half-asleep response was to say, 'Well, I guess I'm not going to work in the morning,' before rolling over and closing my eyes again. Of course, I was promptly woken up properly as calls were made to triage to find out what the next steps were. Still, it was nice to hear about my son's impending arrival while not fully awake as it went some way to removing the panic that can often arise in such a situation.

We'd been asked to visit the hospital at 6 a.m. to see how far along the labour process was. When the waters break, the baby needs to come sooner rather than later, as the risk of infection increases. Mild contractions had been felt following the earlier wake-up call, but nothing too substantial.

We were sent home and told to return to the hospital should contractions become frequent. If not, we were booked in to start the induction process the following day at 10 a.m.

What followed was twenty-eight hours of waiting – and infrequent contractions for Stacey. I remember walking round to the shop at one point to buy a new battery for the smoke detector in our house. It was a strange day.

The following morning, we got up, got dressed, grabbed our already packed bags, and headed back to the hospital for an appointment that would change our lives forever.

I can't say I have any recollection of walking into the hospital. It must have been without incident – a moment of total normality with nothing of note worth etching a memory of. It's funny how we took walking into a hospital – or a shop, cinema, or restaurant – for granted. No masks needed. No social distancing measures. No fear of an invisible menace.

What I do remember is sitting in our room on the antenatal ward. There had been no question that I should be there. As far as I saw, every other birthing partner was allowed in too. Of course, we were allowed to be there. It was encouraged!

The TV in our room actually worked – the only time I've ever experienced that at the hospital – but it was stuck on BBC One. Believe me when I say I searched hard for a remote control. 'Someone probably stole it,' is what I was told when I asked a midwife.

And, in case you're wondering, you couldn't change the channel on the TV. It got its feed through a set-top box without any buttons of its own.

At least my wife was happy enough to be watching *Homes Under the Hammer*. She quite enjoys the BBC's weekday line-up, so the sight of Dion Dublin exploring derelict houses with would-be property investors that had scored a bargain at auction provided a welcome distraction.

As for me, I started games of *Words with Friends* against several friends and family members. It got to the point whereby each time I'd played all of my turns, someone else had taken another go, keeping me adequately occupied too.

Before we knew it, several hours had passed and we still hadn't been seen by anybody. My wife was offered lunch and didn't much like the look of it, so I fuelled myself up before seeing if the hospital staff had any idea of when the induction process might begin. Turned out we'd been forgotten in our room at the end of the corridor and we were seen within ten minutes.

The induction process was explained to us as starting with the introduction of a gel, followed two hours later by hormones, which could take up to a further six hours to do their job. The gel was introduced and it all felt rather routine.

Then, the routine went by the wayside. A few minutes later, my wife said she was starting to feel very warm. When I looked up from my game of *Words with Friends* – a real nail-biter against a mate who's an English teacher – the face staring back at me was the colour of a beetroot. One of the midwives rushed back in, immediately pressed the red panic button and all hell broke loose. The room filled with midwives and doctors who quickly detached all the cables from Stacey's bed and started wheeling her out. With no idea of what was going on, but figuring we were moving somewhere else, I started gathering our stuff.

'Leave it,' said one of the midwives. 'You need to follow her now. Someone will bring your bags.'

I followed the entourage through to the delivery ward and, because our nearest hospital is fairly modern, into our own, private delivery suite. I couldn't get anywhere near Stacey through the sea of medical staff. They moved her into a new bed and I heard talk of an emergency caesarean section. While nobody was talking to me directly, I also gathered that the baby's heart rate had plummeted due to some sort of bad reaction to the induction gel.

It was a strange moment. Like being in a dream. I was just kind of floating there, watching as my world started to crumble while unable to do anything about it. It felt as if I was invisible, a ghost, as nobody spoke to or acknowledged me. Of course, I appreciate – and did then – that everyone's full attention was on making sure Mummy and Baby were OK. It just felt strange that, as the father, you could be left on the outside.

And then, as suddenly as everything had kicked off, it stopped. In an instant, the concentration on the doctors' faces seemed to melt into looks of apathy as they began discussing their weekend plans. When I asked what was going on, I was told that Baby's heart rate had picked right back up and that, although we were to stay on the delivery ward, he would be monitored carefully for further dramatic changes. So much for spending eight hours waiting in antenatal at the mercy of *Bargain Hunt*.

'He's a clever one,' said one of the midwives. 'That baby of yours has gone and found a way to jump the queue.'

Stacey had gone from 1 cm dilated to 4 cm in the space of a few minutes and was hyperstimulated. She was experiencing four to five contractions every ten minutes and they weren't gentle either. With less than a minute between each one, she was largely unresponsive. Gas and air didn't seem to do anything, pethidine should have helped within half an hour but, after an hour, clearly wasn't helping either. With contractions taking place more frequently than not, Stacey finally opted for an epidural as soon as they were able to get one into her. This was something we'd wanted to avoid, but there's a saying about best-laid plans. It seems every birthing plan should include a point at which you tear it up.

After the epidural was administered, the midwife pointed out that the restaurant was due to close at 7 p.m. and that it was half past six. I left to get my dinner, met my parents briefly at the hospital entrance, as they stopped by to deliver the phone charger I'd left at home, and returned to find Stacey no longer curled up in the foetal position. Instead, she was sitting upright and chatting away with the midwife. It was as if she'd been brought back to life.

Beans was born at 3:34 a.m. after an episiotomy – a surgical incision to create more space for Baby's delivery. There had been talk of forceps, which was something else I'd wanted to avoid as I have a scar from my own forceps delivery, but thankfully that wasn't needed. In the hours leading up to the big arrival, I'd napped in a chair at the recommendation of one of the midwives. After all, I'd need my energy to cheerlead Stacey through the main event.

In my defence, I had been awake just as long as my wife at this point, and it was the middle of the night. Also, I did not have the adrenaline of childbirth to keep me awake, and so I slept a little longer than perhaps I should have done. Hey – it's not my fault if nobody decided to wake me up! Still, all that's remembered is that I was in the land of nod rather close to the birth of my son – a fact that's brought up regularly. I'll never live it down. At least I was conscious at the end; that's the main thing, right?

When I first laid eyes on Beans, I could feel the shape my face was making. It was contorted into a look that somehow combined pure joy and terror. Stacey recalls seeing our baby close up for the first time, filled with love, and then looking at me pulling a funny face. It was caused by the sudden realisation that this baby, this abstract idea that had been with us for nine months, was a real, living, breathing human. A tiny human that was going to change our lives in the biggest way imaginable.

***

Fast forward three years and we were living in what at times felt like a dystopian future. We'd spent several months living in lockdown as the Covid-19 pandemic wreaked havoc across the country and the world. Beans was now a cheeky toddler, and his little brother was due to be born at the end of the summer.

As soon as we caught minor rumblings of the coronavirus outbreak in the news during the early months of 2020, we started to get an idea that the pregnancy and birthing process may be a little different this time around.

We had the twelve-week scan that February, back when Covid-19 still felt like some exotic illness you might catch if you travelled to Asia. I'd had to travel to Amsterdam to attend an international event for work the week before the scan, and naïvely thought that to be the most likely way I would come into contact with the virus. Little did I know that a month later we'd all be confined to our homes in the UK.

That first scan went well. It's a funny thing, seeing that tiny, grey creature on the screen for the first time. You gain that reality check – that this little person will change your life all over again. Yet, it's still too early to know much else. Is it a boy or a girl?

Who are you going to be? Is the question that crossed my mind both times we've attended a twelve-week scan. The possibilities are endless.

We certainly lost out on a lot of life possibilities just a few short weeks later. Stacey was sent to work from home two or three weeks before the government initiated the nationwide lockdown – her employer deciding not to take any chances with anyone they considered vulnerable, including those who were pregnant. She wouldn't return to the office at all before maternity leave kicked in almost half a year later.

The following week, I was given the option of working from home too, which I took. What was the point of Stacey staying at home if I was still catching a train to work and bringing home any germs I came into contact with? It just so happened that I'd given in my notice shortly before opting to work from home, figuring that everything would have blown over in the few weeks before my final day with the company – once again, completely unaware of how severe the situation would become. I never did return to that office.

The twenty-week scan was booked in for what would have been the final week of the initial three-week lockdown (how naïve we all were, perhaps). Partners were no longer allowed to attend scans as hospitals did everything in their power to reduce the number of people coming through their doors. Of course, I understood the reasoning for it and although I was a little despondent at not being able to see the baby again, and to be there when finding out the gender, I reminded myself that at least I'd been able to have that experience once before. For those, including my brother and his partner, expecting for the first time, it was likely a much harder pill to swallow.

Upon her arrival at the hospital, Stacey had to have her temperature checked and was quizzed on whether she had any coronavirus symptoms.

There was apparently a little trouble in determining the gender, as the little one had their legs crossed. When they were able to get the right angle, they could finally determine that he was a boy. Stacey brought that information home, playing a guessing game with Beans and me before revealing that she would be further outnumbered by boys.

In addition to revealing the presence of a penis, the scan also flagged up a potential issue. One of his kidneys was holding more water than it should have been and was noticeably larger than the other. Stacey was told that this type of issue is rather common in boys and can correct itself in a lot of cases, although an additional scan was booked in at thirty-two weeks to take another look.

That was twelve weeks away. Surely all this Covid nonsense would have blown over by then…

You already know that it hadn't. We really were clueless as to how long this pandemic would last.

The week before the thirty-two-week scan, at the end of June, Stacey finally attended her first face-to-face appointment with a midwife as all the earlier ones were done over the phone to minimise midwives' contact with other people. Once again, this wasn't something I was allowed to attend, so Stacey was alone in hearing the little fella's heartbeat for the first time.

As for the thirty-two-week scan itself, I would spend that in a car park – foreshadowing what was to come a couple of months later. It was the first week of July and, while Stacey entered the hospital, I took Beans to a nearby garden centre and wound up spending most of the time playing on a grass bank at the edge of the car park. The reason I'd brought Beans out was because Stacey was understandably nervous about this scan, as was I. If I wasn't allowed to be in there, I at least wanted to be nearby, should the findings not be what we were hoping for.

There were a couple of positives to be gleaned from the additional scan, as it provided a chance to see that he was growing properly and generally healthy. The pictures at this later stage of the pregnancy also gave us a clear view of the little man's face, so we could see what he looked like. And boy, did he look like his big brother! The resemblance was ridiculously uncanny.

However, the kidney was, unfortunately, still an issue. I knew this as soon as I heard Stacey's voice on the other end of the phone when she called to say she was out of the hospital. The kidney was still holding more fluid than it should have been and an appointment was being scheduled with a specialist consultant the following week. According to the midwife that called later that afternoon, it may just have been a developmental issue in which the kidney's exit tube wasn't able to drain properly. In many cases, the kidney will fix itself after birth. Of course, it might not. Either way, we were reminded that we humans only need one kidney to live, looking at the worst-case scenario.

While I shrugged off missing out on the twenty-week scan, not being present for this one stung a little. Especially given how upsetting it was for Stacey to hear the news that there was a problem with nobody by her side, no shoulder to lean on.

At the very least, we were informed that the level of fluid surrounding the kidney was about what they'd have expected to see. What that meant is that the kidney did appear to be working somewhat. A worse sign would have been if there was less fluid surrounding it than is normal.

The following Monday, at around lunchtime, we got the call to go and see the specialist consultant. The problem was that the relevant consultant based at our local hospital was on holiday that week, so we needed to travel across the county … and be there by half-past two. Fortunately, my mother-in-law was on hand to look after Beans for the afternoon. Stacey was told, categorically when she asked, that I would be allowed in for this appointment, given its nature. After all, there could be major implications.

We wolfed down our lunch and set off. I sat shotgun for the journey and, distracted by my own wonderful conversation, was too late in letting Stacey know when to turn off the motorway. We wound up taking a detour along a lovely, if not long and winding, country road. It was certainly more scenic than arriving via the industrial estate. We had a laugh about it before I was told not to try anything funny like that when the baby was coming.

Entering a hospital for the first time during Covid was an eerie experience. Not that entering a hospital is ever a fun time. Masks were on, hands were sanitised, and we steered as far clear of anyone in sight as we could. Stacey had been through it already at the other hospital, although we noted that here, at the other end of the county, our temperatures weren't checked like Stacey's had been at our local infirmary.

After making our presence known at reception, we were stowed away in a room by ourselves to wait. This was the first time either of us had worn masks for an extended period. I hadn't realised how damn uncomfortable they could be until then – it felt like my ears were going to tear right off, while Stacey found it difficult to breathe. We soon bought new, much more comfortable face coverings. Who knew how many hours I'd have to spend wearing one during the birthing process?

An hour after our appointment time, I ventured outside the room to see if there was any idea of when we might be seen.

'Oh, we can see you now,' I was told.

It could be a coincidence, but I have a feeling we may have been forgotten about. *Out of sight, out of mind,* as the saying goes. It had happened when Stacey was induced three years previously, after all.

I sat and watched as Stacey, and subsequently, the baby, had an in-depth ultrasound. It was like Ultrasound *Inception.* There was slightly less fluid on the baby's left kidney than there had been a week prior – a good sign, as it meant that it was draining something – however, there was still way too much.

The consultant came in after the scan and informed us that there wasn't much to be done at that point as it was simply a case of 'wait and see'. He noted that kidney issues like this often correct themselves after the baby's born and that they're rather common in boys.

We were told there and then that the little chap would be given antibiotics from birth as a precautionary measure.

While a pin was placed in the kidney issue for the time being, another problem had, unfortunately, revealed itself. As this was a much more thorough scan, more in-depth than the routine twelve- and twenty-week ones, they had found that the amount of fluid on the left side of the baby's brain was higher than they'd like.

What was interesting about this situation was that the fluid levels on the brain were still within the acceptable threshold and we would have been none the wiser had it not been for the detailed examination undertaken because of a completely unrelated matter – the kidney. The cause for concern came from fluid levels on the left side of the brain being much higher than on the right. The consultant told us he wasn't too worried, but that the protocol was to book an MRI.

So, just over a week later, we found ourselves on a commuter train to London, making our way to St Thomas' Hospital.

It was certainly an experience, travelling into the capital during the height of the pandemic. We had to catch a train during what should have been peak rush hour, at about half past eight in the morning. The cost of the tickets certainly reflected that at £65 for two returns to Waterloo East. Daylight robbery, I think they call it! But the actual journey did not reflect the time of day. In fact, when you'd expect a carriage full to capacity with plenty of people having to stand, we found ourselves occupying a carriage with just one other passenger.

It wasn't much different in the city. We walked along the South Bank towards the hospital and it was like the 'Ghost Town' that The Specials sang about. I've wandered along that stretch in the past, at all times of day and night, and I've never seen it empty like that. There were some workmen on a construction project, and one or two joggers passed by, but there wasn't much more in the way of humanity. It was as if we'd arrived in the post-apocalyptic version of London that featured in *28 Days Later*.

Inside St Thomas', we found our way to the MRI area and sat down in the waiting room. We were across the room from each other as most of the chairs were out of use due to social distancing. People came and went, including one gentleman who had missed his appointment from the day before and didn't know what he was meant to do with a test kit they'd sent him in the post. Turns out he was meant to take the test at home the day before the appointment, as per the letter attached. I couldn't help but wonder why he'd decided to travel all the way into the hospital, during the coronavirus crisis, just to ask, and whether he needed some sort of help he wasn't getting.

Half an hour past the appointment time, I went up and asked when Stacey was likely to be seen, as none of the other patients had been there for an MRI. Plus, there was a sign hanging up that stated all patients would be seen within thirty minutes of their appointment time, or would be informed otherwise. However, just as I asked, Stacey was summoned away. Sod's law in action. I wished her luck from beneath a more comfortable mask, and sat back down to read a book.

I read for almost two hours, wondering how long it might take before Stacey returned. It transpired that there'd been a problem with the heating in the MRI room. Stacey described it as having felt more like a sauna. Add to that the fact that Stacey had to lie on her back for an extended period, which was a struggle due to the baby's positioning, and she'd almost passed out. Thankfully, she was fine.

On the train home, a pair of women boarded and one of them removed her mask to speak on the phone. I shook my head and tutted a few times. That really showed her, I'm sure.

Six days later, we made the trip across the county to sit in the same small room once again. We got to know Consulting Room 5B very well over our two visits to this particular hospital, spending several hours within its confines on both occasions. Still, no matter how long the wait, I was extra grateful to even be in there this time as there had been confusion over whether I was allowed to enter the hospital at all.

When we arrived, we put on our masks, sanitised our hands and entered the building as we'd done a few weeks earlier. However, as we made our way down the corridor to the maternity ward, we came to a halt as a young mother-to-be and her own mother were stood halfway down. In front of them was a burly gentleman in black trousers and a white shirt with the sleeves rolled up, exposing a tapestry of faded tattoos. The burly gent, who we'll call Steve in lieu of a real name, had a makeshift desk set up, right there in the narrow hallway, and was explaining to the two women that he was under strict instructions not to let anyone in besides the mothers attending appointments. No partners were allowed as the hospital was doing everything in its power to keep the virus out, including the hiring of a third-party security firm.

'I need my mum... I suffer from anxiety... I can't go in there alone... I'll have a panic attack... I was told she could come with me,' the expectant mother was telling Steve with a frantic cadence that implied she was telling the truth about the potential panic attack.

To his credit, Steve immediately told the mum-to-be that he would find out if they could make an exception and, as he started walking towards the reception area, he set expectations by explaining that it wasn't his decision to make, reiterating that his instruction was that nobody besides the person whose appointment it was – the mother – was to be let in.

While he was gone, I turned to Stacey and told her I didn't like my chances. I felt like a seventeen-year-old trying to get into Wetherspoons on a Thursday night.

Burly Steve returned a minute later and allowed both mother-to-be and mother-of-mother-to-be to pass. It was then our turn to step up to the plate, two metres away from Steve's fold-open desk.

Stacey gave her name and appointment time. Checking his clipboard, Steve confirmed that she was on his list. He then turned to me and said that he was afraid he couldn't let me in.

'Are you sure?' I asked. 'We were told explicitly that I would be allowed in due to the news we might receive during this consultation.'

Steve really was a very reasonable chap, especially considering he had a pretty thankless job to do. I told him I'd understand completely if he ultimately couldn't let me through and that I wouldn't kick up a fuss, but would he be able to double-check given the nature of our visit? He agreed to walk us to the reception desk so that we could find out together.

The receptionist didn't hesitate at all in saying that of course I was allowed in to the appointment. She didn't even check to see what the appointment entailed, which undermined Steve's job entirely.

'I hope you understand I was just doing what I had been told,' he said to us as we parted.

I told him that of course we did and thanked him for helping us. I asked if he'd had many people getting angry with him, to which he replied that he'd been on the receiving end of abuse several times a day. His role at the hospital may have been to help prevent the spread of the virus, but it was still a thankless task.

After several hours of sitting in 5B once again, we had another in-depth scan that revealed that the levels of fluid in both Baby's kidney and brain had remained the same. Both positive signs. When the consultant came in to see us, he reiterated that, hopefully, the little one's kidney would correct itself over time, but that he would need a scan at six weeks old to see how it was developing.

When it came to discussing the MRI results from our trip to London, the consultant began by saying, 'As you know…' before we pointed out we'd heard nothing of the MRI results yet. The NHS had been a little busy, it seemed, which was understandable.

The MRI had shown that baby's brain was working nicely and that all of the proper infrastructures were in place. The consultant added that if we were having a girl, he'd have been worried, but both the fluid in the kidney and on the brain are rather common with troublesome boys.

The appointment ended with instructions put in place to ensure that Baby would have a scan booked in to check his brain once more when he was born, as well as a scan on his kidney at six weeks old, and that he would be prescribed antibiotics from birth as a precautionary measure so that the kidney wouldn't become infected.

By the time we left the hospital, Steve had packed up and gone. It was as if he'd never been there, as the hallway stood empty.

A heatwave followed, making life unbearable even for those of us not walking around almost nine months into a pregnancy. There were no more appointments as there was nothing else to be done until the little fella arrived.

It all kicked off on a Tuesday morning in early September. The temperature outside had settled back down into the early twenties and Stacey had started getting twinges as I went off to what would be my last day in the office for a couple of weeks. Contractions began on Tuesday night and continued into Wednesday, becoming more and more frequent. Then, they became less frequent and rather irregular.

Stacey had a routine midwife appointment booked on that Wednesday afternoon, so we went along to that as contractions were still irregular and infrequent. While she went into the GP surgery, I waited in the car with Beans, as we had his bags packed so that we could drop him off at my parents' house, where he would stay for the next few days. If it was to be a slow labour, at least we could make sure we were prepared.

'We need to go to the hospital; they think my waters might have broken,' said Stacey as she climbed back into the car. What followed was a flying visit to Nanny and Granddad's to say goodbye to Beans, and a quick drive home to grab everything we needed for the hospital. I double-checked that we had a phone charger packed this time around, as the rules were clear in that once I was in the hospital, I wouldn't be allowed back should I leave for any reason, and my parents wouldn't be able to stop by to bring anything we'd forgotten like they had three years earlier.

Next stop: the hospital.

I knew already that I wouldn't be allowed to join Stacey inside the hospital to begin with. I'd only be allowed inside once triage had decided she was in active labour and admitted her to antenatal. I did, however, walk her to the front door before making my way back to the car.

I'd just reclined the driver's seat when a knock at the window caused me to jump back up into a sitting position. I looked out and saw a security officer peering back in at me. I wondered whether he was going to tell me that I couldn't loiter in the car park.

'Excuse me,' he said as I rolled the window down, 'but was that your wife heading in to have a baby?'

A little startled, I replied that it was.

'Go after her,' he told me.

'But I thought I had to wait outside until told otherwise.'

'Forget that,' he said. 'I don't want to see someone possibly miss the birth of their child. Get after her. Run!'

So, I ran.

Stacey was waiting where I'd left her. It seemed the same security officer had spoken with her too. We underwent temperature checks at the entrance, although the staff were hesitant to let me through. When we made it up into triage though, it was confirmed that I really wasn't allowed to be in there. The midwife on duty was apologetic, but of course I understood the situation. These were unprecedented times, after all.

'It was worth a try,' said the security officer as I passed him on the way back to the car. He wished me luck.

I reclined in the driver's seat once more ... and remained there for six hours.

It wasn't all bad. I listened to a podcast, ordered a takeaway, which was

13

delivered to the hospital car park, had a visit from my mother-in-law on her way home from work, and received messages from a range of friends and family, including MFF's Matt Brown.

One message, from my mother-in-law's husband, told me to march right into that hospital and tell them that I was staying with my wife. A noble thought, perhaps, but I figured it wasn't worth the risk of being banned from the building entirely.

Truth be told, I was relatively comfortable there in the car. It was Stacey I felt bad for. While I was eating Uber-delivered chips and sipping cream soda, she was sat in triage, in labour, while they struggled to decide whether her waters had broken, whether they should induce, how they might induce given the issues with Beans' birth, and whether she was far enough along to be admitted to antenatal.

Not only was all of this extremely frustrating, but the six hours it took for them to decide were between 4 and 10 p.m. This meant that because she wasn't yet classified as an inpatient, she wasn't offered any food at dinner time. And it was too late by the time she was finally moved through. The only reason she had even a tiny cup of water was because she had to ask twice. I would have thought that energy and hydration were pretty essential to the labour process.

Throughout the entire pregnancy and birth, I'd been completely understanding and appreciative of every restriction that left me, as 'the partner', on the outside. Even sitting outside while my wife was in triage, although not nice for either of us, I got it. They were doing everything they could to restrict the number of people coming into the hospital, as well as the time spent inside. That, in turn, would potentially limit the spread of the virus.

Fine.

But if a mother is in the throes of labour and their partner can't be by their side, you would expect, at the very least, for her to be well looked after. For her to be made comfortable, checked on regularly, to be fed and watered. While I was upset at having missed scans, this was the only time I felt angry.

As it turned out, there was no need to worry about inducing. Triage took so long to decide that when they checked on Stacey's progress at 10 p.m., it was far too late for that.

When I got the call, I first ripped my jeans, as the belt loop had become caught over the handbrake, and then gathered everything that needed to be brought in. That included bags, snacks, maternity pillows, and a camp bed for me. I decided to lug everything in one go rather than make multiple trips back and forth from the car at that point. I just wanted to be in there.

Admittedly, it might have been a bit much. By the time I arrived on the antenatal ward, I looked as if I might have just given birth myself – sweaty wreck that I was. And no matter how heavy my breathing, the mask that I was to wear for the majority of our stay didn't cause me to suffocate as some anti-maskers might have you believe.

I had my temperature checked again, this time on the ward. I was issued a wristband, which I was to wear for the duration of my stay, to let everybody know that I had been checked.

Interestingly, Stacey had undergone an actual Covid test before being moved to the antenatal ward. However, when she asked if it had come back negative, she was told they wouldn't have the results yet, but that they needed to move her along anyway. It was never mentioned again, and I wasn't tested at all.

When I finally met Stacey in her room on the antenatal ward, I offered snacks right away.

However, the time for eating had passed. She was only in the mood for liquids. I set up the camp bed but had to take it down not long after as Stacey kept on dilating. By 11 p.m. we were in the delivery suite, where I once again set up the camp bed and received a lot of comments from midwives and staff, who thought I was some sort of genius. I managed to get some sleep, with Stacey's blessing.

They woke me up at gone six. I'd been up a few times throughout the night, but this time the baby was really coming. At half past six, Stacey was fully dilated. She was given an hour to rest and let some of her epidural wear off before pushing with all her might.

Half past seven: push time! I predicted 8:14 as a time of birth. I was wrong. But not by much. And I did get to call the time of birth as the midwife couldn't see the clock. That was pretty cool.

The little guy arrived at 8:20 a.m., weighing 8lbs, 12 ounces. We call him Mr Million (as in: one-in-a). When he was placed across Stacey's body for skin-to-skin, I leant in to come face-to-face with the little dude for the first time.

I'd removed my mask on a few occasions – either when we were alone in the room or when the member of hospital staff entering had told me not to worry. I defaulted to wearing the mask though, even when sleeping on the camp bed. As Mr Million laid eyes on his daddy for the first time, all he could see was a pair of eyes looking back. Below them was a black mask, covering my nose and mouth. It was a mask with a valve (which we've since been told are not as effective as masks without ventilation, as the virus essentially has somewhere to escape through) that did somewhat resemble Darth Vader.

'I am your father,' I told him.

We were moved to the postnatal ward and would reside there for a couple of days. We'd wanted to go home that day, but because some checks were needed on Mr Million's brain, we had to stay overnight and weren't released until 4 p.m. the following day.

It was on that next day that Mr Million was taken away from us for an hour or so, for the brain scan. We weren't allowed to go with him due to Covid restrictions. Stacey cried. Ultimately, reports came back that he was super chilled and didn't cause a fuss. And what's more: his brain was deemed completely fine. A huge relief!

One 'first' that we were missing out on was the opportunity to introduce Beans to his baby brother in the hospital. There were no hospital visits at all, which in some ways was a pleasant side effect, as although it's always great to have excited friends and family stop by, it did become a little overwhelming when Beans was born, when all we wanted to do was rest and let everything sink in. It was just a shame Beans couldn't be a part of the story.

Instead, we arranged for my mother-in-law to bring Beans over to the hospital as we left. They met us in the car park that I'd got to know so well. Beans was excited to see us and to discover that with us we had … a suitcase. He dragged it back to the car for us. When asked, he said he thought the baby was all right too.

The story doesn't end there. Life continues on. In the weeks to follow, we had to stagger our visitors to abide by the ever-changing rules and guidelines. Grandparents wore masks as they met Mr Million. The rule of six coming in soon after meant that only couples could visit and ruled out our now-family-of-four from meeting up with any of our friends with kids or in larger groups. It's taken a couple of months for some of our closest friends to meet the little chap, and grandparents have only seen him sparingly. With a new national lockdown coming into effect as I write this, who knows when Mr Million will next get to see any of his relatives? What about Christmas? Will things get better in the new year? Maybe you'll have answers by the time you're reading this. I certainly hope so – for the sake of the kids as much as anyone.

While I played my part as father as best I could during the pandemic and despite the restrictions, I would be remiss if I didn't acknowledge all of the NHS and frontline staff we encountered on this journey. Although I had to miss out on certain aspects and there was confusion when it came to my attendance at the specialist scans and consultations, and despite the fact that I spent six hours sitting in the car while Stacey went without a meal, I am extremely grateful to everyone in the NHS, who were clearly working harder than ever – which is no small feat considering how hard they already worked. I truly am thankful for an incredible service that remains open for us all, no matter our background or bank balance.

Not only did the tireless work ethic of the midwives and doctors impress me greatly, but I was once again astounded by Stacey's attitude and perseverance during the birth and everything leading up to it. Not once did she complain about having to attend an important scan alone, or that Mr Million had to go unaccompanied to his brain scan the day after his birth, even though these things were upsetting at the time. And as for the 'miracle of childbirth', well, I'm not sure my words can do it justice. It certainly lasts a lot longer than the explosion of pain us gents feel from a kick to the balls. What women go through during labour is truly amazing to behold and all I can say is thank you, to my wonderful wife, for bringing our boys into the world.

Mr Million's left kidney currently remains an issue too. Only Stacey was able to attend a recent ultrasound, which found it was still on the large side. However, the follow-up appointment with the consultant took place virtually, online, which meant we could both attend and there was no travelling to a hospital required nor time spent in a waiting room. It was very punctual in fact, even if it did take place three weeks after the ultrasound.

As it stands, Mr Million is set to undergo a round of tests to determine, once and for all, what the problem is. If the tests rule out reflux and blocked tubes, then it simply means he has a 'lazy system', which should well correct itself. If that is the case, he'll be able to stop the antibiotics he's been taking every day of his short life so far. We're holding out hope, as it seems to have shrunk since the prenatal scans. Just like the pandemic, only time will tell.

Chapter 2:

The Things My Father Never Taught Me: Growing up Without a Dad

R.P. Falconer

'Son.'

I turned from the little perch I had made of my window ledge. From 8 a.m. I had diligently kept sentry duty over the car park below, my rucksack strapped to my back, the rest of my bags and belongings by the front door waiting for egress. At 1 p.m. my mother had ascended the stairs and was standing in my bedroom doorway. She wore the look of a woman harbouring sorrow.

We shared a short pause, which in hindsight seemed to summarise everything without the need for words. She broke eye contact and appeared to be looking through me, she inhaled gently then spoke.

'He isn't coming, son… Take your stuff off and come down for lunch. It's OK.'

She turned and left and I watched the space she had just occupied in disbelief. *It's OK*, I repeated in my head. She had said it as if to play down his flagrant shortcomings and assure me disappointment was anything but disappointing. Once was arguably excusable, but to be twice stood up felt tragic to my tiny little heart.

I had promised my friends I was headed to Sandy for the summer. I had made out my dad's house, and its surroundings, were a utopia. A town filled with sand, circled by emerald green forest, teeming with friendly wildlife. I turned back to the window and looked out across the car park below, encircled and trapped by flats. Dirty off-white, asbestos-filled units, constructed from glorified Styrofoam. This was to be my setting for the six-week holiday. This was my life as a child.

My mother didn't even bother giving me his excuse; she was too busy organising last-minute childcare for the following weeks, using money she hadn't anticipated using and, like most working-class single mums, didn't have. In a sense I was arguably one of the lucky ones as my father occasionally wandered in from the dark, did a bit then fucked off for another year.

Only now as a dad do I fully understand how grossly inept he was in performing his duties. So much goes into being a coherent parent, I had to work out being a father without a blueprint or plan. A man raising both a boy and a girl, who never had a father figure at home to learn how.

I believe it is within the last sentence that you find the answer to why so many fatherless young boys have gone astray.

As a teen, I was somewhat a World War II fanatic and I always wondered what was going through the heads of those paratroopers ejected from planes over bullet-strewn enemy airspace. Projectiles, sprayed, sparkling incandescent against the black night sky, tearing through the flesh and bone of those in descent. Many young men died before landing in war-torn Europe. Some landed but in such a battered state they could do little more than wish for a hastened death as they hung cold and alone, entangled in tree branches and parachute fabric, bleeding out into the night.

Some landed behind enemy lines unscathed – luck maybe? Some landed, fought and died. Not so lucky. Some landed, fought and lived to tell the tale.

I always felt my father had dropped my mother and me behind enemy lines. It was only through my mother's work ethic, instilled by both her parents, plus help from family and friends and ultimately the grace of God that my mother, brother and me made it off London's notorious Church Road estate with little to no friction.

My father, light skinned, light eyed and according to the European lens the most handsome of black men, had left a young girl he had promised so much. All whilst he nonchalantly began and collapsed other lives and relationships, leaving nothing but trauma and children in his wake.

My story isn't unique and is far from a tale of yesteryear within the British-Jamaican household. I attribute a lot of my community's woes to families with 'father subtraction' and various other contributing historical factors that, contrary to popular belief, continue to mar my community. During slavery, black men and women were forced to numb their feelings towards siblings, spouses and children, a coping mechanism that allowed them to deal with the horrendous reality that at any time their children or any loved one could be taken, murdered, raped or sold on. All Caribbeans living today have roots that run into the nightmare that was slavery. That slave mentality lives on in many respects. Slavery financially set black people back, and the racism that stemmed from it made and continues to make it difficult for black people living in the West.

The children of the Windrush generation, when in education and employment, were often forced to deal with grossly uneven playing fields. Racism on the streets, racism in work, racism in school, college and higher education, no doubt puts strain on a mind which inevitably has a cascading effect throughout their personal lives. When black men couldn't progress in mainstream society many opted to make money through other means, away from the psychologically draining effects of discrimination, thus we have the possible beginnings of absent fathers, men without care or a real trajectory. This is by far no excuse to play that role, but we have to remember that every person is different and will deal with stress and strain in different ways. Some use it to fight harder, some let it beat the fight out of them.

On my entire estate I can only recall three families that had an involved, active, loving father. Imagine that: just three out of dozens. All the children belonging to those families are doing significantly better than the vast majority of people that I grew up around. I'm by no means saying having a father at home means instantaneous success in life as some fathers are just physically present, but have little to no interaction with their children's day-to-day upkeep, or upbringing.

Do some of these absent fathers know what being absent does to young children? The world is telling these poor kids they're entitled to two guardians but in their reality one guardian doesn't want to know. TV programmes show how it's meant to look but all they see is anything but. No Uncle Phil to offer financial support or bail them out of trouble, no Dan Conner to take them into his hands and show them how they're supposed to do things as a young man.

Like those infantry men we (black people) have fallen from lofty heights. From the Kingdoms of Songhai and Timbuktu, to filling prisons and hearts with sorrow. Men reduced to their crimes, sexual prowess and their ability to entertain, be it sports, dance, music or acting.

Unfortunately, black men in particular are seldom given the mask of humanity to don. We aren't afforded the privilege of vulnerability, or allowed to have excuses for negative behaviours exhibited. Yet many of us are young men suffering from childhoods frustrated by the inaction of adults.

The issues that children face coming from deprived and unfathered households are basic and boil down to two factors: a lack of economic and emotional support. So what happens is, large swathes of boys and girls grow up in families filled with stress and constant tension. Stress surrounding a constant lack of funds, giving way to a lack of liberty and a reduction in time to be free, time to love, time to live and reflect, which causes tension. Now, in order to create twin incomes, the mother may have to take on two or maybe three jobs, making her effectively an absent parent as well. Without support they find themselves having to miss parents' evenings and sports days, or appointments made by the school to discuss their child's slow descent into trouble.

This is worse if the mother has more than one child; now she has to run around the deck trying to plug numerous holes with masking tape only to turn around and find the one just plugged has sprung open again.

Older siblings are forced to become makeshift dads, plunged into a role they've had no training for and shouldn't have to fulfil, given the fact they have a perfectly fine biological father in existence who should be doing the right thing. The role bestowed causes conflict between the child and their mother as they will inevitably get things wrong and make decisions a child naturally would. In many, but not all situations, the older sibling tries to do what their father should be doing, like protect the family and balance the books. Schooling and education now play second fiddle to making money and avoiding becoming a victim in an area filled with pure unadulterated dysfunction.

These young adults seek guidance from older teens on the estate, older guys and girls that are going through the same as them. Effectively, the blind leading the blind. Young damaged men grown without fathers themselves affected by the two aforementioned factors have no business being the sole male reference of masculinity in a child's mind, be the child male or female.

I can give you a prime example of how easy it is to get caught up in the street business. In the summer of 1995, I was twelve and walking through my estate trying to find my friends. A car pulls up beside me. It mounts the curb and the window rolls down. In it is a cab driver and an older guy from my area. He stops me and asks where I'm going. I tell him I'm looking for my friends. We talk for a few seconds before he pulls out a band of notes and hands it to me through the window. Although numerous in total, they are filthy and tatty, varying in denomination and type. Small blue ones right up to larger purples all tied together with no rhyme or reason.

He asks if I want to make money. I say yes, not even caring about the cash, more excited about being seen with a top guy off the block. He opens the door and lets me in. We drive for a while and arrive at our destination. We disembark and the older guy gives the cab-man instructions to wait outside. We enter the ground floor maisonette without even knocking. What I see inside is shocking to my young mind. A den full of drug addicts, the smell of bad body odour and the sickly odour of crack hang thick in the air.

We walk throughout the flat to find the registered occupier, a woman. Her frame so small if I hadn't known better I would have thought she were a child. As they talk I take to looking around at the flat's inhabitants, young children running in and among thinning adults completely strung out. Empty bottles, food bags and containers strewn across the dirty floor. A feeling of deep sorrow gathers within me and I know instantly this isn't for me. I was lucky I had been taught the beauty in empathy and compassion as a child, and my mother never burdened either me or my brother with monetary woes, although she had plenty. I was lucky my brother's dad was active in his life and at times, mine. Lucky that he would help out with funds and childcare, giving my mother a modicum of support beyond the care of his own child.

We drive back from the crack house; and till this day I still laugh at what he did next. He rolls out that filthy bundle of notes and pulls from its middle a miserly five pounds and tells me to have it. For all his troubles present and to still come, he is so broke he can't even afford a carrot bigger than five quid to entice me with. Unfortunately, these are the most visible male figures a young person has growing up on bad council estates. Believe me, if you don't raise your children someone else will. Children need both parents, or stable guardians, period.

Deeper into my adolescence I began to play up at school. I wasn't a nasty child, I was charming towards teachers, never answered back and did what I was told. Well, when I was actually there and not smoking weed, running the streets, getting into scuffles, and being a bad boyfriend to my now wife. My high school was just off Edgware road, so our automatic bunking-off territory was Oxford Street and Marble Arch. We used to ride the open-back route masters and jump off the bus before the conductor could make his way to us. We'd give him crap if he did actually get round to asking for fares.

My mother tried to get me sorted. I remember she once invited a male family friend to attend a parent's evening with us, hoping he could talk some sense into me. When he heard from my teachers what I was doing (or not doing) at school, he tried to give me a lecture but it fell on deaf ears. At the end of the day he said all the right things but he wouldn't be around to oversee the requested changes. Changes in children require examples, care and constant attention. My mother worked her ass off and although I did get her work ethic, she just wasn't knowing enough of the academic system to allow me free reign with my education; she would ask if my homework was done and that's about it.

The above wouldn't be the last time my mother thought it necessary to sub out fathering duties during my ascension into manhood. She once called in a male friend to have a word with me about the birds and the bees, who happened to be from Jamaica, who happened to have a remarkably heavy Jamaican accent. He and I both found the whole thing bizarre and we sat there laughing nervously at his attempt at playing father-teacher, me barely understanding a thing he said and he sweating, completely out of his depth. Imagine a family friend having to be brought in to talk to a boy about something so crucial whilst the boy's actual father runs around town playing happy families elsewhere.

On the same note, I recall showering after PE one Monday afternoon and getting dressed in the changing room. I heard some of the boys cussing each other about washing their penis and I discovered an uncircumcised one should have the foreskin pulled back and cleaned daily. I laughed along with their banter but was too ashamed to admit that at twelve years old, I had never pulled my skin back and given it a scrub. When I got home that night I did and boy, oh boy, did it look bad, not to mention the stink. Little things like this can go unchecked in a fatherless household, maybe a convenient oversight for my mother, who hated talking to me about anything to do with my maturing male anatomy. She would send me out of the room if people even kissed on TV, so there was no way she was going to talk to me about changes in my body or worse, sex.

Years later, at sixteen, I had inevitably left school without GCSEs. Not even one to my name. I remember standing at the results board – God knows what I was thinking even turning up on results day. I was standing by a girl called Patricia; she was in tears. I pinpointed her grades and saw she had an array of As and Bs. I asked: 'What are you crying about, your grades are good enough?' She turned to me and replied, 'No Renaldo, they're good enough for people like you.' I looked at her, stunned, gobsmacked. I had been cussed before, I had been laughed at before but what she said hit deep and it was at that point I began to develop a certain mindset surrounding the importance of academic standards. Oh dear, I thought, look at little Renaldo falling through life, being given lessons in education by a sixteen-year-old schoolgirl.

I walked all the way home that evening, my thoughts and fears roaming my mind like wild rabid animals. The realisation that I was sleepwalking into becoming a statistic hit me square on. I went home to await my poor mother, who worked all the hours God gave to make home the least turbulent it could be. She never asked for much from my brother and me, she always made it clear she'd support us as long as we strived for good grades and endeavoured to get good jobs.

As I stated earlier, my mum knew very little about the school curriculum or what went into achieving 'good grades'. She never had the time to find out either; handling bills and rent on one income is no joke. When I think about the support my wife and I supply our children with to get them as far in this world as possible, I understand how grossly ill-equipped and badly positioned I was to even think about competing with the Patricias of this world. My mother had a good start in life which eventually disintegrated into ruin when my grandparents went through a terrible divorce, leaving her alone with my granddad, who had fallen into a depression upon the separation.

My aunt and uncle (her older siblings) had already left the family home to begin their own lives. My mother's schooling was obviously affected, but what saw her through was her work ethic and the fact she was incredibly focused on any goal set. She was trying her best with her sons, whilst my father barely remembered any of my birthdays let alone my existence.

I got home on results day and sat in silence. What was I going to say to my mum when the only thing she had tasked me with had failed so terribly? She got in and before she could even remove her coat, she came into the living room with a smile. That quickly dissipated upon hearing I had left school with 'fuck all' as she put it on the phone to a friend later on.

I was sent to my room where I waited for the penalty. It never came, just tears. I had heard my mother cry before, but this was different, it was from her pit. A horrendous sob that I can still mentally conjure to this day. 'Heavy is the head forced to wear two crowns,' I say. I had broken her heart and I knew she feared I would end up in jail, or worse.

I fell asleep to her tears and woke to her standing over me.

'You have three options,' she said.

I rubbed my eyes and sat up in my bed. 'One, you go back and redo your GCSEs. Two, you get a trade or a job, or three, if you don't want to do either of the first two, you leave this house and make your own way. I promise you this, though, you won't become a drug dealer or bum under this roof. Make your choice.'

I chose to go back to get my grades, which wasn't easy at all. When I went back to my high school to beg to do my retakes there, they virtually laughed me off the premises. 'Even if we wanted you back, you would need at least four Ds to retake GCSEs,' Mr Morten said with a smile across his face. I couldn't blame him for thinking me a joke after my entire school career could be summarised with a picture of an empty chair.

I eventually got into Maida Vale college after sheer annoying persistence. I rolled up three days on the trot to enrol, only to be told on the first day by the GCSE course entry guy, Michael, that my grades were not good enough to retake GCSEs. So I went home, slept on it and decided I wasn't having that. I went back for a second day to be told the same thing. On the third day Michael laughed out loud when he saw me in the queue again.

'I thought I told you your grades aren't good enough to get you on the courses. Are you crazy?'

We sat and I explained everything, including the fact my mother's heart and my backside were on the line. This coupled with my tenacity and his pity seemed to work, because he miraculously remembered there was another route which involved taking an English and Maths entry exam to get in.

To this day I know I failed the Maths exam, but he knew I was serious and wouldn't let him down. It turned out Michael would go on to be my English teacher. I eventually left college with two Cs in English, one B in Sociology and a D in Maths.

I used the grades to go to another college.

After finishing a media BTEC course at Hendon College, I had only just earned enough UCAS points to get into Kingston University. I had to take a foundation course at Kingston College to get on to the Media Technology degree at the university.

Getting into university felt like I had climbed Mount Everest whilst holding my breath, and was finally allowed to exhale upon my summit. My mother was so happy she told everyone she could. She finally had the GCSE night she had wished for, but better. I made four now – the fourth person (that I knew of) from my estate to go to university, a major feat. But getting in isn't a degree.

At twenty, I was seriously developing a thing for further learning and had begun to realise the life-changing benefits of being educated, be it academic or otherwise. Getting into Kingston was me punching way above my weight, especially given the fact that I left secondary school with no GCSEs. I'd even sat witness to a meeting in primary school between my mother and headteacher, questioning if I had learning and behavioural difficulties and whether I should obtain a Special Needs statement.

My attendance at Kingston University wouldn't be my first time there. Fortunately one of my best friends had done the unthinkable and become only the second person on my estate to begin and complete a degree.

I remember our friendship circle getting the invite to go down to Kingston for the weekend to visit him; we were so hyped getting on a train from Waterloo. Anywhere outside of NW10 felt exotic to us.

You have to understand how small the world seems for people from an estate like mine. There is a comfort in staying ignorant to other experiences, a perceived feeling of safety in staying on the block. How can a young mind expand and grow if all it's ever known is violence, degradation and struggle?

The status quo is kept up in places like my estate by people convincing themselves that education, reading, writing, learning a language or instrument is reserved for nerds or uncool kids. Can you see how dangerous it is for a young impressionable mind to be in receipt of this narrative? Imagine you mix that with a lack of funds or a non-opposing narrative at home? Imagine your perceived father figures are the older guys on your estate who push the aforementioned mantra? Gradually you have young gifted people dimming their light to stay out of the light, so afraid that they may realise they have potential and want to act on it.

Young people on estates and in deprived areas are not dumb or innately stupid, however, many are fatherless, financially weak and, like most humans, they adapt to their environment and circumstances. If we did a 'trading places' experiment with the son of an aristocrat and swapped his life with the son of a poor mum living from hand to mouth on the Stonebridge estate, believe you me, the results would be the same.

Visiting Kingston in my late teens felt like visiting a different world; the people there were so progressive and positive about their lives, they had real dreams and aspirations.

I remember we went to a nightclub and they played cheesy pop music. No one cared about image or status, people were there to have fun. My friends and I weren't used to those sorts of people and places; the kind of places we went out to back home were filled with questionable vibes and turbulent atmospheres – you had to be ready for whatever. But not there. We walked back to my friend's place eating greasy kebabs and chips without the need to look over our shoulders. We all crashed out and in the morning we were woken by birds chirruping. On the last day of our visit, we went for a walk down by the river and around the town, and I knew I needed to be there.

Returning to our area always felt depressing, having to slip the mask back on, smudge the smile and furrow the brow once more. I wanted to make Kingston my reality and I did. I worked so damn hard to get there that I couldn't even recognise the person I was becoming. Not bad for a high-school dropout with suspected behavioural issues.

I lived on campus at first (Seething Wells) then flat-shared with a couple of really good guys in Surbiton.

Being out of an area like mine for that prolonged period of time and meeting people from all over the world does something to you. You begin to expand and outgrow places like Harlesden, Tottenham or Peckham. It's not that you forget where you came from or look down on the place where you were brought up, but that you realise you need more than the high-rise and dysfunction that can occur in those places.

I left university with a 2:2 in Media Technology. God knows how. It involved science – physics, to be exact. I almost cried when I realised. I was so out of my depth, I had to really compensate for it. When others were drinking and partying, I was in the library up to my eyeballs in books and past papers, trying to get things to stick. An 8 a.m. to 11 p.m. library day wasn't foreign to me. Very hard times, my lack of education catching up with me again.

I worked part-time throughout uni but at times money was really tight and at one point I was so desperate I called my dad to ask him to help me. He didn't even know he had a child – the first child in his family in the UK – that was at university. He should have known, and I shouldn't have had to ask him for shit. He should have been calling me to offer aid from day one.

The phone rang and he answered. We did the whole 'how are you' thing, loads of pauses and empty space. I always felt like an echo to him, an echo back to a time he would rather have forgotten about. Although I had spent the odd summer with him, maybe five in total, I'm convinced if I could have offered my father a one-off payment to sever all ties with me, he would have taken it.

Anyway, I asked him for a hundred pounds and he ummed and ahhed about it. It took him a month to get that money to me. By then I had had to borrow from other sources. My dad had two daughters after me (the first of his girls born whilst he was with my mum) by another woman. Two daughters he fought tooth and nail to see. He even went to court to get visitation rights, and here I was with no resistance from my mother and he couldn't have given a toss.

I would often see cousins from my dad's side and we'd talk. They'd ask how come I wasn't at a family gathering (Christmas, birthdays etc.) with my dad and the rest of his children. Gatherings he would have driven an hour from Bedford to London to get to, driving past my estate. The destination taking place a mere twenty minutes' drive from me.

He never once stopped to pick me up or ask if I wanted to go. Not me: I was a child called Inconvenience. Terrible, I know.

My father died in 2007 of a heart attack. I went down there to attend his funeral. I felt a degree of sadness but I can't lie, I felt like an imposter son. I was constantly confronted and comforted by friends of his and family I had never even seen before. They said, 'Oh, you're his eldest son. He loved you, don't worry,' etc., etc.

The truth was that I didn't feel loved and I wasn't worried. He wasn't involved in my life enough to make me feel a profound sense of loss for him in any way. He hadn't earned that. To this day if you paid me, I couldn't tell you where his grave was. This is not out of spite but a sense of – what for? He was the author of his own story and he neither painted himself the protagonist or antagonist in the chapters concerning me.

If I'm being honest, I have friends that if I'd lost, I would have been actually devastated about. Friends that have put their lives on the line for me in the past.

My father's last set of children, after my two sisters, the children he had actually raised, were in pieces. They really wanted me to feel as they did, wanted me in a pile beside myself, but he simply didn't mean to me what he had meant to them.

I have divulged so much to you about me without discussing the positive people, besides my mother, who are, or were, constant within my life growing up.

My grandfather filled in where he could. By the time I was really aware of his input in my life he had passed away at the age of eighty-nine. My mother would take my brother and me round to his house every Sunday to visit him. He'd lift me up with such ease, his huge hands, firm and strong. He'd sit me on his lap, the smell of Murray Mints teased from between his lips, carrying tales from the old world he came from. The world where his current attire was still high-end fashion, a world where his apartment décor and all its contents were still cutting edge.

He was a carpenter by trade and had virtually built the house he had shared with my grandmother before they separated, which split the house in two and spoilt my mother's almost flawless childhood. He would walk with his hands behind his back and I'd follow. He used to take me to the 'bookies' and ask me to pick a horse or two. A silent, loving man, who for some of my childhood collected me and my brother from primary school, allowing my mother to go to work without the stress of childcare.

After fetching us food, he used to sit on the step in my house reading the newspaper as we watched kid's TV till my mother got in. If we ever wanted anything he'd get it without question. He was a good man, and when I got old enough to go and visit him by myself, I would sit for an hour or two in total fascination, laughing and joking with him about everything and anything.

He once told me about visiting Minnesota in the fifties when they still had a racial divide. He was almost given a good beating for trying to buy cigarettes in a 'whites only' shop. He'd tell me about having to work two jobs to get by. He'd tell me about the Teddy boys in London when he first arrived in England and how carrying knuckledusters to work was standard procedure for all black men in the sixties, as you'd certainly come across some racist troublemakers trying to set upon you, coming home in the dark.

He'd tell me about how cold England could get and how a man he was just talking to at a bus stop went silent for minutes and passed away there and then beside him.

I'll sum him up in an act. I used to pass my grandfather's house whilst out with my friends gallivanting and one day he called me over from amongst my gaggle and asked me to do him a favour. He needed to borrow fifteen pounds. I wanted to do it but I also didn't want to lose my friends (this was before mobile phones) who were on their way to another friend's house. I contemplated. If I went to get the money, it would mean me walking all the way to the bank on the high street. Twenty minutes there, twenty minutes back and then twenty minutes back to my friend's house who may or may not even be there by then.

I knew if my grandfather asked me for money, he must really have needed it as he had never done so before. So I split from my group, went into Harlesden, got the last bit of cash I had, got back and handed it to him. He was grateful and told me he'd call my house when he had the money to repay me. I got a call the next day and was told to go round to his to collect what he had borrowed from me.

He opened the door and we sat down watching TV; he got me a ginger beer – both our favourite. We sat talking then he pulled from his cardigan fifty pounds. He placed it on the table and slid it over to me. I frowned and looked to him for explanation. I said, 'But I only gave you fifteen pounds.' To which he replied, 'It was never about the money; I wanted to see what kind of man you were becoming.'

I've never forgotten what he did and said that day; it formed part of me. When he got to eighty-nine years old he had developed Alzheimer's. I'd go round to feed him, wash him and cut his hair. When he died I was devastated. I wish he had lived long enough to see my children; he was the best grandfather a boy could have had.

Another person of great significance was and is my wife who I met in 1996. I was fourteen and she was thirteen. She has always been there for me and showed me, via her actions, what it was to have aspirations and goals. My wife makes me better in every which way imaginable. She's a girl from where I came from, who exceeded the world's expectations and went on to UCL, a Russell Group university. A gargantuan feat. Her standards were set so high I had no choice but to raise my level to try and keep her by my side.

I say the above with maturity in my mouth and in my fingers now, but I didn't always treat her the best as a teenager. With no blueprint of what a healthy relationship looked like, I was possessive. God knows why she stayed through some of my intense behaviour earlier on; maybe she saw I was trying to be a better person and hadn't ever had any guidance on being in a healthy relationship. I think I was the best of a bad bunch. At least I never sold drugs, put my hands on her, and could hold a conversation. I worked a job and had manners towards my elders, so my mother had done a decent job with me in that sense.

But, unfortunately I played games with her heart and was fast following in the footsteps of my father, careless and uncaring, leaving her despondent.

I got a stern wake-up call in my early twenties, when she left me for eight months. She'd had enough of my shit and was done. She was at university realising that life is bigger than what she was used to, and had no place for non-progressive situations or people. I couldn't blame her. She had always been strongheaded; her self-respect wasn't malleable.

I fought for almost eight long months to get her back and I eventually did convince her that I was a changed man. Whilst we had split, a girl or two had heard I was back on the market and attempted to fill the void, but I wanted her back so badly it hurt. I would act as if I was still with her, even telling everyone I was still in a relationship. This was not healthy, and for the sake of a healthy mind, I gave up. After eight months of grovelling I had begun to accept her departure and look forwards but it was in my most nonchalant conversation with her that I saw daylight. I think it was the mixture of me being so chilled out and a mystic palm reader – yeah, that's right – a mystic had spoken to my now wife on the back of a bus and convinced her to forgive me. My wife denied even having a love interest, but the woman knew she was lying.

We are married now, have been since 2008, and have two beautiful children: one girl and one boy, the boy being the eldest. I was at both births and wouldn't have been anywhere else in the world. Saying that, my son's arrival terrified me. The sheer size of the situation, the weight of responsibility so heavy I could see how a person with a weak mind could run and hide. I could see how a young man or woman could bask in the waters of desertion and let it gently drift them away. Having a child or children and doing what you actually need to do to give them the best start in life is difficult, to say the least.

The day we were due to leave the hospital with our son, I remember looking at that nurse and thinking, 'Are you out of your mind? Do you know who I am? I'm a fatherless boy off an estate who just about dragged himself through an education. An, at times, irresponsible man, who almost walked all the way down the wrong path, who's been arrested on several occasions, who has almost been shot twice, who was just playing Xbox last night thinking of colourful ways to squander his wages, completely unable to fathom the role he had just signed up for. Are you nuts?' Are these the sorts of people they allow to take children home? Her answer would have been 'yes'. Although I walked into the hospital all of the aforementioned, I walked out of there a parent – full stop. Next chapter. A parent who would do anything for his child to thrive and live well.

Years passed and my fatherless beginnings were starting to show through. One situation that jumps out at me was when my son began playing football and had been playing for a year.

We moved him into a team where he'd get to both train at a higher level and play Sunday league football. I was a horrible football dad. I would handle my six-year-old son's inevitable learning failures as if he were a professional footballer. I had no chill whatsoever. If he performed badly, I'd berate him because I wanted to win, erm sorry, I wanted *him* to win and be the boy I'd seen other dads parade home off the pitch.

Whenever football training or matches came about, my son would become very distant from me, scared to put a foot wrong through fear that I would become the monster he had witnessed the week before. So what was going on with me? Well, even outside of football, my convoluted impression of what a growing boy should be was being marred by my own upbringing.

I was a tough kid and was prepared to fight if needs be, prepared to do whatever it took to not be disrespected; this was my interpretation of what being a man was. Not being disrespected or losing.

When I think back to certain situations relating to my son, I cringe, and I could cry sometimes. In parks, if a kid pushed in front of him to get on the slide, it would eat me up. I would then have a stern talk with a four-year-old child about not letting anyone push him about in life. Way too heavy a conversation about park play. I needed to lighten up and I couldn't see that I was harming more than helping.

Can you see how deeply I thought about things like this? My wife thought I was off-key and she was right. I was failing badly at the dad thing and one Sunday my wife left a letter on the kitchen counter, the day after another bad Saturday training session.

I picked it up and what I read reduced me to tears. I will not divulge what was written but my wife highlighted what I was psychologically doing to the boy I loved with every fibre in my body. I had become the enemy to his development, I had taken away his freedom to fail and put upon the shoulders of a child, the weight of the world. I felt so shitty. I felt the damage done could never be reversed. We had a good cry and we talked at great length about how I should proceed. Once again, Renaldo barrelling through life; my wife, a woman, showing me how to be a father. 'Jeez'. Thankfully I hadn't lost, but I had learned.

I never raised my voice in frustration outside the realms of positivity at training, or during a match again. And guess what, his level shot through the roof! He could fail without fear. Instead of berating him we would talk about ways of improving his game, an approach I took and applied towards different facets of his upbringing. Instead of being impulsive and rushing in with my initial thoughts or feelings, I would always take a step back and analyse the situation at great length before making a move.

My relationship with him has infinitely improved. My son's Man of the Match medals are numerous. We have great conversations about everything and anything. He's growing up to be a fine young man, top in class in every aspect. I'm so very proud of him and the person that he is. I'm so glad I was alerted to the error of my ways and was able to award myself with a better connection with both of my children.

Can you imagine if I had run and left either one of them? Imagine how much I would have deprived myself of! I'd had holidays, nice shoes, trainers, gone to parties and places with my wife and friends and thought nothing could top those events or moments. I was unable to fathom that having children would put all of the above to the sword.

I look at guys I know who are running around town spraying out kids without looking back, living for the night, women, cars, clothes, and I feel a great deal of pity for them. They are missing out on the greatest gift a person could be awarded.

Those men are my father, and they are the product of his absence. They are that little boy on the rough council estate looking out of the window, hoping he'll come. They are the father who delivers an excuse over a promise. They are the little boy pulling back his foreskin at twelve for the first time ever, and the dad who should have been there to give him the advice at ten. They are the teenagers who flunk class, poor, broke and disadvantaged in every way possible. They are the dad that should have been there to whip them into shape. They are the boys that dim their lights to fit in, as the reality of realising their true potential would be an acknowledgement of how much further they have to stride than the more advantaged kids around them.

When I tell people where I come from, and that I'm a writer and business owner who is happily married and super active in both my children's lives – be the person black, white or Asian – I see the cogs turning within. The pigeon holes allocated don't fit and they can't seem to get their head round it.

I'm hurtling towards a destiny my stereotype shouldn't have allowed me to. I'm breaking his cycle. I may not be the greatest dad of all time, but I'm trying to be best father I can be.

Chapter 3:

Christmas Without the Kids:
When Marriage Breaks Down

Ian

I think it's fair to say that having children recreates the thoughts of magic around Christmas time, the joy of gifts under the tree, that wonderment of opening presents and the excitement that there is the present that is the 'one' for that year.

The joy of Christmas is spending time around our loved ones, with fun, laughter and with copious amounts of food. It's all about everyone having that one perfect day together.

The reality of this can be very different and for many different reasons.

For myself, Christmas as a child was an incredibly easy affair. My brother, sister and I would spend weeks looking through various catalogues, carefully studying the pages to make sure we didn't miss anything. Our Christmas wishlist needed to be just right.

On Christmas Eve, presents were placed under the tree, biscuits and whisky were left out by the fire ready for Santa and we were ushered upstairs to get ready for bed. This was the point where we were allowed to pick a sock from Dad's draw to use as our stocking, so that Father Christmas could fill them with gifts. We always chose the biggest sock we could find: Dad's red football socks. These were placed at the end of our beds and we were told to 'get to sleep or Father Christmas won't come; he knows when you are awake'. So, for what felt like the next hour, we would lie in bed, desperately trying to stay awake to catch sight of Father Christmas. In hindsight, we were probably asleep within the first five minutes.

The morning could not come fast enough and we would wake in excitement to go through our bulging socks to see what gifts had been left. This was normally around 5 or 6 a.m., so we would try to hold off as long as we could. This didn't last long and soon enough we were running into Mum and Dad's room to tell them that Santa had been. Without thoughts of them being half-asleep, we would empty our swiftly repacked stockings on to their bed and go through them again so they could see what presents we had received. They always indulged us before making their excuses to make a tea, let the dog out and grab five minutes to wake in their own time.

This would be followed by everyone going downstairs to find one present that we were allowed to open before church. Personally, the trick here was not to go for the obvious big present, but to get a nice pre-taster to the big event. Even better if it was something you could play with at church. After we had breakfast, walked the dog and arrived home after church, we were back in front of the tree and ready for the main event. Mum and Dad would fix a whisky and a milky coffee and we were all ready. This was it, finally opening our presents as a family. The day would then progress onwards at a rapid pace which involved seeing the whole family and having a huge lunch around one of their tables. More presents would follow before sitting in front of the TV, looking in amazement at our wonderful new things.

I do need to make this clear: we were anything but rich, and our presents, stockings and otherwise were not of great monetary value. But they were hard-earned and bought with a huge amount of love and thought. Christmas was a day that we truly felt spoilt and it always felt like it was over too soon.

Fast forward a few years and Christmas had turned into something else, a much trickier period of the year. Growing up and becoming an adult seemed to bring a very different reality.

The Christmas holidays started to come with many different faces, and not all of them were enjoyable. The pressure of the Christmas season had taken over and had brought with it thoughts and fears around buying the right presents; to be generous without overspending as well as making enough time to spend time with our loved ones. And then there was the question of which loved ones we would see. Some years, Christmas was just about getting through it without another family argument. Christmas had brought an element of tension – unease that was simmering in the background and just wouldn't go away, constantly nagging away at years gone by where the season was wonderful and there to be enjoyed.

In early 2002, I became a father for the first time. This was something that I had wanted from a young age. I always wanted to be a dad and having my own family released the chains around Christmas. It became a wonderful event again, seen through the childhood eyes of my youngest and a release from all the worries and stresses that previous years had brought. In 2004, our second child was born; our family was complete, and Christmas was elevated even further with the children running around and the true magic of Christmas returning. It came with setting new traditions, resurrecting old ones and being able, just for a few days, to get lost within the wonderment of our little family. It became a time when all those little stresses disappeared and playing with the children and watching them enjoy the festive season was an incredible time. The excitement and the laughter returned, as if disappearing down a rabbit hole and returning to a much simpler time in life.

In the summer of 2008, my wife and I decided to separate. Our children were four and six.

Unbeknown to me at the time, Christmas Day would become more painful and lifeless than I had ever experienced.

Our separation had been tricky; we had gone from chatting, discussing and communicating well with great intentions to walking out of rooms as the other one entered. I had decided that I should leave the home for the sake of the family as it was fast becoming a toxic environment full of blame and hurt. I felt that taking myself out of the picture was best for us all. Breakdowns in relationships can be incredibly painful and with children added to that mix, emotions can rocket to new unknown levels.

At first, I would go back to the house and look after the children during the week while my ex worked. I had the kids as often as possible. Sleeping from time to time on the sofa was good enough. This started out well as we both knew we needed to get to some form of workable solution. But as time went on, this proved challenging. I had nowhere to call home and I started to sofa surf at friends' houses. I would spend the odd night sleeping in the car, away from the world and by the sea. Sometimes I would finish work, drive to a quiet spot, park and then just walk until the early hours. My brain was a complete mess, trying to figure out life and where I had got to.

Bills don't change, life pressures don't shift to make things more manageable in these times, they just become more heightened. I was still holding down a full-time management role, working at least ten hours a day and at times it was my sanctuary. I found it easy and it became a switch-off from my reality outside. I knew I was living a life that I couldn't keep up – lack of sleep was a problem but I would stay awake until it wasn't a choice. Trying to find a place to call home became a priority; I knew this wasn't a lifestyle I could hold down for too long. My diet had become erratic and I had started to drink. I can remember waiting and watching the clock for 11 a.m. so I could justify nipping out to get something to eat, and a quick beer. It just became keeping my head above water. My bosses knew that something wasn't right, even asking if I was living in my car, but they allowed me the freedom to do what was required, both at work and outside. My job became my focus point, the piece I had to keep together; I had to earn and support us. But with every penny going to the family to maintain a mortgage, all the while trying to keep life as normal as possible for the children, finding a home was a real struggle. Weekends would become a weird game for me, known only to myself as 'operation somewhere to go for the weekend'. I would pick up the children on a Saturday morning and we would normally end up at my mum's or at another family member's house. On the nice days we would appreciate the freedom of being out, running free and enjoying ourselves. We made the best of the situation; we always tried to have fun. We would do homework, play, play-fight and we remained as close as we could. On the days that I didn't see them, we always spoke on the phone, we remained as close as we had always been and this connection was something I didn't ever want to lose.

Over the coming months, we all started to settle into this bizarre life of the in-between. By now my ex-wife and I had bigger problems. Communication had deteriorated to an all-time low and we both struggled to communicate at all. Our conversations would often descend into arguments. We had gone from a loving family unit to some chaotic shambles. The harder I tried to hold it together, the more it seemed to be breaking away.

It was around this time that the cracks started to show and I started to struggle mentally. Sofa surfing and sleeping in the car, I'd have two boxes: one for my clothes and one for the kids' stuff. Our breakup was becoming increasingly messy. Trying to keep that all inside while dealing with the kids' predicament was taking its toll on me.

Our family, like many others, has a history with mental health issues. My nan had been in and out of health institutions and when I was around four-teen, I would spend time looking after her, and her me, during the school holidays. I loved having that alone time with her; I remember her being such a beautiful lady, so mild and gentle but easily confused and meek when surrounded by family. It was as if a switch went off and this other person would take over. It still hurts today when I remember all the terrible times she had. Seeing her in a mental institution was horrific, but it was my nan. I could not quite understand how it was full of so many people and how they all seemed to be in their own little world. I can remember my dad having similar problems as I grew up and it was always in the back of my mind that one day I may have to face some demons myself. But I tried to convince myself that it was a route I would never travel. Even today, it is something that is very close to me, still affecting our family and always lurking, waiting for a slip-up or a fall.

I would go for long walks at night and would often come to a crossroads of thoughts. Some thoughts were positive and I would tell myself that, regardless of my situation, it wasn't going to define me. And other thoughts were the complete opposite, that maybe I was the problem and life for everyone concerned would be better if I was not around.

It was on one of those downward spirals that I found myself testing my limits to the extreme. It was a dark, cold night. The beach was quiet and I had decided to sleep in the car rather than drive anywhere. I had been walking for what seemed like hours. The moon was full and low in the night sky. The light was shimmering on the sea and had a strange effect on me, luring me to it. As if trapped in its beam, it was calling me to come closer and in some weird out-of-body experience, I could see myself being drawn towards the light and the sea.

I remember entering the water, still fully dressed and although it was a freezing November night, the cold could not knock me out of my semi-conscious state. I felt the water engulf my shoes and before long it was around my knees. The light of the moon still captivated my mind and it wasn't long before the waves were over my waist and had started to engulf my upper torso. I had taken my coat off and left it in the car, my jumper now soaking wet and clinging to me. It was around this point that I could feel the pull of the sea lift my feet ever so slightly off the seabed. The water was around my neck and although the moonlight still had me in its grasp, I remember thinking I could let go, just give up trying to resist and drift away into the dark. No one would know, and I honestly thought no one would care.

It summed up where my life was. Maybe letting go would set everyone else free? This thought lingered over me for what felt like hours as I have no idea of how long I was out there for. I battled with conflicting thoughts in my head while I stood contemplating whether to float away into the cold dark night. I remember thinking about the children and how they would be OK, as they were so young. It had been made clear that being a dad, I would not get much say in their upbringing, if we ever did involve the court system.

But it was thinking about my children that pulled me from the watery lifeless state I was heading for. I knew that being a dad was something worth fighting for and regardless of the walls I would meet along the way, it was paramount that the children knew who their dad was and that he cared. Wading from the water that night, I knew how close I had come and that I could not repeat that; my relationship with the children was bigger than that. Once dry, I slept lightly due to being so cold. I was at work by 5 a.m. with a new determination pushing me forward.

By early December I managed to secure a flat which was a huge step. It was within a few miles of the children's school and home, so picking them up was easy and we had somewhere to stay, to call ours. We had worked out a routine. They would come to stay after school and once I managed to get some bunk beds, they had a room of their own. In hindsight, this was a huge step in so many ways, both good and bad. It gave me and the children some space, some routine back, but it came with life accessories. Bills. Money was tight and I couldn't afford all the upkeep but I was happy to miss out on a few bits for myself just to have a space for the children. It seemed to be working out for us all, much better than in the previous months. It even brought some respite from the arguments, and that was a much-needed relief.

Christmas loomed large on the horizon and presented us with two new problems.

Firstly, the company I was working for went into liquidation, and although I managed to find a job the next day, I had to take a £5000 pay cut, but I was earning and could cover most stuff – just… But the other problem was Christmas Day.

After much deliberation, we managed to come to the conclusion that we would spend Christmas morning together at the family home, and at lunchtime, they would go with my wife to spend time with her side of the family. This was anything but ideal. No stockings, no tucking them in knowing the excitement that we would wake to, but I was desperate to hide my sadness to make sure that regardless of where we were, the kids would still have a great day.

As I remember it, I arrived at 8 a.m., at the family home, excitedly waiting to see the children. I knew it would be tricky for my ex and I to be together for a short period but it would be worth it for our children. So we decided that, if I could be there early, we could try to make it semi-normal. Presents would be under the tree, excitement and happiness would fill the air and I could be with our children to open their presents, spend time with them and enjoy that occasion.

I went to open the door only for my key not to turn. I was caught in that weird moment when your brain struggles to understand the scenario, but once that thought had gone, I realised it had been locked from the inside and the key was left in the lock. My heart sank; I was gutted.

As I peered through the letter box, I could hear the children tiptoeing around, but I could not get their attention. I just sat and waited it out. About thirty minutes later, the door was opened. This was all I had been waiting for, so waiting around didn't matter; it was forgotten and the children became the focus. We managed to enjoy Christmas morning together, opening presents and having fun spending time with each other. Unfortunately, this did not last. It seemed only a matter of minutes before my time was up and I would need to leave so the kids could get ready to visit relatives.

I was heartbroken. There were no words that I could say at this point. The few hours we had weren't enough.

I reluctantly left.

It is hard to put that feeling into words. I remember leaving the house and driving an hour to the coast, parking up in my now normal spot and just walking. I had no idea where I was going, what to do or how to handle the day. I ended up sitting in a busy pub, surrounded by strangers and families enjoying their Christmas together. I was angry at the world and the injustice of it all, that everyone else should get to spend Christmas how, and with whom, they wanted. I was completely broken. The feeling of disappointment, loss and injustice was unbearable. I soon ended up walking again before speaking to my family – my shining light – my mum. She knew what was going on for me and although many offers had been made to spend time with her and the family, I just wanted to be alone. I felt empty and dead inside; I didn't want to be around anyone. I knew I was in a difficult place and was overwhelmed with the feeling of not wanting to ruin Christmas for anyone else.

Slightly reluctantly and not completely sure how, I ended up at my mum's, having lunch and leaving again as soon as I could. I returned to my spot on the coast and continued my walkathon to nowhere. It was just a feeling of being away from the world, not causing anyone pain and dealing with some really difficult thoughts and feelings regarding my worth to my children and myself. Suicidal thoughts had been coming and going since that night at the beach and these thoughts were never far away. They would come and go and reach points that were hard to anticipate.

My fall was swift. I had gone from being comfortably happy and surrounded with family to feeling completely alone and worthless. It was only thoughts of my children needing me more than ever that kept me going. I had not chosen to be a father to give it all up by walking away; my intention as a father was to be a role model, to lead by example, to steer and grow these tiny children into fully functioning happy humans. I completely understand the thoughts about walking away and leaving your children in a happy and settled environment. Sometimes walking away seems the best option, to remove the pain, the problem, so others can be happy. If only life was that easy: no emotion, no feeling.

The festive period was a pretty rough experience that first year and although it took time to get my feelings in check, I was always able to bring it back to the bigger picture. We had plenty of ups and downs, but I think the kids enjoyed their alternative Christmas experience as a whole. New Year's Day was a similar experience to Christmas Day for me: it was more about getting through it and moving forward. I started to look at these big social dates as just another day, and as far as I was concerned, I had lots of days to come that could be special with the children.

As we entered the new year, I thought I was doing OK. I had a new job locally and I was hopeful that the year was going to prove a turning point. Plus, the kids loved coming to stay, even if it was cold. Those heating bills were a luxury I couldn't afford so we huddled around the log fire, curling up together and doing things to get our minds off the cold. I don't think they even cared; they just seemed happy to be there, but you know it's cold when you can see their breath.

But as the months passed, it became clear that I wasn't coping with life and I would sink into a downward spiral after a bad call with my ex, or not being able to see the children. Looking back, I was depressed. I had started to self-harm to deal with the thoughts in my head. It was easier to punish myself than inflict pain on others.

It started one night while alone in the flat. I found myself drifting into the headspace that I was in that night at the beach. I tried to exercise, work and anything else I could do to take my mind off it, but the darkness kept coming. I have no idea how, but I found myself in the bath. I vividly remember having a knife in the bath with me just placed on the side as if that was completely normal and that was where it belonged. I couldn't take my eyes off it. Like the moon, it was as if it was talking to me, dragging me in. I remember playing with it, running it across my arms and forearms. I thought that being in the bath was a good idea as I wouldn't make a mess; any blood could be washed down easily once I had been found. On the other edge of the bath was my phone. I stared at it and wondered who I could call. Family were a no – I did not want that burden on them. I came to the conclusion that I would ring the only person I considered a friend at the time. She was the only person who I felt wanted nothing from me. She did not know how I was feeling and what I was going through; she barely knew anything about me. We had only met a few months before, but that night she saved my life. I have never thanked her – regrettably we lost touch a few years after. But her picking up my call and just chatting, as we always did, seemed to ease the thoughts around the knife and suicide. I wish we were still in touch, but life moved on and I thought it best to leave parts of my past life behind. Not a great decision looking back but maybe for the best.

Although that night I had dodged the urge, it didn't go away. I would cut myself as a way of releasing the pressure that life was bringing to my door. I would always cut my arms; they were easy to cover up. After my first attempt, I switched to a serrated knife. The pain was more unforgiving and I felt more of a release, as if I was righting my wrongs by going through the extra pain. I never once got to the point of suicide again after that; my self-harm being my way of coping.

I know that some people noticed, from strange looks across desks at work, but I didn't care. I only really managed to get it under control when I attended a hospital appointment for an unrelated issue. The nurse stopped and questioned me on the cuts up my arm. I explained that it was to do with some cleaning I had done. I don't believe she bought that at all but it made me realise that I needed help and spoke to my doctor about my state of mind.

It was suggested that I did some talking therapy. I had to fill out a form, asking me how I felt that day, when I last thought about suicide and such like. For me, the therapy did not go deep enough; it was a scratch on the surface and only delayed my thoughts and moods. The other route was to take some medication, and although this may prove a sensible choice for many, this was never an option for me. I could not allow myself to become everything my past had shown me through my dad and my nan. That experience had made me strong and showed me a route I could not take.

The feelings of depression, self-loathing and pain never left until I managed to push life forward the only way I knew: head down, grit my teeth, fight and create a better me.

By now I had left the flat as it had become too expensive. I reluctantly moved out and gratefully moved into one of my friend's and ex-neighbour's houses. Their kids were at university so I was able to move into the spare room.

I can't remember my second Christmas without the children. Divorce was in full swing and proving to be anything but easy. I don't remember seeing the kids. By then it had been a difficult year and it wouldn't have bothered me as much. I had had enough of fighting by then and was just trying to make it through every day. I still saw the children weekly, but it was so hard. For the moments I saw the kids I managed to switch on, like a light bulb. The moment they went, I would hide away in the dark again. Regardless of my outside persona, I had become withdrawn and a little soulless.

I always loved having the children, regardless of the situation. We would curl up in that spare room at night, sharing a single and a pull-out bed, and being together made it all worthwhile. Our friends were amazing, and it helped they knew the children.

By 2010, I managed to secure a better job. I was now housesharing with two others, and everyone was away for Christmas, so I had my own space. The only problem was that I was now sixty miles away from the children's home. I can't remember the details, but I did manage to have the children for Christmas for the first time in two years and that felt huge. Although, that Christmas Eve and Christmas Day were possibly the toughest two days I have ever had them. Having the kids and feeling really pressured to create the perfect day was exhausting. It was perfect for no other reason than we were all together, but I felt a little lost and not really sure what to do; I remember feeling like I should be doing more.

As parents we are now able to communicate and have developed a respect for each other and what we have brought to our children. We now alternate Christmas with the children and this works well for the adults. But I know the children feel differently about Christmas now. It has lost a little bit of its magic and I know they feel the strain of trying to fit everything into the Christmas period. Christmas has definitely changed for me too: it often feels like a lot of stress and comes with a tinge of sadness that those earlier Christmases, where the children were so innocent and untouched by life, will never return.

Christmas represents a time for family traditions and being around loved ones. But often, life doesn't go to plan and we have to make new traditions and try and create positive memories that our children will remember forever.

I was once told by a divorced parent when discussing Christmas, 'I hate having to share them.' All parents hate being away from their children; I completely understand the statement and the feelings and actions that may or not help the situation. But we must remember that when we create a child, we create that child with someone else. As parents, regardless of our circumstances, we have a responsibility to all those parties, and we have the ability to make Christmas a happier and easier time for all. I am so glad that we are now in that place.

Being a dad, a mum or carer at Christmas can be a tricky and lonely time, but it is only one day. It won't ever define your relationship with your children; there will be other days that will be remembered just as fondly. Being a parent is something we choose to take on regardless of what comes our way and it's a lifelong commitment. The scenery may change along the way, but our responsibilities do not. Our actions and behaviours will shape and mould our children and leave something much bigger than ourselves.

If you are not able to be with your children this Christmas, try to be grateful that they are surrounded by loved ones and that they will have a nice day. Soon enough you will get to see them and have the opportunity to make beautiful memories to look back on. Look after yourself and try to use the time to spend on you and your other loved ones. If you suffer from thoughts of loss and depression, try to remain strong and do what you need to do for you. There is now so much support and the world has become an open place where the stigma attached to mental health is subsiding. It's OK not to be OK so pick up the phone and call someone – a family member, a friend, or a helpline. Do not feel that you are burdening anyone: people do care even if you may not at times.

Maybe we should change the message that is brought out every Christmas…

Kids are for life, not just for Christmas.

Chapter 4:

Equal Parenting and Shared Parental Leave: The Challenges and Benefits of Being a Stay-at-Home Dad

Sam Draper

Please allow me to introduce myself: I'm a geriatric trailer, or a 'latte papa' or a stay-at-home dad, or Mr Mom ... you pick the title, and I'm it. One of the lucky few who took advantage of Shared Parental Leave a couple of years or so ago, and supported my family by taking fifty weeks from my job to help look after my daughter and, two years later, a son. Arguably, one good thing to come from the long-forgotten coalition government of Clegg and Cameron – so I'm writing to encourage more families to embrace this opportunity and change the very gender-divided culture of parenting that exists in the UK.

This chapter will simply recount some of my experience, many of the hiccups and challenges, and hopefully 'share' what is possible for families in the UK, without telling anyone what they should or shouldn't do.

To be honest, I never imagined I would be writing anything like this, or be involved in any kind of discussion about parenting or advocating that fathers be more involved in the raising of their children. I hadn't honestly thought about it. Looking back, I went to a comprehensive school, my background pretty straightforward, my parents pretty traditional in outlook and behaviour, with my mum taking time off work to look after my brother and me. My dad stayed at work. Nothing original.

I grew up in Dorset – a small rural community that is wonderfully pretty to visit and grow up in. It was idyllic in many ways, but it's not for teenagers. It was peaceful and, retrospectively, privileged. I didn't have to worry about anything, except when I was next going to get books out from the local library. Seeing the sea, walking through fields and alongside rivers, and generally not fearing for much but a lack of freedom. Everyone knew everything about everyone. My dad was away with the Royal Navy, but always came back. Looking back, it was a simple, stress-free upbringing (maybe not for my mum) and it was a privilege to grow up where I did. However, at a certain age the safe world around you seems a little small, and you want to get out. My options were simple: stay around and be part of the seasonal tourist trade, join the Armed Services, work at the Council, or find a way to move away. Like a lot of rural communities around the UK, job opportunities aren't that varied, and if you want to see the world, university is an option, and I was lucky enough to get grants and fees paid (yes, I am that old!).

I had no clue what job I wanted, or that I might one day choose parenting over permanent employment. I left home for uni and studying books, and then onwards to jobs as a journalist in London. Not very focused and no real signs that I wanted something different from family life. My twenties were a blur of work and life with my wife-to-be, and a life-saving career change to teaching. Once I had settled into my new role, we led a pretty regular existence all round. No kids. We socialised and lived a London experience of work and socialising and events. We travelled and shared ups and downs like anyone else. And still no kids. It just didn't happen for a variety of reasons, some sadder than others. And I can't say that my thirties were any different. Teaching continued, my life involved trying to buy a house, our family included dogs, and time moved on.

I don't think we had avoided the idea of children; it was a conversation we'd had early on as a couple, and it was just something we 'expected would happen'. We didn't avoid making a family to find that perfect time, or look for a moment that it would fit perfectly into our careers, but maybe that's what happened. We didn't plan or decide. We just lived and experienced life without a major plan or agenda. However it happened, nearing our late thirties, we decided to grow up. We got married after over twenty years as a couple, and finally became parents – not necessarily in that order. All through that time, we had friends who had kids as part of their life plan, those who became parents as a shock and surprise, those who would be wonderful parents but couldn't, and those who would be wonderful parents but chose not to. Families of different origin and experience – marriages, pregnancies, divorces, etc. That's life, and that's people. I hadn't ever thought there was a perfect way to become a family, and I definitely don't think there is now. All I know is our situation: we got pregnant, we were ready (sort of), we were happy (absolutely), and we knew we didn't want to replicate the exact arrangement that our parents and many others had put in place when organising our new life with a child. We knew things would change, and we knew we were old enough and happy enough to deal with and cope with these changes. Shared Parental Leave was just around the corner.

A lot of personal reasons brought us to this loveliest of lovely compromises. To put it into context: my wife is self-employed and earns more than my secondary school teacher salary. In financial terms, this makes me a 'trailer' – a delightfully negative term that I've become immensely proud of, as she is absolutely amazing at her job and deserves every penny she gets. Plus, her financial acumen, talent and patience allowed me to train as teacher – a seventeen-year career in a profession I adore. I'm a lucky hubby. That leads me to the geriatric part; we're both over forty, and had our first child when we were thirty-nine – medically defined as geriatric parents to those in the know. So, with these labels trailing behind me, why did we decide to become one of the 1% who take Shared Parental Leave?

The financial situation made it possible for us to take the hit on my salary and still manage. Meaning we could share the childcare in that first year and also maintain my wife's business. It was definitely a big decision to make, and I'll repeat myself by saying that finance will definitely be a big deciding factor in any choices you make regarding SPL. However, behind all these numbers come some properly serious conversations between you and your partner. Do you want to do this? What will it mean for your jobs? What will be the pros for both of you? How will you feel to take a break from your work? How will you feel as a man taking on the stereotypical role of stay-at-home parent? (Even if it isn't for more than a couple of months). Lots of questions and thoughts to consider. All scary and big to answer. In short, we had been together for twenty years and knew what drives us personally and professionally. Shared Parental Leave would suit us. The chance to change my life from the 7 a.m. to 7 p.m. term-time teacher schedule to trying something utterly new was too tempting. It's hard to discuss this in terms that don't sound patronising or condescending to my partner, and all women who have chosen to take breaks from work to have kids and look after them. However, the truth is, I was happy to share the workload, and I was happy that my wife didn't have to choose between pursuing what drives her professionally and having kids. I was glad that we both would be around on a daily basis to see my little daughter grow up. Ultimately, I was comfortable in making the choice to take a break in my career and take advantage of what I could only see as an opportunity. A chance not to be missed.

A massive caveat should be placed here – the bar for expectations regarding fathers is low, very low. So this is not revolutionary or exceptional or even more than should be done. All fathers should be part of the childcare process – depending on finances, etc. – and we should take advantage of any chance to be part of our children's lives, and sometimes that might mean going against the views of all those around you who still think it's a woman's role to look after the children. In addition, the gender pay gap lurks behind it all, with some women earning less than a man in similar roles, and the structures of employment support that disparity. Add to this our own gender expectations, and it is definitely a challenge for society to overcome. Maybe the changes enforced by various lockdowns in 2020 will speed up this change.

So now came the crunch: we'd made the decision, we'd organised our egos, and were ready to begin a new chapter. Firstly, the reaction from friends, family and colleagues was predominantly a positive, but perplexed one. The novelty of our decision was replaced by questions and mostly acceptance of how our relationship worked as a couple, and how SPL just fitted who we were. Colleagues at work and wider family tended to flit between supportive noises of goodwill, and awkward questions. They just didn't have a frame of reference beyond maternity leave for a woman – the career break – and the two-week stint as a dad before heading back to the 9 to 5. When I'm feeling generous, I just think it's about doing something different that needs a bit of a conversation to make everyone get it. When I'm not so patient, I get annoyed about how embedded the gender roles are surrounding parenting amongst some of the most liberal and supposedly intelligent adults. Scratch the surface and the 1950s nuclear family model still exists – or at least the memory of it. Interestingly enough, quite a few male colleagues admitted that they wish the legislation was around before 2015, as they would have loved to have had this time with their now-teenage children. Rose-tinted glasses from those in a soon-to-be empty nest, maybe, but I do think there is a real appeal to some men to try this way of parenting. Sharing the load in a more in-depth and hands-on way.

Only one male colleague actively snarked about who the 'breadwinner' was in our relationship. I retorted 'My wife!', but I don't think he got it. Expectations about what we were doing seemed to override the why, or even the how. The actual process of SPL is pretty normal. My wife went through the same pregnancy symptoms as other mothers, and we had the same midnight trawl to hospital to welcome our daughter into the world, as many others. You choose a date that you want the parental leave to start – based on due date etc., just the same. You say goodbye to work colleagues and get ready for your new arrival. I guess that is where it all changes.

Fathers who take Shared Parental Leave still get two weeks' paternity leave, which you can start as and when you like in that first year. But other than that, you have the exact amount of Shared Parental Leave you want. Take it all in one go – nine months from birth onwards, or break it into chunks/ shared with your partner. You make the practical decisions about when you or your partner want to return to work. This is all part of your planning and should give you a bit of structure around which the rest of the chaos fits. My wife was self-employed, so her return to work was purely based on how she felt physically after the birth. She could choose as and when she was ready to return, much to the shock and surprise of many other mothers. It was an interesting experience to find seemingly strong women who would claim to be feminist turning around and being critical of how soon another woman returned to their profession. Ironic, maybe. Outdated, definitely. The 1950s parental attitude was never far away.

Ask yourself this: In a world of emails and smartphones, how much of your job can be done remotely, and would that allow for a more shared parenting experience? It did for us. The last year (at the time of writing), and lockdown, has challenged this even further. I chose to step away from full-time employment because it relied on my presence in a classroom and school building. Other jobs are not so narrow in scope. The lockdown experience we've all shared proves that it can be done. Presenteeism is not necessary. Options are definitely out there. So here's hoping that more employers and industries explore this flexible working as we create our new normal.

Looking back at the start of my SPL, the months that followed were a blurry wondrousness. Hard work, sleep-deprived, world-overturning, but wondrous. We took turns with the childcare, as the pressure to return to work was postponed. The hectic and chaotic learning process of being Mum and Dad was ours and shared and felt like this was the plan for the rest of our lives. We organised our weeks – who was where when – and more often than not, we could be a three. Much more than we expected, and absolutely the main reason for recommending that other parents take SPL. Shared Parental Leave allowed my wife to return to her work and keep her business going. It gave me time away from the long hours of a teacher – something I didn't miss as much as I thought I would. I love teaching, and missed the buzz and constant interaction with students teaching a subject I enjoy. But now that time was given to something else – my daughter. It was a definite change of pace, and not without an adjustment period, but I loved it. The pace of parental days is different to working days, and I enjoyed that. We shared a unique few months that we will never get back, and I got to be a fully functioning part of it – not a babysitter, not just a tired participant rushing home for bedtime, but a full-on morning until bedtime parent. Not a choice for everyone, but a choice I will never regret. So why is it still seen as a novelty?

The reality is that I think that all aspects of the parenting industry don't attempt to confront stereotypical expectations placed on mothers, and they don't really consider the fathers as anything other than a bit-part player. From advertising, branding and product development, things we buy as parents are gender-specific and directly aimed at women being at home and men being at work. Money is made creating a need for mothers to purchase products or services, and fathers aren't the target market. Each family should make their own choices, and who am I to suggest otherwise, but in practical terms, after birth, much of the day-to-day looking after of the child can be carried out by both parents. The burden and joy should and could be shared. Typically, it isn't always, and the lack of uptake for SPL demonstrates this. In the short- and long-term, this creates an imbalance, in attitude, in psychology, in expectation. The assumption is that Mum will do it all, and it becomes a self-fulfilling prophecy for all involved. Feeding, sleeping, bathing, cuddling and comforting, can all be done by the dad too. What's the barrier? I'm not going to address the breastfeeding vs formula debate, because it's your choice, not mine. As a dad you are the ally to your partner – the mum – the biggest and best support they can have, and they choose what they want to do with their bodies from start to finish. All I will say is this: a man or a woman can hold a baby bottle to a hungry baby's mouth, and why does one of the parents have to be forced to spend all day physically tied to a space and time at the demands of the newborn? It seems so unnecessary after the first few weeks of nutrient-rich breast milk. I'm not some crazy anti-breastfeeder, but I'm sure we can find a way to help both parents be involved and neither one having to feel the pressure to be 'the parent' above and beyond the other. You will find your own way to do what feels comfortable, and this will and should adapt over time. We learned as we went along. You will make your own choices, but both parents can wake up in the middle of the night to sooth a hungry child. For example, any disturbance from Tiny before 4 a.m. was mine, anything after was her mum's – practical, stupid, arbitrary, but liberating.

It also led to a total reframing of what we wanted to achieve as parents and as career-minded adults. SPL made me face the reality of full-time work, and I found that what I missed in the passion and engagement of teaching in a secondary school was replaced with a different arrangement. I stopped full-time, tried part-time teaching, tried facilitation as a freelancer, set up my own business as The London Bookman (a job I could fulfil during nap times and with my pram, travelling around bookshops). We looked at what could fit with childcare, both financially and for our own sense of worth and well-being. SPL broke the routine of my full-time employment, and opened up the possibility of flexible working with a variety of different hats. A few years later, and with a second child in the mix, I am still running The London Bookman and balancing self-employment with childcare, and supporting my wife and kids to have a balanced and quite time-precious existence. We see a lot of each other – more so during the lockdown – and we are still 'sharing' the work of caring for our children and working at our careers. A curious phenomenon occurred when the first lockdown came, in that our lives didn't radically change as we both worked from home and both shared looking after our children. This last year has been horrific because of the many difficulties people have suffered, and the horror of the human cost it has caused, but the challenge to traditional employment standards and the model of full-time office work must be a good outcome.

Underlying everything I have experienced about Shared Parental Leave is that gender roles have to be tackled. The cliché of a man heading off to work each morning and leaving his wife and newborn at home may have to change. It is absolutely why Shared Parental Leave is important. After all, why should it always be the woman at home, and the man returning to work after a cursory two weeks of 'helping out'? I'm not renowned for my feminism, but I never understood how much we accept about gender roles and stereotypes until we had our first kid. Who do doctors, midwives and health workers direct their questions to about the welfare of our child? Who do family and friends direct questions to about day-to-day baby routines? It almost becomes an expectation that the father is a secondary player to parenting. (On another day, I'll write about the awful gender stereotyping of children's clothes, but I'll need a few more pages).

There is a strange set of expectations around the role of both men and women in parenting, but for women the expectation and support is both all-pervasive and overwhelming. For men, it is a strange acceptance of the role of support worker. We don't even speak about taking part in that first few months of having a child. It's not a consideration when applying for a job – how many women are informally overlooked for jobs or promotions because they are of a certain age? Parental leave for the father is not part of the HR set-up for most businesses. And we don't talk about it. What are the expectations for men as parents, and do we recreate exactly the nuclear family gender behaviour that went before? It's not that it is idyllic for women to take on 100% of the maternity time. The constant refrain I heard at the mother and baby groups was how the little one would only settle with the mum, not his daddy. 'How do you do it? My little one just won't settle with Daddy.' Bear in mind, this is said with the beatific look of a burning martyr, and not a sense of irony. The pressure on women to live up to this expectation is ridiculous and all-encompassing; from birth onwards, a woman is supposed to live up to the pressures of being 'mother'. But what about 'father'? Can the father be seen as part of this equation? Should they push to take on more and relieve that pressure to be in absolute control that is placed on mums? I am absolutely the clumsiest, most impractical man you are likely to meet. But in those first few months, when you change over thirteen or fifteen nappies a day – they don't tell you that in the baby books! – I got better. I managed to avoid dropping my child (regularly), and we've worked on not knocking her over when she was toddling and used to following right behind me. Now, we have a four-year-old attending reception and a two-year-old son to add to the mix – so the battle is ongoing. We have tried to share everything. Bedtimes, feeding, bathing, dressing, playing – everything. Not because we are some New Age pioneers of parenting, but because we wanted to. We wanted to have our cake and eat it. We wanted to share our professional needs as a family with our personal needs as a family. We looked at the practicalities of our lives and decided to share what is a wonderful time in a parent and child's life. We are very lucky, but we work at it constantly.

It isn't easy. Compromise is key. My life as a full-time teacher changed radically, but we've made it work. Strangely enough, the attitudes of those around us have been the most depressing aspect of it all. The remark, 'Oh, you're heading back to work so soon?' has never been so loaded, especially when it is one woman questioning another woman's motives. Beyond that, the idea of a father looking after a child is always diminished. A man taking Parental Leave is 'playing' or 'skiving', not caring or looking after. And yes, this was said to me, without irony, on more than one occasion by mothers and grandmothers of varying ages. I understand it is a novelty, but would you say that about a woman looking after their child? I'm not a martyr to my child, but I attempt to look after my daughter and son in the same way as my wife would. Food, drink, nappy changes, play and sleep. Does being a man mean that I obviously sit back, crack open a beer, whilst my unchanged baby and I watch *The Walking Dead* on TV? It's a complex set of value judgements placed on men and women looking after a child, but we're not making it easy for fathers to step up, or mothers to share this important role. You don't have to scratch very deep to find some very old-fashioned views hidden below the liberal psychobabble of a modern parenting discussion.

Very simply, if you're having a baby or adopting a child, you and your partner can apply for Shared Parental Leave (SPL) and Statutory Shared Parental Pay (ShPP). Which means you can share up to fifty weeks of leave and up to thirty-seven weeks of pay between you both. It all has to start within the first year after your child is born or placed with your family, but you can use the SPL in chunks between work, or in one go, and stagger the pay – the choice is yours. So far, so straightforward. So what's stopping people? Just google SPL or visit the gov.uk website for information.

If this is something you're interested in, then the first thing you should do is check your employer's policy, or at least speak with the HR person. It might cause them a surprise – I was a delightful novelty for the HR Officer in my workplace, but they enjoyed the chance to talk through the policy with me and consider what the options were. I'd been a full-time teacher for over sixteen years, and was grateful to have someone explain the details and what was possible. This was one of the most important things to make this whole process possible, taking me from simply an idea of what might work, to some actual detail about payments, dates and logistics. We'll consider the why a bit later, but now just focus on the practicalities: finance, and how to go about SPL.

Financially, it was a no-brainer: my job was the lesser earning of the two, but arguably the more flexible. I was a teacher, I felt I had a solid CV behind me and had no doubt that my return to teaching would not be hindered by this career break. I knew my pension could be deferred. I knew that after working full-time since the early noughties, a change in my work patterns wouldn't be a negative – I quite looked forward to a different pattern to my days. It was all pretty convenient.

I know this is not always true for many couples, and typically, the gender gap in pay seems to be a large barrier for men taking up SPL. But my wife runs her own business, and that meant our choice for me to take the full leave was made. I was happy, she was happy, and my employer was great. I opened up the dialogue early, so my head teacher knew well in advance. The novelty of a male employee going through this process caused some excitement in HR, and all options were discussed professionally and without underlying pressures. You can take Shared Parental Leave in chunks, and they don't have to be equal for each parent, and at present, the father still gets two weeks of Paternity Leave as well, so use that as you will. The legislation is in place, the will and the desire are not. Since 2015, only 2% of those eligible to take SPL have actually taken up the offer – and that hasn't changed. Maybe we're not as liberal and broad-minded as we might think.

The physical recovery after pregnancy, the share of the childcare role, the financial implications, the emotional and psychological impact on the individual, all of these are important factors to consider. The choice of who and how you may take the SPL is tricky for most couples. The gender pay gap in the UK does tend to make it impractical for men to take large chunks of SPL as they statistically earn more. However, that's part of the reason to encourage other parents to take up this option. The traditional expectation that any female employee will at some stage take maternity leave, and the lack of any consideration that a male employee might, is at the root of the gender pay gap. If a few more parents switch around this convention, then maybe a more equitable approach to salaries will happen. Pipe dreams – maybe? But that's an underlying thought for the politics behind all this.

Don't get me wrong, it wasn't all easy. I definitely question whether I would have been so enthusiastically and stubbornly determined to do this in my twenties. I personally think my age and the confidence I feel from my achievements as a teacher, mean that I had less to prove in my career, and I felt more calm in making this change. However, I still had moments when I felt slightly less 'manly' because I wasn't earning, and sometimes the over-whelming sound of gender stereotypes drowned out my better self. These were passing and generally related to a lack of sleep or my insecurities about my quality as a dad. They didn't last long, and didn't stop the overall sense of well-being I felt from being part of my daughter and son's early lives. Not struggling to find the time, but just juggling a family life filled with chaos and fun like every other mum and dad who get to take this time away from work to be with their kids.

One last caveat: these are my opinions and I'm no expert in anything. However, I'm happy to be a proud father and husband who took fifty weeks of leave from his 7 to 7, five-day-a-week teaching role, to share the care of my baby daughter and then my baby son. It's my proudest career choice to date. More families should consider how they could do it, more employers should discuss this as an option for their teams, and more men and women should address a few old-fashioned gender stereotypes that they probably didn't think they had. Shared Parental Leave should be shared.

If you are considering Shared Parental Leave, here are some things to consider:

1. What is the SPL policy at your work? Find out and see whether it works for you financially.
2. Have the conversation with your partner. How do you both feel about sharing the load in such a different way from the traditional expectations?
3. How do you want to share it? Think about how you want to divide the time before you both want to return to work.
4. What are you both up for? Keep having chats about what you want day-to-day life to look like. How do you want to share and compromise to make this work?
5. Are you ready for the outside world? Prepare for some weird views from a lot of different sources – don't let it get under your skin.

Chapter 5:

A Journey to Gay Fatherhood:
Surrogacy – The Unimaginable, Manageable

Michael Johnson-Ellis

Elton John, Tom Daley, Ricky Martin, Nicole Kidman, Sarah Jessica Parker and Kim Kardashian have all created their families through surrogacy. Some think that surrogacy is just for the rich and famous but in actual fact our story demonstrates that this is not the case and that surrogacy can be accessible for all.

We're Michael and Wes – we're a married couple that live in Worcestershire, and like all the other men before us in this book, we're dads too. Our journey to fatherhood was a little different, and at times felt like a minefield, leaving us unsure what steps to take in our pursuit of fatherhood.

We've been together since June 2012 when we met at Birmingham Pride. We got engaged after six months because it just felt right, and we were married two years later – the year gay marriage was legalised in the UK. We gave our vows in front of our friends and family on 9th August 2014 in Shropshire, including Wes's daughter who at the time was almost ten years old. Wes and I are no strangers to straight relationships either as we've both previously been married to women. I got married when I was just twenty; I thought

56

I was in love, but I now know only too well that I was just trying to fit in, to conform, to not be made fun of. I'd cringe when I heard people talking about someone being gay; I feared it was me they were making fun of. It tormented me daily and had done so since I was about thirteen. Growing up in the eighties and nineties had its highs – nineties Dance and R'n'B was one of them – being a closeted teen wasn't.

Another coincidence to mine and Wes's relationship is that we both have one brother, who also happens to be gay. Our parents are otherwise known as the 'Gay Makers' to some of my friends. Either way, they have always been supportive of our situation since we came out.

I guess for some families it's hardly ideal, but this is us; this is who we are.

As a young child, family life with my parents was healthy, loving and fun for the majority of the time. I was born and raised in Wolverhampton – a really happy childhood, living on a regular mixed estate in a place called Wednesfield in the heart of Wolves. Life was pretty good minus the odd bit of bullying from the older crowd. They didn't get me – I think they got pissed off that I was hanging around the girls of their year group. My love of amateur dramatics was quite the magnet, clearly – who'd of known, eh? As a teen I swam; this was the main way I kept fit. I love water, love the ocean; I get lost in the motion and feel safe when I'm underwater, weirdly. Swimming was an escape for me. Throughout my childhood I always had a fascination with cars, and I'm desperate to get the kids their first Scalextric. Now at almost forty-two my obsession hasn't left me: I'm still a petrolhead, it's just become slightly more expensive.

As I got older, and into my late teenage years, the guilt of who I really was riddled through every part of me. I disliked who I wanted to be, which ultimately meant I had an unhealthy relationship with myself. This isn't uncommon. As we know, more men commit suicide than women in the UK, and it becomes even more heartbreaking when you factor in the LGBTQ community. Suicide is the second leading cause of death among young people aged ten to twenty-four[1]. LGB youth are almost five times as likely to have attempted suicide compared to heterosexual youth[2]. The issue within the trans community is even more of a concern. In a US study,

1 CDC, NCIPC. Web-based Injury Statistics Query and Reporting System (WISQARS) [online]. (2010) {2013 Aug. 1}. Available from: www.cdc.gov/ncipc/wisqars

2 CDC. (2016). Sexual Identity, Sex of Sexual Contacts, and Health-Risk Behaviours Among Students in Grades 9-12: Youth Risk Behaviour Surveillance. Atlanta, GA: U.S. Department of Health and Human Services

40% of transgender adults reported having made a suicide attempt. 92% of these individuals reported having attempted suicide before the age of twenty-five. Varying factors will play a role here. For me, I felt as if I would be disappointing those that love me, for not being true or honest. I also didn't know any gay men. TV and media in the eighties and nineties often mocked the gay community, which only added fuel to the fire. I completely empathise with teenage and young gay men as I understand only too well how fragile their mental health is.

When I came out to Emma, my now ex-wife, we had already been separated for around six months. It was her decision to leave me, based on a number of reasons, mainly personal to her. She was obviously upset and angry, and naturally she assumed I had been unfaithful in our marriage – which I hadn't. When I started writing this chapter I messaged Emma to ask if she minded me mentioning our life together. I haven't messaged her in years – we don't have a need to stay in touch – but we each know the other is there if needed. She has remarried too, and has children of her own. This was my message.

> **Me:** *Hello! Hope you're well? Ex-husband here, out of the blue message – I know … I wanted to check something with you.*
>
> **Emma:** *Hello, Michael. How are you? Yes, it is out of the blue, how can I help?*
>
> **Me:** *I've been asked to contribute to a book about fatherhood and my chapter talks about my surrogacy journey for Talulah and more recently our son, Duke. There's a paragraph about our marriage breakdown, and I use the name 'Emma'. I wanted to see if you objected. I talk about me coming out and then I move on to another stage of my life. I thought it only fair to ask.*
>
> **Emma:** *Well I don't mind as long as that is the only identifier. For me it wasn't a breakdown per se, rather than a series of realisations but I'll keep that for my book ☺. It's good to hear from you and it's lovely that you are sharing your story (no pics of me though please). (This bit made me laugh and I remembered her sense of humour, and her laugh.)*
>
> **Me:** *Yes, it's the only identifier. (That's held back for my other book. My Memoir!) There are no pics. ☺*
>
> **Emma:** *I feel that we found each other and in our relationship we gave each other the courage to discover who we both truly are. I will always be grateful for you and your family for that. It was really lovely to hear from you. I wish you and yours all the best xx*

I sent her a picture of my children and we exchanged a few more messages, just closing off our chat. It was nice, and she was right. We found each other at a time when we both needed it most.

I came out when I was twenty-two; I had a couple of serious boyfriends and then I met Wes when I was thirty-three. He was thirty-five. For him there was no 'outing' as such. There was no big shock, no cause for a massive announcement. Wes is a private person, so he didn't feel the need to please others, he simply wanted to continue living his truer life.

Wes was brought up in East Hull, living in pubs most of his life. He was destined to work in the hospitality industry, following his parents' love of all things catering, and he did. Who'd have thought years later he'd be playing a key role running the event of our lifetime, when London entertained the world in the summer of London 2012 – my favourite summer on record, not only the time we met but the moment the world saw what our country could showcase, showing all as a nation what we do best: culture, sport, and everything British. As a result of our chance meeting in back in June 2012, I later got to see some of the most memorable sporting events I think I'll ever witness, from the opening ceremony through to seeing many medals throughout Super Saturday, witnessing Jess Ennis take gold at the heptathlon, Greg Rutherford take the long jump and then minutes later Mo Farah take the gold in the men's 10,000 m – everyone celebrating Team GB at its finest. A moment to be alive.

So back to me and Wes. We're far from athletes but in my opinion we're our own heroes in the dad arena, and I've certainly learned everything I know from Wes. He's a superb dad to Katie, his daughter. Always putting her first, always fair but secretly and subtly using an invisible pedestal (just so she doesn't notice it and use it to her advantage!). I wasn't introduced to Katie until we'd been together for three months, as he wanted to protect her as much as he could as I was the first serious boyfriend he'd had – and would later become the only one he'd ever tell her about. In fact, one September afternoon, whilst being driven to her mum's, Katie, an astute seven-year-old, just asked her dad outright. 'Is Michael your boyfriend?' she said casually. Wes panicked, but thought this through – now was his moment. He could continue to lie, or hide – but chose to be true to his seven-year old's question. 'Yes, yes he is.' Silence followed, for what Wes said felt like minutes, but in fact was more like five seconds. 'Oh, OK, cool,' she said. And the matter was never discussed ever again. Wes had just 'come out' to his seven-year-old daughter; if only adults could behave with the same degree of respect, love, tolerance, innocence and acceptance.

Wes and I have two children together. Talulah was born in October 2016 and Duke was born in August 2019. We didn't adopt our children, despite what society assumes 'us gays' will do. As a same-sex family, you get a whole host of weird and personal questions thrown at you about how your family unit was created. When we tell people about our lengthy journey to fatherhood, and the intricacies of surrogacy, not to mention IVF and egg donation and generally the challenges faced to create our family, one of the first remarks is often, 'Well, why didn't you just adopt; there's tonnes of kids in care, and it's free!' As if our parenting options simply came down to the list price of a child, the cost of a life, the price tag of happiness. Sounds appalling, doesn't it, yet we hear it constantly. This rather crude and personal question cuts us deep. Yes, it may be free to adopt, but it's certainly not an easier journey to take. We know several same-sex and heterosexual families that have adopted and it was never smooth sailing. It can be a rollercoaster of emotions, several meetings of interrogation, prying questions and interviews and this is all before you've been matched to a child. I have so much respect for anyone who adopts a child; I think it's an incredible thing to do, it just wasn't our first choice in creating our family.

So, once we'd had the chat about wanting kids, the research into surrogacy began, and I took the lead. It became three long years of research – surrogacy is a complex form, and unless you know where to look for information it can be a maze of data, often frightening and off-putting.

In the UK we have something called 'The Surrogacy Arrangements Act 1985' – sounds dull, doesn't it? Thankfully, it's currently under reform as it's outdated and not fully reflective of modern families, the needs of intended parents (IPs) and surrogates. More and more couples are opting for surrogacy based on their fertility diagnosis or, like us, same-sex couples can now access surrogacy as a route to parenthood. Surprisingly, it was only in 2010 when the UK law changed, allowing same-sex couples to become the legal parents to children born via surrogacy, via a process called a parental order, which is obtained through the courts.

The Law Commission and Scottish Law Commission have released a proposal outlining a 'new law' which closed in October 2019 after a lengthy and highly engaged public consultation. We're proud to have played a part in these meetings and in October 2018 we were invited to the Houses of Parliament to give our account of life as two dads via UK surrogacy – adding our lived experience to what hopefully will help create a new law that is better equipped for UK surrogacy. It was around this time that we made the decision to blog about our fertility journey and life as a two-dad family. We set up www.TwoDadsUK.com and TwoDadsUK on Instagram and Facebook, documenting our life and our parenting but also as a reference place for UK surrogacy.

One of the issues with UK surrogacy which frustrates everyone is linked to the birth of your child. The thing is, when your child is born the surrogate is legally the child's mother, and here's the crazy shit – if she's married – her husband is also the legal father. Bear in mind, most surrogacy journeys in the UK are gestational or host surrogacy arrangements, which basically means the surrogate is not using her own eggs and only hosting the pregnancy – yet the law states she is the legal mother and her husband is the legal father. This issue often drives intended parents to the States, where IPs are recognised as the child's parents from birth, adding some protection and security – removing any risk.

In the UK, for an intended parent to become the legal parent of their biological child they must apply for a parental order, but this can't be done until the child is six weeks and one day old and before the child is six months old, as the surrogate has a right to withdraw her consent for the parental order (something which has been significantly reduced in the new proposal). Arguably, should consent even be there at all, given the intention of the surrogacy arrangement? This 'power' is in the surrogate's favour and makes intended parents very nervous.

Generally, the remainder of the current law is fairly workable but the changes are welcomed by all – it's now a question of how controversial the changes will be, and when the changes will be discussed in parliament, approved and implemented. It could be as late as 2023/4, which was the date discussed at the opening announcement of the Law Commissioners' proposal in June 2019.

Frustratingly, surrogacy can be made even more complex by the fact you're a gay couple as not all countries allow same-sex couples into their surrogacy programmes. You either have to lie, and make out you're married to a woman, which didn't feel right to us, despite some of the Indian clinics telling us, 'It's what everyone does, it will be fine…' Wes and I have a mantra, and it goes back to the day we met and how it felt during our whirlwind few months: 'It felt right,' so when it doesn't, we listen to it. As we began to explore each country, we were discovering challenges, if not for our sexual orientation it was the conditions the women/surrogates were 'kept' in. Some of the countries, in our opinion, were exploiting women, and this wasn't what we thought surrogacy was. Costs in some of the countries were low, and this was clearly the appeal to many. Some international surrogacy programmes were costing around $25,000 in India, for example, versus $120,000 in the US, where surrogacy is far more professional and closely regulated. Whilst our research continued, several countries were being investigated for their practices into commercial surrogacy. In 2015 commercial surrogacy was banned in India – so that was no longer an option (it wasn't for us anyway).

Thailand was always a popular choice for UK couples, cleverly marketed as a 'surrogacy destination' but short-lived. Commercial surrogacy was banned there in 2015 following two main cases which hit the headlines, the largest being the 'Baby Gammy' case where the intended parents returned to Australia following the birth of their twins with only their daughter. The other child was born with Down's Syndrome, and was left behind. This naturally caused the Thai government to restrict the commercial Thai surrogacy process, and international commercial surrogacy was banned. The only people that can complete surrogacy in Thailand are married heterosexual Thai couples.

We spoke to Mexican clinics, but we were underwhelmed by the lack of couples exiting with their children. We heard that some couples had to wait up to twelve weeks for a passport or travel document – the longest we spoke to took six months – again that didn't feel right to us either. I travelled to fertility conferences in Spain and met with agents from clinics all over the world, but this too just didn't feel right. I left feeling deflated and thinking I'd never become a dad, that my darker thoughts of my younger self were right. Was I chasing something that wasn't a viable option? I had two paths back in 2001 when I eventually came out – I could stay married, have kids but not live to enjoy them, as the demons of my true sexuality consumed me. Or trade – be honest with everyone, be the real me, live my true life with a man, but understand that I may never become a dad (as I never knew any gay dads) – but I'd be happy. That was exactly how I played it over and over in my head, weekly actually – it tormented me. I almost felt like my sexual orientation was 'owning me'. That was the hold it had. It was making me infertile, which I know sounds dramatic. It was a curse and a blessing to be this happy and comfortable now. Watching friends settle down, meet partners and go on to make a family was wonderful to see, but weirdly sad. It was a painful reminder that being a gay man, and wanting children was, and would be, a challenge to achieve. That much, I was certain.

Once I was back in the UK following the fertility conference in Spain, Wes and I spoke about what we had discovered over the last year and we realistically weighed our options. We couldn't afford the US route, which felt the safer route – we just didn't have £100K sitting in the bank. We had just planned a wedding and had bought our first home together which was being built, so funds were tight. The Canadian option too was out of reach financially – and we also struggled to find enough about it. We knew it was an altruistic model, which means it's not commercial like the US; surrogates are reimbursed expenses for their services and are not 'paid', which we liked. It almost felt like the surrogates donated their uterus, and didn't profit from the journey. The commercial models for us at that time never really sat well – this is purely our opinion and I understand why couples opt for this route of parenthood. One by one the other countries were no longer for us.

We were like rabbits caught in the headlights in the beginning, and we didn't see the differences between commercial surrogacy and altruistic surrogacy. We were merely looking at surrogacy as an international venture as we knew little about what the UK offered. In fact, like most people, we thought it was illegal – but, as we've explained, it isn't. I felt we'd been thorough, we'd spent a year researching international options, talking to agents in Thailand, Nepal, India, Canada, America, Mexico, Northern Cyprus, and Ukraine. None of these options were working for us, they didn't suit our situation and I wasn't prepared to lie or hide my sexuality – I'd done enough of that. So we decided to explore the UK to build our family through UK surrogacy.

But back then, we had a tonne of unanswered questions – is it legal? What does it cost? How do you find a surrogate? How do you get them pregnant? Home inseminations or IVF? Whose sperm would we use? How do you choose an egg donor – the list goes on.

We always had a vision when creating our family that we'd be present at the conception (which may seem odd to most of you!). We wanted to witness the embryo transfer, witness the positive pregnancy test in real time and be at every hospital scan and appointment. Watch our baby grow and feel them kick, let them hear our voices and see the birth of our children. How very heteronormative of us! The more and more we thought about it, the UK was the only option that ticked these boxes.

We began scouring the Internet for UK surrogacy and wanted to see if there were any agencies or any bodies of advice that could support us. We found a number of not-for-profit resources, the main ones being: Surrogacy UK, Brilliant Beginnings and COTS. We contacted all of them to understand their registration criteria, costs and details of what services they offer. Surrogacy UK and Brilliant Beginnings seemed better equipped to deal with us as a same-sex couple – however both organisations weren't at that time (2014) accepting new intended parent registrations due a shortage of surrogates. We began talking more with Surrogacy UK and got to understand how they support the surrogacy community and we liked their ethos, which is

'Surrogacy through Friendship'. Whilst we couldn't register, we loved their approach and decided to embark on an 'independent journey', but using the principles and the guidance that the not-for-profits suggest. Such as:

1. Taking the time get to know your surrogate. Don't rush into an arrangement as this is where the horror stories of surrogates and intended parents make the headlines.
2. Get legal advice (most clinics insist on this).
3. Produce an Intention Document with your surrogate once the expenses have been agreed (whilst not legally binding, many clinics ask for this before treatment can begin, as do the courts for your parental order).
4. Background checks on surrogates and IPs (DBS – Police Checks).
5. Health screening (full bloods – usually carried out by the clinic where the IVF takes place, for traditional surrogacy arrangements, and full sexual health tests for home inseminations).
6. Implications counselling for all parties (standard and free in a clinic environment).

Whilst all this is fabulous, when you're not using services of the likes of Surrogacy UK or Brilliant Beginnings to help you connect to surrogates, where do you meet these mysterious, selfless women? Is there a magical place they all hang out spreading love and positivity, whilst offering to donate their uterus to childless couples desperate for a family? The problem is that the law states it is illegal to advertise for a surrogate, so you have to know where to network and build these relationships.

What astonished me back in 2014 was the sheer scale of UK surrogacy, and the massive community that existed completely out of sight of the general public. There are forums, closed Facebook groups, hidden Facebook groups and surrogate networking sites – all useful in their own unique way. On the whole, it's a supportive community, made up of surrogates and intended parents on the journey or who have completed it. The wealth of information and friends I built as a result of these groups helped me understand the do's and don'ts of surrogacy. So, in the winter of 2014, we were officially looking for a UK-based surrogate, and I had begun playing an active role in around eight surrogacy forums online, as well as building an intended parent profile on another site. In the Spring of 2015, I was contacted by a first-time surrogate based in Lancashire. Her name was Caroline. She was the same age as me, had four children of her own and was married. Her husband fully supported her wishes to be a surrogate, and we immediately hit it off on email, with several exchanges. It felt exciting, but I felt like I was cheating on my husband as I didn't tell him she'd messaged us; I didn't want to get his hopes up. After a few more emails discussing our timeline for a child and our preferences for our pregnancy (gestational surrogacy, not traditional), I felt we were on the same page and moving in the right direction – it felt right.

I shared all the emails with Wes and we agreed to meet up with Caroline and her husband. When the time came, the meeting felt so relaxed. Although we were nervous, it felt like we had always known her, which I know sounds dramatic but that's how we felt. Over the next few months, we met every few weeks. We drove to them and they came to us until the time came to introduce their kids to Wes's daughter. After all, surrogates' husbands and their children play vital roles in surrogacy and it was so important to us that we all clicked – and thankfully we did. After four months, we considered ourselves 'matched' and the quest to find an egg donor now began.

Finding a UK clinic was easier than we thought. For us, choosing a clinic close to our surrogate was important as the tests she would endure in the early stages were plentiful. So, we found a clinic that had experience of same-sex surrogacy based in Manchester, and again we really gelled with the team and we began being educated on fertility treatment, the success rates and what to expect. The clinic also had a decent egg donation programme so our requirements were discussed. It was always going to be my sperm being donated for the treatment as this is what we agreed as Wes already had a biological child. Therefore, it was important to us that if Wes and I could have children naturally, the egg would need to reflect his physical characteristics. I'm classed as a brown/brown donor: I have dark brown hair, brown eyes and olive skin – therefore I can produce blue and brown-eyed children (and everything in-between). Wes is classed as blue/blonde – fair skin, blue eyes and dark blonde hair – his genetics could only produce blue-eyed children; therefore, my genes are the more dominant. Having a child that resembled Wes's features was important – on many levels, not least bonding. So, after six months of searching, the clinic called us one September morning telling us we had a donor match. Shit was about to get real.

Egg donation in the UK is classed as non-anonymous, which means you only get non-identifiable data about the donor, and when the child is sixteen, they receive information about the donor if they wish to seek it. Then at eighteen they can get full disclosure of the donor if they want to. In the meantime, my sperm had been tested, re-tested, bloods taken, taken again, and taken again. In late Jan 2016, we were now ready for our surrogate to begin her hormone injections to ensure her menstrual cycle synced with our donor. The eggs were retrieved, and we only got five which is low, but we were always assured her eggs were excellent quality. I donated my sperm, and the eggs were cultured in the lab.

Those that have endured fertility treatment will know only too well how nerve-racking the calls are. You are called on Day One (the following day after fertilisation) and you're told how many eggs have fertilised. Most have 50% fertilised; we had all five. Our next call was the following day, and all eggs were still developing well, four of them showing normal cell division. On Day Three we had three strong embryos; the other two had taken a back seat and didn't look like they'd develop past Day Three, and they didn't. However, the other three all reached Day Five – a blastocyst. The best possible outcome, most likely to attach and become a foetus. Day Five fell on Valentine's weekend. We were ready to transfer our little Blast (we even have a video of this cell), later to become our daughter, splitting and dividing as if it was dancing with the most beautiful rhythm. The clinic opted for a fresh transfer rather than a frozen embryo transfer, which suited us and our surrogate's womb lining which had been chemically manipulated for the optimum implantation. Our surrogate was now being prepped in theatre for the transfer and we were by her side, as was her husband – just as we planned. This was a team effort.

What followed is known as the 2WW or the two-week wait, an agonising period where you are advised not take a pregnancy test, until day fifteen. The day after the transfer, Katie, Wes and I flew to France to go skiing for a week with members of my family. All I could think of was the test. Was Caroline OK? Was she resting? She kept in touch with us whilst we were away; she was having painful cramps and even some light spotting which terrified us, but we persevered. Then on day five post-transfer, we received a message. 'I've taken a test; I'm sorry I couldn't help it.' My reply was instant... 'Well?'

'You're going to be daddies!' the next text announced.

We cried.

The fourteen-day wait came, we tested and it remained positive. You're always nervous due to the risk of chemical pregnancies, common in IVF treatment. We advised the clinic of the test result, and we had our first scan a few weeks later. We were around six weeks pregnant. We saw our baby's heartbeat – it was incredible. I remember squeezing Wes' hand and Caroline's shoulder (as she was being scanned internally and I was at the head end!).

This moment of seeing my child had been played in my mind for most of my adult life. Wondering when would it happen, how would I feel. Well, it was finally happening, and it felt magical.

The time arrived where we'd tell our close family. We told my parents first. My mum is one of eleven kids, and my dad is one of nine. My mum was the only one missing grandchildren and it pained her, I could see it. She had two gay sons, so I guess, like I did – she had written the chances off. She knew the journey we were on; she'd seen the struggle and knew how hard we'd been saving, and she remained hopeful, supporting us. Telling her and showing her our clinic ten-week scan felt incredible, again another announcement I never thought I'd make. One I'd seen countless friends and cousins make, the Facebook posts, the well wishes – I'd seen and read them all – just never thought I'd be writing them myself. Mum was beyond excited. She cried, we cried, and we hugged. I knew then I had given my mum a purpose to fight harder against her crippling COPD.

The twelve-week scan arrived – this was our first taste of the NHS. Seeing the looks and the stares when three men all stood to accompany Caroline to be scanned was priceless. The look of confusion, and the desire for them to ask about our situation could almost be heard from inside their heads. The hospital was well briefed and well prepared for our appointment. We were given standard policy protocol; at this time this NHS trust hadn't had a positive surrogacy experience and it was evident in their lack of policy and lack of understanding of what surrogacy actually looks like. The needs of Caroline and us as parents were totally overlooked – and this felt disappointing. The consultant came across as inflexible and inexperienced with these types of pregnancies. We felt like freaks, like we were doing something wrong. The hospital's policy didn't support us; it was inflexible and unfair – and, more crucially, discriminating against us.

This moment in my head was meant to be joyous. It should have been exciting, the moment we announced to the world we'd had our twelve-week scan; yet we came away deflated, unsupported and concerned. We called Bev Jones, the lawyer we had taken initial advice from, and we told her what the trust had said about our treatment plan, and the care of our pregnancy. More importantly, we told her about the plans for the birth, which we couldn't be present at as we're not legally the parents. Bev wrote to the trust and issued an Intention to Sue on several counts of discrimination under the Equality Act. Several emails and letters later, we were assigned a new female consultant to look after our care, and a birthing plan equal to a heterosexual regular pregnancy. We just wanted to be in the room when our child was born, and meet them together. We understood that hospital policy wouldn't allow us both into theatre as Caroline was having an elective C-section, so we wanted her husband with her as this was more important. Wes and I decided that if only one of us could see our child being born, then neither of us would.

The pregnancy continued smoothly. We attended all appointments and scans, we saw our baby kick and wave on the numerous scans, and even managed one of those weird 4D scans too. The time had come to decorate the nursery, and before we knew it the bag was packed and in the boot of the car. Our baby was being born at thirty-nine weeks, so the date was set for 19th October. However, at 3 a.m. on 16th October Wes's phone rang and it was Caroline's husband: 'Her waters have broken; get yourselves to Burnley Women's ASAP.'

We darted out of bed, changed and called Wes's dad. Katie had had a sleepover so had friends staying over, so we couldn't just leave. Wes's dad arrived and we made the 120 mile journey north. All along the route we were getting calls updating us. Finally, we arrived at 5:15 a.m. We dashed upstairs and were greeted by a well-briefed team. Wes and I had our own side room; we were delighted. We saw Caroline just as she was being prepped for theatre, gave her a kiss and then we went to unpack. Her husband followed her into theatre, scrubs on and looking apprehensive – this was his wife having major surgery all for us. The next time we'd see him was when he'd be bringing our baby into us.

At 5:50 a.m. there was a knock on our door – he was there, but no baby. 'Is everything OK?' I asked.

'Get some scrubs on, they're letting you see your baby being born – hurry!'

I've never undressed and dressed so quickly. We dashed into theatre and the first incision was being made. After what felt like a couple of minutes, we heard a cry. We looked over and this beautiful baby was wriggling their way out of the neat cut on Caroline's abdomen. 'Congratulations,' our consultant said, 'you've got a little girl!' Tears were streaming, a girl – my first thought was my mum. She'd always wanted a girl and I know secretly she wanted a granddaughter. Our baby was beautiful, weighing in at 8 lb, born at 6 a.m. on the dot, our Talulah. She was perfect.

After all the checks were carried out, we walked out of theatre and into our room, where we had skin-on-skin contact and were both in awe of this gorgeous little human – our daughter; we were a new family.

I called my mum first – no one knew we were at the hospital as it was too early to call, so I called them at around 6:30 a.m. and told her the news.

'Really – it's a girl? Promise me… swear on my life,' she said. I then heard a cry, a sound from my mum that I'd never heard before. She'd been waiting for this moment. She needed this, more than we knew. That's the thing with infertility: whatever guise or shape it comes in, it affects family life in so many different ways. My mum had almost grieved for the grandchildren she thought she'd never get.

That moment will stay with me forever.

We were discharged after five hours. After some time with Caroline, we got our bags together and left. Unlike the original plan, there was no 'handover' of our child in the car park. We left the maternity ward like any other new parent – car seat, hand in hand and a balloon. Sadly, however, many intended parents are unable to challenge the NHS like we did; some just accept the conditions, as they've longed for a baby for such a long time. Some have even missed the birth of their child, or are told that the baby must be given to its parents off hospital premises, often in car parks. This is something we're determined to change, and have already made progress. The car journey home was eventful – I basically couldn't stop bloody crying, I don't know what came over me, I was a complete mess!

The next few weeks passed quickly, but I think that was best for us. I remember the sleep deprivation was intense and something I was not prepared for. We were new parents, for many the first time they'd seen two men with a baby – so we raised a few eyebrows and the questions began. In fact, we now know the questions never actually stop.

'You giving Mum a rest?'
'Surrogacy – is that like buying a baby?'
'Whose sperm did you use, then?'
'Who's the dad?'
'Who's the REAL dad?'
'How much did she cost?'
'Will you raise her gay?'
'Why didn't you adopt?'
'Children need a mother!'
'Did you feel bad, taking her from the mother?'
'Who does the mum jobs?'

All the above actually happened – some more than once. It seems people are obsessed with our sperm – and love to talk about it. In the most random of places. We've even been asked it in a supermarket – by a stranger!

The 'Giving Mum a rest?' is one of hardest questions. I find myself often lying as I'm having to 'come out' to strangers at least on a monthly basis, in crowded lifts, at the tills, a situation that I need to assess before I respond. So, most of the time I lie and say, 'Yes, yes I am.'

Our next milestone was looming, though – the parental order. This was to be submitted at six weeks and one day; we submitted exactly to the day.

We had decided to ask our lawyer to complete all the paperwork, which involves an application form to the family courts, which then triggers a CAFCASS inspection/meeting. Essentially, a safeguarding check, ensuring we're suitable parents and ensuring the welfare of the child is paramount. We met with the CAFCASS officer – her name was Emily. She was lovely, really supportive and interested in our journey to become parents. That's the thing, you see, this is a journey. Financially it's a journey – our first pregnancy cost us a total of £32,000. £12,000 of that covered our surrogate's expenses, the rest was treatment, eggs and legal costs. The planning, research and preparation that goes into a surrogacy journey requires commitment, and you could see Emily understood this. That's the thing – there are no accidental children born to homosexuals – these babies are always planned for, and always wanted.

We had our court hearing on 30th March – Wes and I went to the magistrate's court; my Mum was looking after Talulah. We arrived at court and it felt bare, the occasional person called to one of the many rooms. Our CAFCASS officer met us there and soon enough we were called through. There were four magistrates, I think, and someone taking notes. They looked confused as soon as we walked in. 'Shit!' I thought.

'Where's Talulah?' one of them asked – should we have brought her with us, did we miss that part of the form?

We explained she was at home, well cared for by her Nanny – turns out they had a teddy for her and a card. These courts often take children off parents and place them into care, so to grant a parental order for them is an occasion to celebrate. The hearing lasted ten minutes – they wanted to hear all about her, her likes, her personality – they made us feel human. And there it was: the legal document was drawn up – Talulah was legally our daughter on the 30th March 2017 – five months after being born. We now needed to apply for new birth certificates naming us as her parents.

In 2017 we established @TwoDads.U.K. The idea behind this was to help normalise families like ours and also raise more awareness about UK surrogacy – helping couples in the process. This very quickly became my new-found passion, and before I knew it I was advising others about the route to parenthood and even got to help influence new guidance for healthcare professionals when it came to the treatment of surrogates and intended parents, realised by the Department of Health and Social Care in February 2018.

It was always discussed with our surrogate that we wanted a sibling for Talulah, a pregnancy that Wes would help create this time. Caroline had offered to do a sibling journey for us, so when Talulah was nineteen months old, the cycle began. Though this time it wasn't a smooth run.

Firstly we had to find another donor as Talulah's donor suffered a medical condition which meant she couldn't donate again. This was a massive blow as it meant there wouldn't be the genetic thread to our family, however since having Talulah we've learned that it's not biology that truly makes a family. Wes's bond and love for Talulah is no different than his love for Katie. Just hearing Wes talk about Talulah you can see the admiration and love for her. Rewind back to the egg donor selection criteria, too. Talulah is blue/blonde (I'm still the odd one out) and strangely looks like Wes and Katie. In fact our neighbour often comments how she's 'Wes's double', which genuinely brings me joy as I believe this helps in the bonding process.

So, this time the criteria for the egg had changed, as we were now matching to me. We wanted a brown/brown donor. Again, after a few months one was found. Treatment began, and the gruelling hormones for Caroline had commenced. Eggs were retrieved and Wes went to Manchester to provide his sample. We had eight retrieved, five fertilised, and four of them were looking great, so we froze them and transferred one. It was strange because I knew instantly that it had failed – I just had a feeling, so at the 2WW it wasn't a surprise to us that we weren't pregnant. And worse than that – all our embryos, the precious cells we created, didn't make the freeze. Some unexplainable catastrophe – and just like that, all our hopes on this round of IVF were gone.

£11K vanished, and our surrogate was as devasted as we were. She felt responsible that she didn't keep the embryo where it needed to be. It hit us all hard.

A lesson learned from this unfortunate event was seeking donor eggs that have proven fertility with the clinic; in requesting this you have an idea of how the eggs perform in the lab, the quality and crucially if any previous donations have resulted in live births. We requested another cycle, but the egg wait was six months – and we just didn't have this. Our surrogate had a life to get back on track, and this was interfering. She was still a mother and a wife outside of all of this – and we had to respect that.

We did the unthinkable – we changed clinics. After a three-month break allowing our surrogate's body to remove the hormones and rest briefly, we started again. We removed the emotion and the attachment to the first clinic, and chose to work with the UK's leading clinic with the best statistics. They were in London, so unfortunately, it meant more travelling. Caroline was on board – so off we went. The matter of eggs was also dealt with differently. This time we had a known donor, a close friend named Fran, and fertility expert herself, who donated her eggs to us. She also matched our profile too: a brown/brown donor. She began her hormone treatment, which was a success, and led to her producing ten eggs, and seven fertilised by Wes. Excellent-graded embryos and blastocysts – it felt right again.

On 17th December 2018, we transferred one embryo, and froze the rest. We were present at the transfer again; we saw it being carefully implanted into our surrogate for safe keeping. The 2WW fell on 31st December 2018 – brilliant! This was either going to be a year to celebrate or one to quickly see the back of. Day Four she tested – negative. Our hearts sank. Not again, surely? She tested again on Day Five – a faint line, Day Six, a prominent line, Day Seven – we were pregnant! We were actually pregnant.

Again, the pregnancy progressed well with no major issues, although it was harder on Caroline and her family this time. We were all a little older, and I think she felt the strains of pregnancy more this time. All our scans came and went – the funny looks in the waiting room at the hospital hadn't changed. We also had the same consultant and midwife as our first pregnancy, which was a relief – and the care and treatment of us all was exceptional; first class, actually. One thing was different, though. Something I was more conscious of with this pregnancy. How was I going to feel in comparison to the love I have for Talulah, who is biologically mine? Would I feel the same? Would I love this baby just as much as I love Talulah? These thoughts intensified, and with about six weeks to go I was beginning to feel more anxious.

The time came to meet our baby. The section was booked for 20th August 2019, and we were first in theatre. We put on our scrubs, gorgeous peach-tone oversized garments – not the most attractive outfit I've ever worn. We sat in a waiting room with other dads-to-be, all looking like extras from Teletubbies with our peach blancmange-coloured garms.

Unlike the first pregnancy, this was still an elective C-section, but Caroline hadn't gone into labour. Every minute waiting to be called into surgery felt like an hour, the nerves were incredible, and the mood felt tense. This time around the hospital policy had been changed to allow intended parents in theatre along with the surrogate's partner too. Something born out of our first experience, and a proud moment for us all – a legacy.

More interestingly, this NHS trust had rewritten its policy and other trusts now look to them for guidance and advice when it comes to surrogacy pregnancies.

The theatre felt icy cold, and was lit in bright white lighting, ginormous dustbin lid-shaped lights framing the huge operating table. As we entered theatre number three (the same where Talulah was born) Caroline was all hooked up to the monitors. I'd forgotten the sheer volume of people involved in the procedure. I counted seven healthcare professionals all invited to wish our child Happy Birthday, but more importantly they were there to protect Caroline; all eyes were on her. Machines bleeped, Caroline's husband held her hand, our consultant, Miss Clarke, checked if Caroline was OK. Caroline confirmed with a smile she was good to go. Miss Clarke turned to us and simply smiled and said, 'You ready to meet him?' We had non-invasive genetic testing carried out at ten weeks' gestation, which also told us the sex of the baby, so we always knew we were having a boy. But hearing Miss Clarke say it hit us hard. Here he was. Here comes our son. Duke was born at 9:16 a.m. weighing 7 lb 4.5 oz, screaming and healthy. Our boy. I instantly melted as I saw his squashed, grumpy-looking face – he wasn't happy he'd been evicted; he was cold and screaming. He was healthy, and we were blessed once more. Happy tears fell. I kissed him, then kissed Caroline – thanking her for everything she'd done, everything she'd been through to complete our family.

There was no doubt that I fell in love with him. I felt a similar force when I held him for the first time in our side room on the delivery ward as he lay on my warm, naked chest, sleeping – with his signature pout.

The weeks that followed were challenging, to say the least. We quickly discovered Duke wasn't much of a sleeper, and he also had milk protein, wheat, rice and oat allergies – which was a new experience for us. And one that would test us and our marriage. I was the primary carer for Duke as I'd taken time out of work, and I also wanted the time to bond, just in case I struggled. Which I did, and I'm not ashamed to admit it.

This feeling I had wasn't because I didn't love him, because I did. I was simply exhausted; sleep deprivation plays the evilest of torturous games with our thoughts and our mental health. I felt inadequate and put this down to the fact I wasn't Duke's 'real dad'. I snapped at everyone around me, I resented anyone that had more than three hours' sleep a day, in fact I resented everyone that slept. Period.

After around six long months, I cracked. I felt done, I felt invisible. Invisible as his dad and invisible to my husband. I didn't like myself much but we had to talk. I poured it all out. Wes was amazing. We cried, we talked, we cried some more. Wes shared how he had moments of darkness with his own parenting journey with Talulah; most of this was new information to me. He referred to something which triggered his own low mood, or depression. It was the use of other people's innocent words. To him they cut deep. I knew exactly what he meant. Even hearing people tell Wes how much Duke looked like him made me feel less of a dad, a fraud almost. And he experienced that too with Talulah, which weirdly comforted me. At around the same time, Duke's sleep pattern steadily improved, and the night feeds began to ease. After seven months I was back in my own bedroom, my own bed! This was bliss. Sixteen months on, there are still challenges with Duke's allergies, but it's manageable. My marriage is stronger as a result.

Looking back, in 2014 when I was fresher-faced and had a tiny bit more hair, our research into UK surrogacy began. Like most, we struggled to find even basic reliable information on gay surrogacy which tackled the needs of intended fathers. Our journey to fatherhood wasn't very straightforward, and neither is the emotional support, but here we are. We survived it and came out stronger, and our babies are none the wiser. A journey spanning several years of planning, invested time, money, research and commitment to building and creating our family through surrogacy. What felt impossible, was absolutely possible. Two healthy babies, a new set of forever friends, our surrogate and her family in our lives, always. Like many gay men, we just weren't able to find the information we needed in order to create a family through surrogacy, and no one was solely fighting our corner, no one understood the challenges. Which is now why we've dedicated our work to supporting other intended fathers on their pursuit of parenthood via @TwoDads.UK. We've built emotional support packages for non-biological parents and we're working with accredited fertility counsellors to implement this unique and much-needed counselling to a community of intended parents. We've even launched a new not-for-profit organisation called My Surrogacy Journey, with the aim to change the landscape of surrogacy, through greater enhanced emotional support. We strive to make change with the Surrogacy Law Reform and continue to educate healthcare professionals all about UK surrogacy whilst ensuring the NHS amends and updates policy to protect the rights of IPs and surrogates.

So, as I finish this last paragraph, my final message to you is this: We all matter, we all play a role, or a part in brightening someone's day. Words also have such a crucial role to play. Celebrate the smallest of wins, and learn from the losses. A good friend of mine sent me text a few days ago, after I reached out to check in on them, and this is what they wrote, which I later learned was a Nelson Mandela quote. I love it and I hope you do too.

'If you talk to a man in a language he understands, that goes to his head. If you talk to him in his language, that goes to his heart.'

Chapter 6:

Widowed at Forty:
Raising Young Children, While Dealing with the Death of My Wife

Alec Grant

Introduction

Up until going through my own experience of being widowed, if anyone had asked me what image came to mind when I heard the word widow or widower, it certainly wouldn't ever have been a 40-year-old man. Plus, it definitely wouldn't have been one with a newborn baby and a three-year-old child to look after. But that is exactly what happened to me. A story that I would never have hoped to be living or retelling. Yet here I am, eight years later, having learned to adjust to the hand that I've been dealt and embracing all the challenges that have come with it.

From dealing with the immediate emotional and psychological trauma of the death of my wife Hazel, to the everyday challenges of the life of an only parent. There have been many ups and downs over these last eight years. In the first few years there were mostly downs. Or, at least, it felt like it at the time, because it was too hard to see the wood for the trees. It's safe to say that the balance has now swayed and although a dark cloud occasionally pops up, our life is definitely moving forward in the best way possible.

So the following is a brief insight into my life and the challenges of being a widower and an only-parent dad. This account is by no means meant to be comprehensive as it would be hard to capture the magnitude of challenges that we have faced in a single chapter of this book. But I hope that my personal view will both inspire others going through a similar experience or other challenging time of their lives; as well as give a greater understanding to those on the outside looking in.

Background

I guess it makes sense to tell you a little bit about myself before getting into things. I hope that it will provide some insight into who I am now and why I have been able to make some of the decisions that you will read about. Hopefully, it will show you why for some reason I have been resilient and why I embrace the path that has been dealt to me. Even though there will be others that have gone through similar challenges both in childhood and/or as an adult, my experiences are unique to me. Not only that, but I can see that despite what I've been through, I have decided consciously or otherwise to view my experiences in a particular way. To use the challenges to empower myself to do better, be better and become better. I was going to say that I don't know where that desire for self-improvement comes from; but I feel that in part it comes from my grandmother who you'll read more about soon enough. I've also in the last year or so come to realise something about myself that I previously didn't have a label for. In the past twelve months, I've discovered stoicism, or rather, I've spent time looking into it and understanding what it's about. It soon became clear that a number of stoic principles really resonate with me on a deep level. I certainly don't know where it comes from but it has enabled me to find strength when I didn't think it was possible. When we use the word stoic to describe someone, the context is often related to a person being unemotional and never showing weakness. But as I've read up about Seneca, Marcus Aurelius and Cato and others, it's become clear that; it isn't that they weren't emotional or didn't suffer great loss. They went through many difficulties in their lives and were very much impacted by them. But what they were able to do was not let those challenges define who they were. In today's terms we would associate it with sayings like 'if you get knocked down eight times, then get up nine'. That seems to have been my natural position in life.

I was born in Birmingham in the early 1970s. Growing up, I lived in a typical two-up, two-down end-of-terrace suburban house, in a town called Handsworth. What it lacked in monetary wealth, it made up for in its richness of diversity and culture. My childhood was mainly full of fun but not without lots of challenges. The largest contributor to that being that neither of my parents were around. Both had decided to absolve themselves of their parental responsibility. So much so that from the age of one I was raised, alongside my two older siblings, by my grandmother. She did the best she could, given the circumstances. Looking back though, things were difficult and I don't know how she managed to do many of the things she did. With that said, although things were difficult there was one thing that we weren't short of and that was love. We might not have had much in the cupboards in terms of possessions, but there was plenty of love in the house.

It was my norm and I guess it's only in hindsight, when I look back at my life, compared to pretty much most of my peers at the time, that I see things differently. Even if they didn't have both parents, they had at least one parent looking after them. In some cases they had a stepparent too. It felt like my life was quite a bit different to theirs. I didn't get to experience some of the things that I later on viewed as being part of a typical family life. There were times when this felt more acute. At birthdays, Christmas and other celebrations throughout the year, I felt that everyone else and their families were having the best time. Don't get me wrong: I don't have memories of having a torrid time, as my grandmother did a great job of making me feel special. But when I saw other kids doing things with their parents, it was hard to not be affected by that. How my grandmother managed to shield us from all the things that must have been happening at the time, was miraculous. She was and still remains to this day, my role model, my inspiration and my superhero. To come on her own to England as a black woman, during the mid-1950s, in order to find and make a better life for herself and her children, just simply amazes me. To then in her sixties take on raising three grandchildren single-handedly, without (as far as we were aware) so much as a grumble, definitely deserves admiration and gratitude.

As a young boy growing up, I seemed to find myself in two camps. I loved learning and at one stage I couldn't get enough of it. Especially maths. Although that love of learning later waned, it re-emerged in my mid-twenties and has continued until the present day. My other love was sport. I just seemed to naturally take to lots of different sports. Even though

I was never the best player at any of them, I was always good enough to get onto all the teams. So throughout my secondary school years I did football, cricket, athletics, basketball and gymnastics right up to the age of eighteen. School was thus mainly a good time for me, and my love of learning set me up for life.

In 1987, though, my grandmother died. After an initial misdiagnosis, it turned out that she had throat cancer. It was terminal and she was too frail to survive the chemo. We just had to watch while the cancer took a grip of her and eventually took her from us. This had been going on for well over a year when she eventually passed away at home. I was devastated. My whole world had been turned upside down. What would I do without my grandmother? She was my rock. Even though at the time I didn't understand her Jamaican style of parenting, I would rather have had that from her than nothing at all. She had put her hand up to do the job neither of my parents were willing to do. What compounded the situation in her death, was that throughout the whole time no one ever really asked me how I was doing. I was a young teenage boy and was expected to just carry on as normal. There were no discussions about her after she died. No reflections on past times. No celebration of her life on the anniversary. Just nothing. I went back to school pretty much straight away. I don't even recall the school doing much, if anything at all. My mother had come back from abroad a few months before my grandmother died. She'd been living overseas ever since she left me with my grandmother. This was the third and last time that I would ever see my mother. In some ways I had hoped that in light of the circumstances she would have stepped up. But she didn't. It was almost as if she couldn't leave quickly enough to get back to whatever life it was she was having. The reality is that even if she had stayed, we wouldn't have got on. In fact, my life probably would have gone further downhill in light of her – let's just say – unique parenting style. Shortly after my gran died, she pulled me to one side and said that I was going to live with my aunt and uncle who lived a few miles away. It was a difficult four years living with them but at least I had someone to look after me. Many children in my situation don't have that and I don't know where I would have ended up otherwise.

At eighteen I went to university. At the time it wasn't so much to get an education as it was to get away from Birmingham. So many difficult memories were now associated with my home city that I had to get away. Make a clean break. Start again. Be somebody that wasn't carrying around the weight of the world with them. I made lots of friends. Threw myself into Manchester's vibrant social scene and started to figure out who I wanted to be. The one thing I did know about myself from the off, was that I didn't want to settle down. That was for much further down the line, if at all. I always wanted children, mind you. But I wanted to have children on my terms or as best as possible on my own terms. Both of my parents were crap. That's the reality of the situation. For some reason I felt that when/if my time came, I wanted to be able to give my children the things that I didn't have. I don't know how or why or where those thoughts came from. All I remember is that it was something that I realised from an early age and that always stuck with me deep in the back of my mind. It wasn't something that I had ever discussed with anybody either.

Going to university away from Birmingham was a big decision that allowed me to have the clean break I wanted. The next big decision was at twenty-seven when I moved to London. As a software engineer with a couple of years' experience under my belt, there were plenty of career options available to me in London. The plan was to work down there for around five or so years, save some money and return to Manchester with the deposits to put down on a few flats. What I hadn't accounted for was the fact that within a year of moving to London I would meet Hazel and that meeting her would completely change my life.

Settling Down and Family Life

I wasn't planning on settling down. So it was a surprise when I realised what Hazel and I were building was potentially for the long term. It wasn't that we sat down and discussed it or anything. But it just seemed to be something that was understood between us. We were so comfortable in ourselves and our relationship, why wouldn't we just keep building on it and see where it took us? We were both in our late twenties, on similar career trajectories and with lots of shared interests. But I think that one of the contributing factors to the success of our relationship was that we each had our own lives and we didn't live in each other's pockets. We had amazing lives as individuals and an amazing life together. That doesn't mean we didn't have any ups and downs. Of course we did. But the disagreements were far and few between. Also, if we did fall out it wouldn't drag on. We simply didn't have time to be upset with each other when there was so much else that we would miss out on if we did.

Seven years into our relationship we got married. We always knew we would get married but we weren't in a rush to do it. It's funny, though, how other people like to label your relationship so that it fits in neatly with their idea of how things should be done. We had bought a house together a few years earlier and a number of people would make comments about getting married and having children. But we were clear in our minds that we would do things in our own time and not anyone else's. For us it was absolutely the right thing to do. Including it being the right time and stage in our lives.

Just over a year after we got married, we had our first child. Up to that point I'd imagined the type of father that I wanted to, or thought I might be. Clearly, you can have all those plans and ideas, but the reality is that you don't really know anything about parenting until you're actually thrown into the deep end of it. There at the coalface dealing with the dirty nappies, the sleepless nights, feeding routines, visits to the hospital in the early hours and everything else that comes with it. Our son was born via C-section and that wasn't something that I had accounted for even though I was aware it was a possibility. His heart rate had dropped during labour and they wanted to make sure that he was OK. Thankfully, he was just fine. I had been told to scrub up and support Hazel in the operating theatre, while the doctors and nurses did their thing at the 'business end'. I remember being quite nervous, mainly for Hazel rather than myself. She didn't like needles. Even just going for a jab prior to a number of foreign holidays had her in tears. So I knew this wasn't going to go down very well. All through the pregnancy she had been adamant that she wouldn't have an epidural. But right up to going into the theatre the labour pain had progressively increased. It was now at the point that she knew she needed to have something, so she reluctantly agreed to having an epidural. I was proud of the way that she stood her ground on wanting the birth to be as natural as possible. But also in her realising that ultimately what she wanted and what was possible just didn't come together at that point in time.

In the end, the C-section didn't take that long and shortly after entering the theatre, our eldest son was born. After a few checks, the nurses handed him over to me. There aren't many truly inspiring, breathtaking moments in life that fill you with so many emotions. But this was certainly one of those. I kissed him and immediately took him over to Hazel while she was still lying on the operating theatre table. She smiled, we both smiled, we kissed him together, we kissed each other and we broke down in tears of joy. Hazel and our son stayed in the hospital for two nights so that he could be monitored. It wasn't great going back home on my own those two nights. But I used the time to get everything as ready as I could for when they both came home. Two days later we were all at home starting the next chapter of our lives together as a family. I had taken two weeks' paternity leave over the Christmas period when he was born and so ended up with three and a half weeks off work. Clearly not lots of time given where things are moving towards these days now. But it was enough for me to help establish some routines, start to bond with my son and to make the most of our time together as a family.

As ever, those first six months were a baptism of fire that nothing could have sufficiently prepared us for. That said, on reflection there were a number of things that we could have put in place prior to his birth that would have taken the pressure off. It's not that they would have made the parenting part any easier but they would have definitely made all the other day-to-day things a lot easier. Anyway, despite those whirlwind first six months, we eventually got to twelve months and then eighteen months feeling like we got this. Don't get me wrong: we weren't saying we had parenting nailed. Just that we could deal with whatever challenges it brought our way and come out the other end OK.

Soon enough we decided to try for another baby and by the middle of 2012 we were expecting again. As with our first, we didn't want to know the gender of this child until it was born. That was one of the many things about our relationship that we were completely aligned about. When we got engaged and married there were approximately twelve weeks between the day I proposed and the day of the wedding. We didn't believe in long, drawn-out engagements, and having been together for a number of years, it certainly didn't need to be drawn-out. It was the same when choosing the names of our boys. With both pregnancies I don't think it took more than an afternoon chat for us to have come up with options for boys' or girls' names. That included backup choices, just in case somehow once born, the baby didn't fit the name! We couldn't understand how people go through a forty-or so-week pregnancy term and still not have a name for their child. What had they been doing the whole time?! Being in a relationship where simple things like that matter, was important to both of us. So to be going through a pregnancy together again and to be making plans that would change family life for us going forward, was something that we were both excited and nervous about.

We had decided some years ago, that once we had a family, we would start planning our escape from corporate life. It's not that we didn't enjoy our jobs and the people we worked with. But we felt that we had to achieve a balance that didn't involve factoring family life around work. After my childhood, I knew that I needed to provide the emotional parts of my kids' lives that I didn't have. It's not that I didn't also want to give them things that I didn't have; but it was already clear that they would have more than I ever did growing up. Even now, there are still things I'm learning about parenthood due to the fact that my frame of reference is based on not having either parent around. It's a hard thing to accept. Especially when I see the relationship that I'm building with my boys and how much I want to nurture and guide them to become whatever they want to be. Accepting that my parents didn't want to do that for me and my siblings has been very difficult. But it became something that was necessary in order for me to not let that hold me back or prevent me from becoming the type of father that I wanted to be. When we looked at the options for building a different and better family life, we decided that I would give up working in London and start setting up a business. From a practical perspective, it was a no-brainer. After all, I was already doing at least a three-hour round trip commute every day. All that dead time travelling and me spending twelve hours out of the house every day. It just didn't make sense to us, for me to keep doing that. With me working in technology, we believed that it had to be possible for me to find a way to work flexibly and remotely and to earn a decent living. Tech start-ups were on the rise, co-working spaces were getting traction and flexible working was finally, albeit still slowly, becoming a thing that companies were considering. Hazel only worked six miles away from our home and we thought that it didn't make sense to change that for the time being.

We had set ourselves a deadline of me quitting and leaving my job before our eldest son turned three in December 2012. Then when we were expecting our second child, it crystallised those plans further. I didn't want to be dependent on my company dictating how much time I could spend with our second son. I wanted control, and following paternity leave with my eldest, I knew that anything less than complete autonomy wasn't going to be acceptable. We had been talking about these plans for years and now it was finally happening. I was working on setting up a business although we had no expectations for me to actually earn anything to speak of, for a couple of years. There was no rush as we'd been saving for quite a while. Plus, I wanted to make sure that I was around for baby number two in the way that I wasn't able to be for our eldest. I wanted to get that time with both our children without rushing around during the week. Or trying to fit in as many family time activities as possible over the weekend. At the time it felt really strange talking to other couples about this, as almost all of them didn't really get it. It was the norm amongst our closest friends who were all striving to build better lives for themselves and their families in the more typical way. This isn't a criticism of them at all, though. But an observation of how we'd all been sold a dream that the way to achieve happiness, success and financial freedom was through having a work/life balance that prioritised the work element above everything else.

Becoming a Widower

Some months early into the pregnancy we'd been told that Hazel had contracted group B strep. A bacteria that rarely affects the carrier but it would require our baby to be given a course of antibiotics immediately after birth. We had been preparing ourselves for this, along with also potentially needing to have another C-section. If I remember rightly, when you've had a C-section, any future pregnancies have a high chance of also being likely to require a C-section. I can't remember the reasons why but it was something that was clear in our heads and so the date for a planned C-section had been discussed earlier on in the process.

Having got to week forty in the pregnancy, there was a sense of comfort in knowing that in at most two weeks' time we'd be having our second baby. The following day Hazel had woken up at about 4 a.m. and was feeling uncomfortable. We figured this was the start of things and that what were mild contractions, would develop into us having a baby that day. We were excited and decided to take the day as it comes and do what we would normally do, until it became clear that we'd need to go to the hospital. So I'd gone into our garage to exercise. Quite a while back, we'd decided that going to the gym was too much effort to organise and not the best use of our time or money. So we bought several different types of exercise equipment and ended up with a rowing machine, a punch bag, weights, a mini trampoline and so on. I had done my usual hour or so of exercise when I went back into the house. Hazel wasn't feeling right at all and she needed to go to the hospital. We asked her parents, who lived a few miles away, to look after our eldest son while I took her to the maternity ward.

After waiting a little while to be seen and getting some checks done, we were told there was nothing to worry about. We sat in a room at the hospital for a few hours and were hungry as it was lunchtime and we'd not eaten anything yet all day. After getting the best that the hospital cafe had to offer us, we were told that Hazel would be induced, as labour still hadn't started. When it finally did start, everything seemed fine but progress was very slow. A few hours later, though, at around 6 p.m., it all began to go wrong. She'd had an abruption, which is when the placenta comes away before childbirth. They rushed her into the theatre for a C-section. I'd assumed, like the last time, I would be allowed in too, but I wasn't. I was sat in the room we'd been in on my own, wondering what was happening. I was concerned but not overly worried. Eventually, Hazel gave birth in the early evening. We'd had our second son but I wasn't able to see him or Hazel yet. Our son would need to spend some time on the NICU (neonatal intensive care unit) ward so that the antibiotics could be administered and he could be monitored. Hazel finally came out onto the maternity ward for recovery but her health deteriorated very rapidly and she passed away five hours later.

The hospital believed at the time and several months later the inquest confirmed that she had suffered a rare complication called Amniotic Fluid Embolism. The research and data available on the condition is very limited, especially in the UK. Over the years most of the information that I've found about it has come from the US and mainly from an organisation called the AFE Foundation. Clinicians are aware of the conditions in which AFE can occur, but they are still unaware as to why it happens and how to prevent it from happening. I won't go into the details here of what happened but if you go to the AFE Foundation website it will explain the details for anyone that is interested in knowing more.

Within a day I had gone from being very excited about our growing family and moving onto the next chapter of our lives, to having been dealt a blow that knocked me completely off my feet. There are no words to adequately convey how I felt when hearing the words that Hazel had passed away. It was surreal and like I was watching somebody else, seeing the doctors come over to me knowing what they were going to say, but not wanting them to say it. I was expecting the three of us to leave the hospital together. For Hazel and I to be taking home another bundle of joy with us. To face another round of long nights, dirty nappies, making up bottles in advance for overnight feeds and all the other responsibilities that go with having a new baby. Yet I left the hospital after being there for nearly seventeen hours, alone, widowed and a sole parent.

Even now while writing these words, my eyes are filling up thinking about it. I can see myself walking out of the hospital in a daze not knowing exactly what had just happened. Those first few minutes, hours, days and weeks were a complete blur. I just kept thinking that this must be a dream and any moment soon I would wake up and everything would be as it should be. At that point in time I didn't want to accept that this was my life, and at any rate, it was too hard to accept it. Despite that, my overriding feeling was that I needed to do whatever I could to get through every day as best as possible.

Somehow I had to find a way to do the best for both my boys. For them, for me and for Hazel.

I didn't know how I was going to cope with the needs of a newborn baby while trying to explain to my three-year-old son why his mum didn't come back from the hospital with me. He saw me leave with her for the hospital and was excited about seeing us all come back and him beginning his life as a big brother. This is one of the hardest things I've ever had to do in my life. I remember not even having the words to explain to him what being dead meant. How does a three-year-old begin to grasp death as a concept? A few days after Hazel died I found out about Winston's Wish, as a close friend of ours had brought some information and booklets over to the house. After going through the information, I started to understand about how grief affects children. The answer to my previous question was that death isn't something that is even possible to grasp in some way until at least five. Even then the permanence of death is not realistically understable until closer to seven. Don't forget that this is a generalisation and thus a guide rather than a hard and fast rule for every child. The Winston's Wish website has a lot of information about this and includes age-range specific guides. While it was hard having to go through all of the information, it did provide me with what I needed in order to come up with a way that I could tell my son that his mum had died. Over time, it also made me realise that this was a conversation that I would continually need to have with him throughout his childhood, as his mental development progressed and his ability to understand increased more and more. There would be many questions over the coming years. Right through to eighteen and beyond. I would need to prepare myself for each stage so that I could give him the right answers at the right time, in a way that would be relevant and appropriate for his age and level of maturity. I also soon found out about Child Bereavement UK. They too have a lot of information and I took in as much of it as I possibly could. I'm an information person at my core and I tend to first look at the available information to guide me to the action that I need to take when faced with a challenge. In this situation my son was hurting. He was grieving and would continue to grieve in his own way for many years to come. As much as I needed to surround him with love, care and attention, I also needed to do right by him and be guided by those organisations who deal with child bereavement every day. I needed to learn from them so that no matter what else happened I could say to myself that I did the best that I could for him.

Looking back at this now, I can see that I was really hard on myself. The burden of responsibility weighed heavily on me. There was no one to share the load of raising two boys with. The person who I should have been leaning on and turning to was no longer here. There was to be no time out from parenting; no tapping out when things got hard so that I could pause, take a deep breath and tap back in again.

Close friends and family were there in an instant and some still are now. You can't get through the aftermath of something like this alone, especially when you can't see the wood for the trees. So many people stepped in to pick up a lot of the slack on my behalf. Some managed my daily calendar or filed the probate documentation, while others would even come and stay to do the overnight feeds for me so I could try to get some sleep. I still didn't really sleep for about seven months, but it gave me a break during the night. The sad thing was that some of those around me just couldn't get this. How could they really get what I was going through, when they were looking from the outside in? None of them had been through anything like this. But it soon became clear that it was more than just that. In some cases, it was clear that the expectations were that I was a man who would be incapable of looking after my boys and meeting all their needs. How could I possibly be capable of running a house and raising kids? The thing is, though, I was staying on top of the boys' routines and things that needed to be done around the house, even though I wasn't doing many of them myself in those first six months. I was instructing those around me that were helping, on the things that I wanted them to do and what they should prioritise. I was also really clear on feeding routines, a sleeping plan and all the things that are part of having a newborn baby. These are things that Hazel and I had anally planned in advance. So it wasn't like I had to think about a lot of it. What was required was to follow the instructions that we'd written down and/or for me to remember what we had done with my eldest and to do the same things this time around. This is obviously not everyone's way of doing things but it was what worked for Hazel and me. We liked having a routine as it helped us focus on what needed to be done. Even though we needed to change things that either didn't work at all or that were no longer relevant after a few months. All those things became even more important to me now that Hazel wasn't here. I wanted to ensure that things were done in the way that we had planned. I didn't want to let anything slip as I felt I owed it to her. Clearly it was an overly ambitious expectation, but it was my way of still holding onto Hazel.

This is in addition to dealing with sorting out all the ensuing admin and paperwork that is required to be completed after someone dies. In other instances, because I was open with showing myself being vulnerable, it was as if I wasn't allowed to be that way. I understand that the cultural norm in the UK is that we don't talk openly about a lot of things. But that doesn't make it right, and from my own experience and what I've observed of others, I have to question whether it does more harm than good. Grief brings a particular aspect to this. People don't know what to say and many don't know what to do. Even if people initially give you some latitude, it doesn't last for long and it feels like as a man it is even more pronounced. You get asked how you're doing as a pleasantry, but most people don't really want to know how you're doing. So a lot of people within a few months of Hazel dying just withdrew. Her friends, my friends, joint friends, some of her family and some of my family. I was a bloke and I should just get on with things and not show my emotions regardless of the fact that I'd just been dealt a life-changing blow that would continue to be felt many years in the future. One of the things that made it even more difficult at the time was that some of the people in our lives were actively going around, openly criticising everything that I was doing, to anyone that would listen to them. I wasn't doing this or that right. I should be doing things in a particular way. Some of it was so vitriolic that I lashed out. In no uncertain terms I made it clear that if they weren't going to support me as best as possible, then there was no place for them in my or the boys' lives. At this point, those people soon became the victims and it was now I who was the one treating them badly and not the other way around. Once I realised the impact that this was having on my well-being, I set about finding a way to distance myself from the thoughts about this and make peace with the fact that those people may not be part of our lives ever again. It was very hard accepting that at a time when everyone that this impacted should come together; some were doing their hardest to be as divisive as they could. I wrestled with this for quite some time. I don't remember exactly how long. But I do remember that I was able to fully make peace with my decision about them when I started to talk to other young widows and widowers. In fact, what became very clear was that this was common. I couldn't quite believe it at first. The number of conversations in our group chats about the types of things that friends and family had done to people in the group was unbelievable. Could people really behave like this after a bereavement? I know they say grief affects everyone differently but these things were on a whole different level. People were arguing over wills and estates, possessions and things that in the grand scheme of things weren't that important after having just lost someone. It was horrible, brutal and a very stark reminder that you only truly know certain people when you go through difficult times.

With my three-year-old son I was following the guideline information from Winston's Wish and Child Bereavement UK, and taking from it what I felt was relevant for us and adapting it accordingly. I sent him into nursery school a few days a week, so that he could have some consistency in his life. After doing some research, I found out that every school class in the UK has a child who has lost a parent. Even now I still can't get my head around that statistic. At the time it did provide some reassurance that we were far from the only ones going through this situation. For days, weeks and months in the immediate aftermath of Hazel's death we sat and talked. In fact we probably cried together just as much as we talked about what happened. I still don't know how he did it. When I look at how young he was to where he is now, I feel so proud of who he is and how resilient he has been. He's my hero.

The advice from the bereavement organisations was clear. When discussing death with a small child, you need to be truthful and clear about what has happened. Don't use any ambiguous phrases, like 'she's passed away'. Your language will inform how a three-year-old is going to understand death, so you should be honest and explain it as soon as possible in a manner appropriate to their age and character. Hazel died in the early hours of the morning and I'm not sure how, but by the following afternoon I had told my eldest son that his mum had died.

My son and I cried and grieved openly together, lots. I don't know why but I felt that in not doing so, I would have reinforced the outdated male stereotype that it's not OK to be upset or to show your emotions. There were times when I was overcome with sadness and my son came to put his arm around me, and vice versa. Somehow we got through it together.

As a family, we looked at and still look at photographs and video footage of Hazel all the time. I tell my son that whenever he wants to talk about Mummy, then he should let me know and we'll sit down to talk about her. While this was initially hard to do, I knew that it was the right thing for us. It did eventually start to get easier to do and I repeated the process when my youngest son started asking lots of questions about Hazel too. Right now, he probably asks more questions about her than my eldest.

Doing right by my boys was imperative; but it became clear that I couldn't deal with the psychological aspect of grief all alone; I needed professional help. The hospital Hazel passed away in had a counsellor who worked in what they called a birth reflections unit. We'd spoken to her previously and it felt OK to be able to speak to someone who knew Hazel and still had memories of her. This was a big help to me in the first few weeks and months after Hazel died. To have an outlet to talk about all sorts of things without being judged, had a stabilising effect on me. I'd also been given some information from someone about an organisation called Care for the Family, who had a grief service called Widowed Young Support. This organisation and the support offered was outstanding. Amongst the help that they provide, is a peer-to-peer support offering. I was matched with a guy who had lost his wife six years prior to me. For two years after Hazel died, he called me to check how I was doing. At first he called every few weeks, and over the two years, the time between the calls got longer until I didn't need that level of support any more. It was comforting talking to someone who could relate to what I was going through, and it was a great relief to have someone to vent to, who could understand whatever I was experiencing. Around eighteen months after Hazel died I contacted an organisation called Widowed and Young, a nationwide charity that provides support to those who are widowed while under fifty. They provide online groups and regional face-to-face meetups for people to be able to directly share their experiences and provide peer-to-peer support. They are another amazing organisation without which there would be many people in my situation thinking that they are all alone and no one else is dealing with the same set of challenges that they are. Everything from meeting up for meals out, going for walks, getting a coffee, bike rides, hosting meals at a member's home and more are covered in the set of things offered. While I didn't connect with many in my local group outside of us having being widowed in common, I did become and remain very good friends with someone who lives just a few miles away from me. To this day, we still meet up for coffee, meals, nights out at the cinema and more.

By engaging with various support groups and, in particular, groups that were focused on men, the most consistent observation I have made is that many of us found it hard to talk about bereavement, grief and our emotions. Some of the guys in the men's group wouldn't join the mixed-gender group because they didn't feel comfortable opening up in front of women even when the groups were online. Across both genders we were all hurt from going through a similar experience, yet some of us men still felt that we had to portray an image of masculinity that was strong and resilient. We had, in the main, all subscribed to a model of our role in society for so long, that we didn't know any different. I could see that the pattern had repeated itself, having been passed down from and through our grandfathers, dads, uncles and society in general. Whether through nurture or nature, we were conditioned to not show weakness, regardless of the situation. I even had someone in my extended family say to a friend of my wife that I should 'man up'. As men and boys were not allowed to cry, show vulnerability or do anything less than being what a 'real' man is. I couldn't do it. I wouldn't do it. I had to break free from this role that society expected of me, regardless of what others, including and especially friends and family, might think. I needed to switch it around and be able to feel that there was no shame in sharing vulnerable feelings. It became clear that this was essential for my own well-being in order to be the best dad that I could possibly be for my boys.

I was blessed that I had and still have friends and family who supported and stood by me, though. From the groups that I was part of, it was clear that some of the other widows and widowers didn't have the same level of support that I did, especially the men. I started to feel that not only should I help myself but that once I was in the position to, I should use what I have learned to see how I could help other widowers too.

They say that when you have a child, the first six to twelve months are a blur. We certainly found that with our eldest son. But having a newborn baby, a three-year-old and dealing with grief for us all, took this to another level. For some reason I decided to journal certain things. I'd realised very early on that my brain had turned to mush and that I wouldn't remember much of what was happening. I also thought that as my boys get older and more aware of things, they would start to ask more and more questions about what happened and why. I had presumed that by the time they had matured enough to ask more challenging questions, I would have long forgotten some of the reasons I did particular things. At the time my wife died, there was so much noise going on from all over the place, that it ended up being cathartic to get it all down on paper. I've not read any of it for years. But for the first few years I would reread it quite regularly. It was as if I needed to remind myself that this really wasn't a dream.

It probably took two years for it to feel like maybe there was a new life out there for us. I was actually able to start thinking about a future for the three us. At sixteen months I booked us on to a flight to see some relatives in Scotland. I wasn't really sure what I was doing but I knew that I had to do it. One of my friends and someone in my family offered to come up with us. But this was something that I had to do alone. I needed to start to be able to do regular things on my own with the boys without relying on someone else. It was daunting and I wasn't sure how I was going to manage with a sixteen-month-old and a four-year-old on a flight; but I had to do it. It then still took another year before I was able to start finding some regular proper time for myself. In that period I took up meditation, yoga and started to exercise again. That seemed to be the catalyst for a number of things in being able to move forward. Now eight years later, I'm doing a lot more things for myself and the challenges of parenthood have become easier to manage. I don't know what the future holds but I know that my boys and I have a bond that is unbreakable. That doesn't mean that we don't have wobbles, whether individually or collectively. Sometimes we need to have time out from the world and just retreat into our own world, regroup and go again. I don't have a problem with that, though. Things could have been even worse for us, as strange as that might sound. I think that's my stoicism coming out again. There are widows and widowers I know that have even further challenges to deal with than I did/do. So I take time to show gratitude every day and to recognise that, I have a certain privilege. As hard as parenting can sometimes be, it's a privilege that Hazel didn't get to have. I get to see my boys every day develop into the amazing young boys they are now and I won't ever forget to appreciate that.

Chapter 7:

And Then What?
The Challenges and Rewards of Being a Dad
of a Boy with Autism

Danny Herbert

Before setting off on a recent trip to visit our family in France, my son Charlie refused to get out of bed. Typical teenager, you might think. But he wasn't being a typical teenager, and beneath his rage lay a crippling anxiety which is sometimes associated with autism.

As a father of two in his early fifties, with a pretty good job, living in Walthamstow, I've come a long way from my mischievous childhood by the seaside. I think I've achieved a measure of success despite many struggles and setbacks. Clearly, as with all other dads, being a dad is not the only thing that defines me. I grew up in Brighton with my mum and brother; my dad moved to France with my stepmum when I was eleven. When I was in my twenties, I was thrilled when my dad and my stepmum had two kids and I gained two little sisters, something I'd always wanted. Mum and Dad always got on really well right up until my dad died a few years ago. One of the most important things in life for me are the raucous gatherings of my large extended family. One of my uncles was a massive influence on me, a big character, full of mischief and a lot of fun. When I was about eight he came to visit but we were out, so he went to the shop and posted twenty Mars Bars through our letterbox and won his place as my favourite uncle. When I was older he frequently provided my friends and me with 'beer' money. Mum and Dad were also big influences. I've inherited Mum's calm, kind approach to problems and Dad's passion for film, dance and politics. I grew up going on various demonstrations, including the great Rock Against Racism ones in the 1970s; I often tell people I saw The Clash at one of them, although I was only ten. I describe myself as a left-wing libertarian and driven to fight injustice, sometimes with a tendency to be a bit ranty/shouty, with a passion for film.

Aged about seven, I discovered I could write poetry, encouraged by a fabulous English teacher, and it's something I've done ever since. Poetry helps me express my emotions and frustrations. I went through various youth-cult phases from punk to casual in my teens, but the one that stuck with me was the mod scene and through that grew my lifelong love of soul music. These days the most important things in my life, outside family, are spending time with friends (usually in the pub), music, reading, film and dancing; northern soul keeps me going.

A Long Time Ago in a Maternity Ward Far, Far, Away

Well, actually it was Hackney. My wife and I decided to have children when we were both in our thirties. We'd had a pretty full and fun packed life up to that point and had been together for about eight years. It wasn't really a difficult decision. I'd always wanted to be a dad so it felt right for me.

As far as I know, it was a fairly normal pregnancy, during which we both read the books and discussed each stage in detail. We became 'experts' on pregnancy (our second child was an entirely different experience because we didn't pay her much attention due to the demands of having a toddler to look after). My wife went to hospital to be induced because the baby was two weeks late (perhaps the first sign of a resistance to change). The labour and birth were far from easy – fourteen hours of feeling helpless and watching my wife go through agony. It transpired that the baby's head was in a difficult position, and all sorts of horror stories flashed through my head. After a few attempts, they wanted to take her for a caesarian but we pushed them for one more attempt at a 'normal' birth and they agreed to try with forceps.

Suddenly they pulled something out and I stood feeling confused, looking at…*Oh my goodness, it's a baby!* After a brief panic when it looked like he was not breathing, there was the unmistakable cry of a newborn and I found myself face to face with my son. I cried and felt an amazing surge of joy and emotion. There really is nothing like that feeling.

The Dark Side

Charlie was always a 'difficult' baby, having trouble sleeping, feeding, and he never seemed satisfied. We read all the books and tried to do the right thing. But it often felt really difficult and I sometimes wondered if I was doing things wrong. I got annoyed with myself for not knowing what to do. My wife and I bickered over what we should be doing from time to time but we always got through it and remained close. Then, shortly after his first birthday Charlie had a series of fits. I was off work looking after him and had to get the doctor to come but he had another fit while they were there, so they called an ambulance. I was terrified but tried to keep calm throughout. I called my wife and she met us at the hospital.

We spent a terrifying week in the hospital while all sorts of tests were carried out on our baby boy. He particularly hated the EEG scans which involved sticking lots of sensors all over his head, and no matter what we did to try to distract him, he pulled at them and kept crying. I remember sitting in the canteen with my wife and feeling completely helpless. I think the experience made us stronger as a couple because we built up a powerful sense of solidarity going through this awful thing together. But there were many moments where I just wanted it all to stop, those soul searching 'why me' moments.

When you find out your child has a condition like epilepsy, I think it is common for there to be a period of denial, adjustment and finally of acceptance. I certainly felt it. The future you thought your child would have was now going to be something completely different. My thoughts were all over the place but included 'the hand I've been dealt' and 'not what I signed up for'.

So, once again, after he'd been diagnosed, we found ourselves at home with our baby, not knowing what to do. We were both very anxious, continually checking for signs of another fit for a long while after getting home. Charlie was prescribed various different epilepsy medications which were a nightmare to give to him twice a day, every day!

For the next few years, we learned to live with the fact that our son had epilepsy and actually he didn't have another full fit but did have the occasional absence fits. However, Charlie was very difficult, he often had tantrums, he didn't play in the same way as other kids and we worried about his behaviour. Sometimes we disagreed on it and I quite often sought to find excuses for it – 'he's just tired' or 'he's hungry'. But one thing we both discussed was whether the medication he was on was causing his behaviour.

There were many signs of autism early on but we didn't know much about autism so missed them. For instance, Charlie often asked, 'What are we doing today?' And the reply would be, 'We're going to X,' to which he would say, 'Then what?' We'd respond: 'We'll have lunch', and he'd say, 'And then what?' This could sometimes go on until you had listed all the activities for a week. We thought it was funny at the time but looking back, it hinted at the need for routine and anxiety about the unknown. He also had several 'special' interests including helicopters, trains and anything yellow. While on a camping holiday in Dorset we heard a helicopter in the distance and Charlie said, 'Six Chinooks.' Then over the hill came exactly six Chinooks. Charlie has a remarkable sense of hearing, which can be problematic when he is somewhere noisy. One of my dad's friends wondered then if he might be autistic, to which my reaction was, 'No, of course not. He can recognise emotions,' again demonstrating my very limited understanding of autism.

The School Strikes Back

We'd raised our concerns with the SENCO (Special Educational Needs Coordinator) several times while Charlie was at nursery and in year one. But our concerns were dismissed with phrases like, 'Oh, I think I would know if there was a problem.' This made my blood boil and I had a few run-ins with the SENCO. From nursery to school his behaviour got more and more challenging.

While all this was going on, my wife and I decided to have a second child, and when Charlie was three and a half, our daughter Lola was born. For both of us this was a bit of a revelation because she was so easy compared to Charlie, and I know you shouldn't compare your children but we just couldn't help it.

By the time he reached year two, the problems with Charlie's behaviour got significantly worse. Other children would egg him on to do things and he would end up getting into all sorts of trouble. Fortunately, by this time there was a new SENCO at the school who was much more understanding. She was the next person to suggest the possibility of autism. I was absolutely sure he didn't have it and was terrified of the idea of him being autistic (he wouldn't be able to love or have emotions, I thought in my ignorance). As the behaviour got worse, Charlie had begun to hit teachers and have tantrums. If there was a helicopter he would have to get up and look out of the window no matter what; he was disruptive in class and assembly. They gave him his own little workspace, kept him back from assembly and stopped him from doing PE, effectively excluding him in a mainstream setting. Then the school started to call us to collect him at lunchtime, which impacted on my wife's job; she was nearest so it was usually she who had to pick him up. I was furious with the school but also got angry with Charlie. I couldn't understand what the problem was or why he couldn't behave.

Also around this time my stepdad passed away. Charlie was very close to him and shortly after, Charlie developed a fear of street cleaners, which turned into a debilitating phobia and often meant it would take at least an hour just to get him out of the house. I used to have to carry him on my shoulders all the way to school. Again, with my limited understanding of autism, I thought it must be linked to grief and loss. But actually, it was linked to him being hypersensitive to noise and other stimuli, so the sound of the brushes hurt his ears and terrified him. We'd been referred to Child and Adolescent Mental Health Services (CAMHS) for support, but this 'support' was rather poor. The school had suggested getting some sort of diagnosis from them, so we asked. Following a very shabbily run session and us chasing a letter that wasn't sent, we received the diagnosis for 'Global Development Delay', *whatever that means*. When the SENCO heard, she was fuming; she knew that he did not have Global Development Delay.

The behaviour, the exclusions and the phobia all got progressively worse. This all took its toll on my wife and she became quite depressed. At one point she rang the CAMHS service desperate, in tears telling them she felt like she was having a breakdown and pleading for their support. I was staggered, and furious, when my wife told me that their response was to tell her, 'If you think like that, you will have a breakdown.' She ended up losing her job, although her boss made her redundant. But this all added to our stress levels and put a strain on our relationship. I found myself getting very angry at the system and the lack of support we were offered. We bickered quite a lot; we often had different approaches and ideas about Charlie and how to support him. I was a bit more confrontational with the system than my wife. Stress often presents as anger in me, whereas it is much more in tears with my wife. Sometimes we'd argue over lots of little things like household chores in disproportionate ways, all our feelings about Charlie submerged like an iceberg. I hated my anger and felt really guilty whenever I'd had an outburst. It reached a point that I sought counselling, which has helped to varying degrees. I have a tendency to reach for drink when I'm feeling stressed or down and that certainly put a strain on things sometimes. However, I believe we have a really strong and solid relationship and we have managed to get through all these difficulties by talking (usually instigated by my wife) but also by taking time out for 'us' e.g. going out for dinner/dates and dancing.

After more pushing from us and from the SENCO, and a letter to our local MP, we finally got another diagnosis. This time it was at a different clinic and was done properly. Charlie presented various autistic traits at the diagnosis session, including flapping his hands. He was given a diagnosis of ASD (Autistic Spectrum Disorder).

So, what is Autism? I've learned a lot about autism over the years from researching websites, participating in training and workshops and from being Charlie's dad. There are lots of definitions out there but they all share the same ideas. Autism is a lifelong condition that impacts on the way the person communicates with others and interacts with the world. Autism affects people in many different ways. People with autism may have heightened senses and find places too noisy or too bright, they may take longer to process information, they may have heightened anxiety, dislike change or like routine, they may be literal in their communication and find 'unwritten rules' difficult to understand. What I think is less understood is what causes autism, but it has been proven that it is not caused by any vaccination, or parenting or diet. Autism is not an illness and certainly not something to be 'cured'. When I explain it to Charlie, I sometimes tell him that his brain works differently, not better or worse, just differently.

There is a wealth of information available about autism, including on the National Autistic Society website, Ambitious about Autism, and the NHS website.

There are different definitions of autism and there are different conditions described under the autistic spectrum and there is much more information on the National Autistic Society website. But for me, Charlie's is all about communication, emotion and sensation.

There are lots of myths and misunderstandings about autism and I wanted to dispel a couple:

Firstly, 'Autism is a spectrum, we are all on it.' No. The spectrum is a moveable thing. For example, sometimes when he is stressed, my son displays obvious autistic traits, but when he is calm he displays far more neurotypical behaviour and as such moves on the spectrum. To say we are all on the spectrum suggests we are all autistic and this is just blatantly not true. While we may sometimes display autistic behaviours, we are not all autistic. My son is autistic, I am not. If we are all autistic, it implies that the problems are with people who are 'more' autistic and society doesn't need to change.

Secondly, 'People with autism are geniuses.' No. Only a tiny minority of autistic people are 'savants'; some people with autism struggle in education, for various reasons. My understanding is that the brains of people with autism work differently to neurotypical people, but with just the same varieties in intelligence and ability.

So now we had the diagnosis and once again found ourselves coming to terms with my son having a condition. I went through the same sort of denial, adjustment and acceptance process that I'd experienced when he was diagnosed with epilepsy and I worried about his future.

At the same time, the exclusions continued and it became clear that the school didn't want Charlie there. They just didn't know how to handle him, which made me wonder why they called themselves an 'inclusive school'. While he was there they excluded him within the mainstream setting and now they had decided to exclude him completely. But they wanted to do it so 'it would not show on Charlie's record', or theirs! The SENCO was very supportive through this time and pushed with us to get Charlie a Statement of Special Educational Needs which guaranteed a level of funding and set out what Charlie's needs were. She also visited some schools with us while we decided which one to name on his statement.

The process for getting a statement, or Education, Health and Care Plan (EHCP) as they are now called, is an exhausting trip through various bureaucratic hoops and just another thing we had to endure to help Charlie. At one point, near the final stage of the process, I had a massive stand-up shouting row with one of the officials who was insisting on keeping certain wording in the statement which was clearly not about Charlie. She wanted it to remain as 'Charlie has difficulty making friends'; I kept making the point that it should actually be 'Charlie has difficulty maintaining friendships' – obviously two very different statements which might require different approaches. She was also insistent that Charlie had mobility problems, which we assured her was not the case. The woman refused to change it, saying the doctor and other 'professionals' had put it in there. I kept insisting that it be changed and that as his parent I had a better understanding of Charlie. It was a ridiculous situation and neither of us was willing to back down. Eventually, some sort of compromise was agreed which was more or less the wording I wanted. So we moved on. I think having the confidence to challenge professionals is a really important lesson and something I've applied often as a parent – you know your child better than anyone and you know what is best for them.

We agreed, somewhat reluctantly, to send Charlie to a special needs school chosen by the borough. Another bit of denial and a big thing to come to terms with. I didn't want my son to have to go to a special school. I wanted him to be gifted and doing really amazingly in every subject and in a mainstream school. We kept saying to people that it was only a temporary thing and insisting that he would integrate into mainstream after a while. This denial probably went on for the first year or two, but it eased quite a lot, and when we saw the progress Charlie was making and how happy he was at school, we realised it was absolutely the right place for him. That for me was the key: it doesn't matter where or what sort of school it is, as long as your child is happy and learning. They were amazing at the special school and I often thought it would help all kids to do some of the stuff they did – *all* schools should be like that.

Help Me, Andreas Arnmar – You're Our Only Hope

After Charlie got his diagnosis, lots of support suddenly became available to us. I felt a bit confused by what we might need and it was really hard to get anyone to understand. Then, Andreas Arnmar from an organisation called the Hamara came round. He was the first person to really talk to Charlie properly. He really understood Charlie and reassured us that Charlie did have autism; we still didn't understand it properly at that point and sometimes we questioned the diagnosis. Andreas found someone to look after Charlie and give us some respite. He really put a lot of thought into who on the team could support Charlie effectively. It was all about Charlie and his needs instead of the needs or egos of the services/professionals involved.

Around this time, and with the help of our MP, we received an apology from the heads of the local Child and Adolescent Mental Health Services (CAMHS) for their various failings, and someone advised us that we could insist on getting a referral from our GP to the Tavistock Clinic. When we got the referral to the Tavistock the support was fantastic; they really helped Charlie with some of his phobias. My wife and I also had some sessions and our daughter was offered some support as a sibling of someone with difficulties. It really helped us and made and big difference. Again, I found myself wondering why all local provision and support wasn't at that standard.

Andreas had set up a group to support dads of kids with special needs, and after a few unsuccessful attempts found that by holding the sessions in a pub, dads were more likely to attend. It was brilliant and great to talk to other dads honestly about our experiences and how we felt. When I first went, only two or three other dads would turn up, but that gradually increased over the years. When the Hamara closed down, Andreas secured funding from Waltham Forest Parent Forum to continue with the dads group, but it had to move from the pub to meeting in an alcohol-free environment to make it more inclusive. We started to invite guest speakers which generated some really interesting discussions. What was great about this group, was the way we could share experiences and feelings. It helps you to realise you are not alone and all the difficult stuff is not just happening to you. I remember one dad talking about how guilty he felt for getting angry with his autistic child and shouting at them and I thought, *I feel the same way sometimes.* We talked through the anger and how it made us feel and it really helped me both understand his feelings but also helped with my temper. We were able to talk openly about how our kids with special needs affected our relationships, how it was difficult to talk to other parents, and we offered each other advice. There is something very empowering in being part of a community.

Charlie also started attending various clubs for kids with special needs – mainly autism – and making friends. This was a real relief for me because I really worried about Charlie's ability to maintain friendships. Charlie used to become very fixated on one particular friend, which could sometimes be very difficult if there were any problems like the friend moving away or falling out with each other. Friendship is something I value very highly and has been one of the things that has helped me through the difficult times, so I'm really keen to ensure that Charlie has a wide network of his own. My wife has done loads to help facilitate some of Charlie's friendships outside the clubs, driving him all over town to hang out with mates – 'Cleo's Cabs' as we jokingly describe my wife's car ferrying (I don't drive).

When, if, and how to tell Charlie about the fact that he was autistic was an issue my wife and I grappled with and argued about for a while. We swayed between thinking it was really important for us to talk to him so we could help him understand, to not making an issue of it. At what age was he old enough? How should we tell him? What exactly should we tell him? Then, on a trip to Legoland I saw an opportunity. We'd taken Charlie's disability living allowance claim so we could get a 'Ride Access Pass' – these are provided for various reasons including for neurodivergent people who find queuing very difficult. We had been very anxious about the trip because family outings like that could and would often end with meltdowns. So, we put the wristband on and my wife and I agreed that this would be a good time to tell him. We just explained that: 'You have something called autism that means your brain works a bit differently to ours and sometimes you find things like queuing difficult. This wrist band means you won't have to queue.' By the end of the day he was walking around waving his wristband-clad arm in the air shouting, 'Autism, autism, no queues.'. So in that way the first time he found out about his autism was a positive thing and I think that has shaped our, and his, engagement with it ever since. When Charlie gets angry about it, it is more directed at the neurotypical world making it difficult rather than autism being an issue, and he is quite right about that.

As Charlie settled at school we began to learn more and more about autism and my wife and I both looked back in amazement at how many signs there were when Charlie was younger. His autism explained so many things about his behaviour. The school offered some training called 'EarlyBird' and this provided us with a more in-depth understanding and how to support Charlie. The thing that has stuck with me from that training is the phrase 'allow for the autism', and when I remind myself of that, things can be a little easier. Why is that? Well, primarily because it can be easy to forget that Charlie has autism, when we are just getting on with life.

Charlie struggles with transition, and one of the biggest struggles for us over the years has been the transition from bed to getting out to go to school or college. When he went to the specialist school Charlie was also provided with school transport, which was great and very helpful, however it meant being at a pickup point by a certain time. Charlie has a different concept of time and one thing guaranteed to stress him and trigger tantrums is rushing. Some of the drivers were really understanding and supportive but others were very difficult, which added pressure. When he was younger we used to get him out on time with the promise of feeding the geese; we live very near to Walthamstow Wetlands. One of Charlie's 'special' interests was birds and particularly geese. He loved to feed them, so our tactic was: 'If you want time to feed the geese...' This worked very effectively for a few years but then one year the bus started picking him up outside our house, a change which made Charlie very angry (well, pretty much any change makes Charlie anxious and angry). I used to get stressed because Charlie couldn't get ready on time and the bus would be outside beeping its horn, with a very impatient driver. Charlie processes information differently to us; he needs quite a bit of time. That was another thing I learned from the training. The trainer suggested counting in your head after asking your child something, so I tried just calling 'Charlie' then counting, usually to about twenty, then he would respond, 'Yeah?' It's amazing how long it takes. Sometimes, evidently, each instruction or bit of information needs processing time. The trouble is, in a neurotypically run world, when you are in a rush, you expect quick answers and actions, which are pretty much impossible for Charlie. Sometimes I would shout at Charlie in the mornings, forgetting to allow for the autism and then I would feel guilty and like a shit dad. We have done lots of independence training with Charlie and he is now able to get himself to college, but it still involves getting him out of the house on time. This is fine when my wife and I are not working or working from home but if we have a meeting to get to it can cause huge amounts of stress.

Revenge of the Dark Side

A year or so after getting his diagnosis and all the additional support we received, the election changed everything. The ConDem government imposed its vicious austerity agenda and we soon discovered that the first services to go were those to vulnerable children and adults. First the funding to charities like the Hamara was cut. I was furious and couldn't believe how heartless the government and the local authority were being. I began campaigning against the cuts, put a social media group together and managed to get the local press involved. I was featured in our local newspaper and this caused a brief reprieve for the Hamara. They managed to soldier on for another couple of years until finally folding under the financial pressure due to the cuts.

The council decided they would no longer fund our support from the Tavistock Clinic. All the support for siblings offered locally disappeared, and gradually over the years we've seen the support available to Charlie and ourselves shrink to almost zero. I was so angry and kept thinking, 'My son didn't cause the deficit, that was the bankers and all their greedy political pals. So why the hell is he paying for it?'

The cuts continued to bite, and as a teenager Charlie has faced a whole new range of challenges but a lot of the support is no longer there. So it has been really hard to deal with all the adolescent stuff Charlie is going through with the added anxieties and difficulties associated with autism. Particularly concerning are the vicious cuts to CAMHS, which Charlie needed to access as he reached post-sixteen. Charlie has suffered with bouts of depression and once again we have had to battle to get him the support he needs. I've found it really hard to deal with some of his mental health problems, not because I don't want to but because I feel so powerless, not knowing what to do. It has had an impact on my mental health and sometimes I can't get the worry out of my head and that impacts on my work. It is a horrible feeling, to feel unable to help the people you love most. The core of being a parent is that feeling of responsibility for someone else and the ability to help them. When you can't help, you feel inadequate and like a failure. All these feelings come out in anger for me and most of my anger is directed at the state for the way it has cruelly turned its back on those with the most need of support. What sort of country doesn't prioritise the most vulnerable citizens, but instead focuses on the needs of business, of the wealthiest?

I helped to set up and have been actively involved with a local group campaigning against all the cuts our children face. This included outrageous cuts to school transport services which has had a huge impact on many vulnerable children. We managed to get the council to backtrack on some of the cuts and to issue apologies for some of the problems.

During this period I lost my dad, which was devastating for me but also it broke my heart to see how upset both my children where. They were both really, really close to him and he was such a huge support for all of us. So in some of the worst points of the cuts I was also dealing with my grief and probably channelled some of my feelings into campaigning and generally ranting and raging about the impact of austerity.

There have been times during these years when my wife and I have been really tight and strong in solidarity with each other. But there have been darker times when our relationship has been really strained. I have a tendency to lose my temper when I'm stressed and I get really snappy with my wife. The thing that saves us in these times is making time for each other. Getting a babysitter, going out and having a bit of normality.

Not a Jedi Yet

I am by no means an expert, however over the years since Charlie was first diagnosed with autism I have learned an incredible amount and I think it has changed me for the better. I understand so much more about autism and realise what a loud, busy, bright and overwhelming place the world can be. I've learned some really helpful stuff about change management and how important it is to explain each stage of what might happen and to avoid the unexpected as much as possible. I've discovered that sometimes people move around on the autistic spectrum, that it's not a fixed thing, so phrases like 'high functioning' aren't always very helpful. My union, PCS, has been one of the leading trade unions in relation to neurodiversity: they have run training courses, established a network of neurodiversity champions and at our annual conference we debate a whole section under the heading 'Neurodiversity'. I am very proud to be involved in such a forward-thinking union. When I told Charlie about all the things PCS are doing, he said 'really' and gave me a massive smile. I have tried to use my knowledge to suggest improvements to the workplace and to things like recruitment. I've also become an experienced campaigner.

Sadly, Andreas decided to leave the country after the Brexit vote, so I volunteered to run the dads group because it has been such a fantastic support over the years. I've learned a huge amount about autism, being a dad and coping, from all the dads who attend that group. All the dads are amazingly open and articulate about their fears and feelings and there is a real sense of supportiveness between us as we help each other navigate the world of parenting a child with additional needs.

We are lucky that Charlie was diagnosed in a time when awareness of autism was increasing at a fantastic pace, thanks to the National Autistic Society, Ambitious about Autism, some trade unions and all the people with autism and their parents who have campaigned and shared their stories with the world. This gives me a real feeling of hope. One of the things that has improved is the way airports support people with autism.

A Long Way

I've discovered a lot about my personal resilience and the things I need to do to ensure I'm coping. Music is probably one of the best therapies for me, listening to it and dancing – alas, I was never able to master an instrument. So, something that keeps me going is regular northern soul nights, which combine hanging with friends, music and dancing. At home I can often be found in the kitchen, music blaring out while I dance and cook dinner.

We have come such a long way since Charlie was first diagnosed, and the support we've received over the years has at times been outstanding. We've been through many, many battles, won and lost. We have come to terms with Charlie's autism and understand so much more about it. The journey has taken us to high peaks, terrible lows and a constant, steady state of perpetual worry.

Charlie has achieved so many things over the years and I am immensely proud of him. He is an amazing swimmer and has won medals for the school, despite the fact that he hates competition. Once we get him over the initial reluctance to go to swimming competitions, he pretty much always wins. That is probably the reason we can get him to go.

Charlie has a range of special interests. He is an expert on Star Wars and his knowledge outweighs mine a hundredfold. I love the fact that he is such an expert and has such a passion for something that I love. Unfortunately, Charlie hates going to the cinema, even to special screenings for neurodiverse people. When *The Force Awakens* was on we booked tickets for us all to go as a family and we made Charlie go; I was convinced he would be fine. He wasn't. He hated the experience and it took us all our resolve and patience to get him in but he wouldn't go into the screen so he and I sat in the corridor with the door held slightly open, until someone complained and the manager made us leave despite me explaining. But I did manage to persuade him in to see the last fifteen minutes of the film, which made me very proud. Since then we haven't tried to take him to the cinema again, although I remain hopeful that he will one day go with some of his mates.

I get really frustrated sometimes with some of Charlie's abilities because he is a really good guitar player; he has been learning the bass for a few years. Charlie has a natural ability; he taught himself to play 'Hey Joe' on his own. But he is reluctant to play, preferring to spend his time on his Xbox or looking at YouTube on his phone. I've been really keen to keep the lessons going and live in hope that one day he will thank me and might even play in a band. The other thing I'm really proud of is Charlie's love of nature, particularly birds and how he can identify them by their song, something my dad loved. I've learned more about birds from Charlie than my dad was ever able to teach me. Again, there is a lot of frustration with Charlie's reluctance to engage with this interest as he has grown older. We do try to get Charlie out into nature and when we battle through the protests and his guard drops he still loves it.

There is one thing that, over all these years I have grown really proud of and that is the fact that Charlie is autistic.

So, after much coaching and cajoling, and a little bit of shouting, we managed to get Charlie into the car ready to go to France. We realised that we probably hadn't done enough preparation but that is not always easy when you are working in busy jobs. Once we got into the airport with Charlie still feeling anxious, we headed over to the additional needs desk to collect a lanyard for Charlie. With that, we were able to fast-track through security which made so much difference for Charlie. Queueing and all the noise and activity is really hard for him. Which meant when we boarded the plane we were all relatively calm. We had a fabulous holiday with Charlie's aunties and a trip on the Petit Train Jaune, yellow is still his favourite colour. While I will always worry about Charlie, I also have a strong feeling of optimism that he will be OK, and maybe become the YouTube star he wants to be, all in yellow, of course.

Chapter 8:

Finding a Way:
Healing After Miscarriage

Andy Kapadia

Although time is a great healer, I still find it hard to talk about the miscarriages we have had and, in writing this, I realised that even after counselling and the birth of my second child, I still have not fully processed the events.

We have two children, but my wife has been pregnant five times. And to my shame, this is something I sometimes forget. I do not know if it is my subconscious protecting me, because when these thoughts do return, I become overwhelmed by a maelstrom of emotions that feels like having a thousand waterfalls poured into the centre of my chest and being drowned from the inside. I have developed ways to cope with it and I guess ignorance may be one. The counselling helped, but as with many things in life, some wounds persist.

I was never the sort of person who had their life mapped out or indeed cared for the details. I had an idea I would follow the basic template – meet a girl, get married, have kids, and the rest would work itself out. My wife and I met when we were seventeen and although we were young, we were sensible enough to take things slowly.

Not that I was cautious in many other aspects of my teenage years. I had a rather all-consuming passion at the time, and that was music. I was obsessed with guitar-based indie music and would spend any spare penny on a new tape, band T-shirt or going to gigs. The first gig I saw was Carter USM supported by The Sultans of Ping, aged fifteen. Somehow, I managed to fool the bar staff to serve me (Asian genes gave me a rather resplendent bumfluff tache) and the heady mix of alcohol, mosh pits and very, very loud music got me hooked.

My approach to relationships was formed by my parents' troubled marriage. They married young – my mum was sixteen and pregnant, and my dad was twenty-two at the time, having recently emigrated from India via Kenya. Their marriage was a tempestuous one which came to an inevitable conclusion after fourteen years. The clashes I witnessed left an indelible mark on me and I was determined that my own relationships would not be like that. I developed a cautious approach to relationships, and the opposite sex in general, so much so that my first serious girlfriend, Susie, ended up becoming my wife.

Susie and I decided to go to different universities to experience life for ourselves. We agreed that it was important for both of us to be individuals and not become one of those couples who are one entity, rather than two separate people. We felt our bond was strong enough for us to stay together and try to make it work. Looking back, I think those early years built the foundation of our relationship that was instrumental in helping us to find the strength to get through the pain and sorrow of losing three babies. We moved in together when we were twenty-four and, not being people who rush things, got married when we were thirty. We had our first child at thirty-two, and that was a relatively trouble-free pregnancy and birth.

Overall, we seemed to be following a very happy path, but experience has taught me that fate often has other ideas. I never considered that miscarriage would come to define certain moments of my life because, ultimately, who does? But in reality, it happens to more people than you might think and is more common than I could have imagined.

According to the charity Tommy's, as many as one in four pregnancies ends in miscarriage. I still find this statistic heartbreaking and whilst there is certainly a little sense of solidarity in knowing more people have experienced this, more strongly there is a feeling of sorrow that so many others have experienced what we have. I still have many questions about our own experiences. We had three miscarriages, and I knew at least twelve people who had successful births. Why did we have to have their share of miscarriages?

It felt, and it feels unfair. I struggle to understand it, to find a reason. What had we done so wrong that meant we had to suffer this? The truth is we will never find out why.

***

The NCT states that the chances of having a miscarriage decrease as the pregnancy progresses: the overall probability of a pregnancy ending in miscarriage in the UK is 25% at four weeks; 5% at eight weeks; 1.7% at twelve weeks; and 0.5% at sixteen weeks.

Our miscarriages were identified as 'missed miscarriages' at twelve weeks, five weeks and eight weeks, so no pattern there. And the nature of missed miscarriages usually means that finding causes is difficult. The Miscarriage Association describes a missed miscarriage as being 'one where the baby has died or not developed, but has not been physically miscarried. In many cases, there has been no sign that anything was wrong, so the news can come as a complete shock.' [1]

Not knowing what the causes of the miscarriages might have been was one of the hardest parts to deal with. Sometimes there is just no reason. Most of the time, with medical problems, there is at least some justification. But miscarriage remains one of those things that seems unsolvable. The NCT states that: 'Despite the fact that approximately 25% of pregnancies end in a miscarriage, we're mostly still in the dark about why.'[2] Reasons such as age and previous miscarriages are cited as factors that could make it more likely. All this despite sex education classes at school leaving me with an impression you would get a girl pregnant even if you *thought* about having unprotected sex with her. So why, when we wanted to have a baby, was something stopping us? I suppose getting pregnant was the easy part, so they got that right. The hard part was the rest of the process.

***

Our first miscarriage was detected at the twelve-week scan. We had told family our news beforehand which may have been seen as tempting fate. But this was going to be our second baby, so what could go wrong? The pregnancy tests were positive, and my wife was experiencing all the usual symptoms. So why would we not tell anyone? We were excited as

---

1 https://www.miscarriageassociation.org.uk/information/miscarriage/missed-miscarriage/

2 https://www.nct.org.uk/pregnancy/miscarriage/miscarriage-your-questions-answered

we really wanted a second child and it had taken us longer to plan and get pregnant this time around.

Our first child, our son, was a textbook planned pregnancy. Checking dates for the 'right time', eating the right foods, having the right sex, my wife fell pregnant quickly. No complications during pregnancy, straightforward birth – like I said, textbook stuff. So why would we not think the second time around it would be just as easy?

My memory of the very moment we were told there was no heartbeat to be found is sketchy. I do remember the sterile whiteness of the room and the tear that rolled down my wife's face when the sonographer confirmed it. I was hit by what felt like a thousand different emotions all at once. Anger, confusion, fear, shame. Thoughts racing through asking why it had happened and why it wasn't the same as the first time. After all, we had done EVERYTHING the same. The thing that sickens me when I think back to that moment, is that, in my ignorance there was a part of me that blamed my wife. The demons roared in my head, 'It must have been her, SHE did something wrong.' The demons were screaming at me, tearing my mind apart. My demons had to be pushed to one side and dealt with later, because the centre of my world was hurting in many more ways than I could possibly imagine. I managed not to listen to them and follow the other part of my brain that told me to just hold her because this loss was not just mine.

I guess people are well-meaning: the support offered from colleagues, friends and family always began with 'Well, thank God you already have a child'. I can only imagine the trauma for people who have multiple miscarriages with no success at all, it must be horrific. We do thank God that we were so lucky first time around, but the sentiment from others did not make things any better; there was a sadness I had never felt before. It felt like someone had left a weight on my chest and refused to lift it. No one could say or do anything that could help, but I knew that I had to find a way to carry on with normal life as my son and wife needed me to. Whether it was manly pride or denial, I don't know. But I felt I had to carry the burden of my sadness. Normal life had to continue and after all, it was my wife, not me, that this had happened to. I felt like I had no right to feel sad about how things had turned out. All of the physical pain was experienced by my wife, so she had that as well as the emotion of grief to deal with. The creation and loss of a life happened to *her* body not mine and this made me feel that my feelings were invalid.

My determination to be the pillar for my wife and boy kept eating away at me, no matter how hard I tried to push it to one side. The darkness kept growing in my soul, and ignoring it was becoming a less viable option. I became very withdrawn and numb to what was going on around me. Instead of providing the support for my wife, I was making things worse between us. The little things bothered me more but instead of talking about them with her, my tactic was to bury and hide my feelings, I just let them fester. I couldn't sleep and ended up drinking more and more heavily in order to anaesthetise the pain and help me drift off at night. The idea of intimacy with her made me feel sick. Nevertheless, I persisted with burying my head in the sand until the darkness grew and grew. Looking back, I think I was being hollowed out from the inside, just becoming a shell. My wife had noticed and tried to encourage me to talk about how I was feeling but my unfounded belief that I would burden her with my grief meant that I didn't. This in turn manifested itself into anger and resentment and for a period of time it felt like we were simply co-existing with each other rather than being the partnership we once were.

I did not realise at the time, but what I was experiencing was mourning. I had never experienced true grief over losing someone. People I knew and family members had died, but I never truly knew that crushing feeling of loss. My father-in-law died sometime after our first miscarriage and I recognised the feeling of grief. This made me wish I had been a bit kinder to myself after the miscarriage. I realised then that I should have allowed myself to acknowledge this and mourn the loss in the same way I grieved when one of the most important male role models in my life had passed away.

***

I woke up one day and thought: this needs to end. My relationship with my wife and boy seemed stretched to a point where it could snap, I needed to take a new approach. My wife had been attending counselling sessions and suggested that I should try to do the same. I was resistant to this, but that morning when I woke up and decided I needed to address this, I accepted my employer's offer to seek counselling, and I will be eternally thankful that I did.

My counsellor helped me to understand why my approach to dealing with the situation was to ignore it, and we explored other things I could do to try to move on. They suggested having a look at the support offered from specialist organisations but I found the support available for partners was limited to short pamphlets and the odd article online. There was, however, an article from The Miscarriage Association which I found particularly useful, as it spoke about the role of partners in miscarriage. It helped to know that

I was not alone in experiencing this and that I was not the only person whose reaction was to shut it out: to be silent and strong. The counselling forced me to be reflective and think about the miscarriage, in essence starting the wheels of processing the event. I now know that this is one of the first steps towards working through the grieving process.

I think the most significant thing the counsellor and I discussed was the importance of speaking to my wife about how I felt. At the time, I did not realise just how vital taking this very simple step would be towards healing, yet it seemed like the hardest. I feel quite ashamed to admit this. Why couldn't I talk to the person to whom I had so publicly committed my life? The person I had spent all my adult life with and promised to share the good and bad times. So why was I frightened to discuss my hurt with her? I kept coming back to the idea that I was protecting her, but ultimately, I knew my silence was doing more harm than good.

The counsellor suggested that I didn't just sit my wife down and offload it all in one talk but rather open up slowly with the aspect I felt comfortable talking about. I cannot remember what the initial talk was. I think it was me admitting I was sad and affected by the miscarriage, and we took it from there. If the truth be told, I don't think my wife and I have really ever fully talked things through. Partly because of our personalities, and partly due to life forcing us to move forward. A lot of what I have written here will be stuff she will be hearing for the first time, and I can only apologise to her for not speaking about this before now.

***

As part of the healing process we needed to discuss whether or not we wanted to try again. I think the assumption was that we would, and even though I felt trying again would be the best way to move on, it was tinged with a sense of apprehension for me. We tried again and my wife fell pregnant, but unfortunately we had another missed miscarriage. This time, at five weeks. Because of the earlier miscarriage, we were under a lot more observation and as such, it was detected earlier.

It was just as heartbreaking and upsetting as the first time, and we both really began to wonder what was wrong with us. What had we done differently since my son was born? The second miscarriage was hard, but we were more prepared to handle the outcome. Certainly from my point of view I was not drawn to the darkness in the same way as before. I was much more prepared to process and move on, and crucially, willing to try again.

We were referred to a specialist to investigate what was going on and various tests were conducted, all of which were inconclusive. We were both healthy and there was no indication as to why it happened. We tried again and suffered our third miscarriage. When we found out my wife miscarried for the third time, there were tears. But the most saddening thing was the sense of normality of the situation. This was how our life was: my wife would get pregnant, we would get excited and then she would miscarry. It sounds quite macabre, but I began to feel a comfortable familiarity with the hospital ward that was responsible for treatment following a miscarriage. I began to know the ins and outs of the process and this in itself made me sadder still. What did it mean to feel at home in a place that is responsible for the clinical process for getting rid of what should have been my baby?

With each miscarriage we did not learn a reason for our loss or find a meaning to the process but what we did discover was resilience. In each of us we grew and discovered a strength that we didn't think we had, a sense of determination and a stubborn hope. Next time it might be different, we thought. Next time we won't have to come here. Each time we would go home and we would look at our beautiful son and we would remember that this was possible, that maybe we just needed to try again.

We now have a little girl who turns four this year. I feel a little guilty admitting that when my wife was pregnant with her we did not allow ourselves to fully embrace the idea and get excited. We were fearful and cautious, tempered by our history.

After each antenatal appointment and each confirmation that everything was all right, I felt a little more relieved and a little more excited. But never to the point of allowing myself to be too carried away; I held back, just in case. Maybe that is the way things go with subsequent children, maybe nothing is ever as exciting as the first time. Or maybe I was just protecting myself because of the miscarriages, I didn't want to get hurt again. Who knows, but the rush of love and joy I felt when my daughter was born was something that I will never forget or experience again.

I guess our story is one of persistence and belief, but I think what I have learned and am still learning is the importance of communicating with my wife and being more open about how I feel. I wish I had been more open with her from the start. I still find it difficult to talk about these experiences and a lot of this will be new to her. I think perhaps if I had opened up sooner, I would not find it so hard to talk about it now.

Chapter 9:

Fitting in to Stand Out:
Set-ups and Setbacks of an Immigrant Dad

Philip Robinson

Do you ever sit and reflect on the string of unexpected circumstances and decisions that brought you to this moment and place in time? Are you amazed and hopeful or at times filled with despair and regret? Hindsight is a privilege and a curse. It informs and sheds light on our next steps, with knowledge and experience, but can also blind and bind us, creating boundaries around safety, relevance and benefit. I write this from a place of hindsight. I never intended to be an immigrant, furthermore an 'immigrant dad', raising kids in an unfamiliar land. My kids were meant to grow up on breadfruit, cou cou, flying fish and mauby, as I did in Barbados, surrounded by siblings, cousins, aunties, uncles, grandparents and friends who looked very much like them, but here I am: married, two children, living in south Manchester in the United Kingdom, a long way away from the Caribbean. I have lived a life of happening upon opportunity and challenge, having at times to commit to a 'yes' or a 'no' on the spot or at least overnight – note that I am not speaking about marriage here, I thought long and hard about that one. Barbados is a paradise that attracts royalty and celebrities, given its sun, sea, sand and various products of sugar. Why would anyone leave? Another peculiarity I find when I reflect on who and where I am is my varied interests. I studied computer science and chemistry, worked in technology for almost twenty-five years and even taught courses in software engineering, yet much of my free time is not committed to coding, scripting and tinkering. I am also a songwriter, a worship leader within a local Christian church, kids' book author and blogger on topics about community, culture and parenting. The worlds of technology and artistry seem very separate – one based on logical precision and the other on emotional expression. Yet I find satisfaction exploring, navigating and switching between these worlds instead of being confronted by conflict. In hindsight, this is my story of home – fitting in, understanding the culture and people wherever I am, but then seeking to stand out, innovate and present new thoughts, ideas and possibilities.

This is Home

When I initially left home, Barbados, I expected to be away for twelve months. Two decades later and, through a series of experiences within and beyond my control, I now have a different impression of what it means to be at home. Raising children in a culture different to the one in which we were raised continues to be a real test of parental adaptability for my wife and me. We were both born, raised and educated in Barbados, moved to Germany once we were married, migrated to Northern Ireland some years later, where both our kids were born, and are currently settled in south Manchester, United Kingdom. We have been through a series of cultural shifts over the last twenty years. Culture is defined by the ideas, customs and behaviours of a certain set of people. The ideas established in a culture influence how we view ourselves and the world around us. They shape our expectations and ambitions, impose limitations on our endeavours and prioritise the things we value and pursue. The customs and traditions we are born into seem normal and we have no reference or past experience to judge them otherwise. An outsider observing a foreign culture is more likely to identify and question practices, foods, styles and behaviours than someone for whom these formed their first impression of what it means to be alive. Like our parents, and their parents before them, we raise our children within a cultural framework that we believe is best for the place, time and purpose we live. The culture of a family may not directly reflect the wider, majority culture of the society in which they live but it does heavily influence perceptions of safety, community and access to resources and opportunities.

As I think about my story of changing localities and places I called home, I see trails of evidence of how changes in culture impacted my worldview and perceptions of opportunities and limitations. These changes have significantly impacted my approach to parenting, which now looks very different to how I was raised. Watching and learning from different people and now having kids of my own, I am convinced that parenting, like medicine, is a practice and not a set of skills acquired from a handbook. We deal with changing knowledge, understanding, health, relationships and circumstances, drawing daily on our own intuition, skills and experiences, and those from others. When you develop the resilience to deal with change, the meaning of home is no longer bound to a particular place or culture, but is a mindset that allows us to plug in and thrive wherever we go. In my aim to develop more resilience as a father, I find the following three reminders useful, when faced with new circumstances or people:

- **Be humble.** Do not expect that I need to know everything and do not hold my parenting skills above others.
- **Be relational.** Get to know my wife, children, teachers and neighbours better, as well as play a role in raising my kids.
- **Be determined.** Never think that I am not equipped to be a father. Always aim to acquire knowledge but not to doubt, deny or denigrate my deserving of being a father.

This mindset has helped in my journey of fitting in and finding community in a culture where I am labelled as an ethnic minority and a foreigner. My wife and I now endeavour to use this foundation of fitting in to raise children who stand out as citizens and contributors to the land of their birth and the world, confident that they will always know the true meaning of home. We want that they experience many positive set-ups as a result of their ethnicity but are aware of the setbacks that they might encounter, just as we have on our journey as immigrant parents.

The Missing Mother-in-Law

One of the first setbacks we faced as new parents was not having our own parents in proximity, advising us every step of the way. While to some this might seem like a gift, given the stereotypical notion of an intrusive, meddling, opinionated 'monster-in-law', we experienced daunting knowledge gaps and moments of anxiety as we were expecting our first child. These might have

117

been alleviated by having our parents' wise and present counsel. Yes, they were only a phone call or Internet chat away, but technology can never replace casual drop-ins, random meals and extra hands. In the UK, a survey by age. uk[1] of 5 million grandparents showed that 12% looked after their grand-children at least once a day, 18% four to six times per week and 38% two to three times per week. Having grandparents nearby brings many benefits in the early years and beyond.

Three months before our daughter was born, my wife suggested that we would need help and that her mother should come all the way from Barbados and stay with us for a while in our cosy, three-bedroom, semi-detached house. My man-mind immediately thought that we should avoid having another person in our house and just enjoy the experience of being a family unit, figuring it out, adapting, evolving and innovating along the way. Certainly, we were equipped to look after our own baby. How hard could it be? We didn't consult her mother about conception, at least not to my knowledge, so why should we suddenly need her help? Surely this was an opportunity for us to lean on our intuition and develop a parenting style that suited us and our baby. Long story short, that same evening we arranged to have my mother-in-law come over for the birth and first few weeks of our daughter's life, and eventually did the same some years after when our second child was born. This made a significant difference for which I am always grateful.

I recall the first time we had to bathe our newborn daughter. I was like a fish out of water. It is hard to imagine the complexities of holding a tiny, helpless human being in a tub of water sufficient to drown them, while their soft, slippery, soapy skin makes it seemingly impossible to stop them from going under. As my mother-in-law observed us awkwardly fumbling, panicking each time our daughter slipped from our grasp and making bath time into a tedious two-person task, she intervened and demonstrated to us the grip. The basis of the grip is to secure the child with a reverse, under-arm embrace, supporting their back and leaving one hand free for soap and washing. Lightbulb! We went from anxious slips and splashes to calmly soaking, soaping and enjoying the experience of bath time. It dawned on me that my wife's mother maybe recalled the first time she had to bathe a baby, as she watched us, and was able to share a technique that was passed on from generation to generation.

---

1 https://www.ageuk.org.uk/latest-news/articles/2017 september five-million-grandparents-take-on-childcare-responsibilities/

My mother-in-law eventually returned home and left us for the first time to figure out parenting on our own. Having now earned our certificate of competence in bathing, dressing, cleaning and feeding a baby, we could now think of the wider picture of raising our infant daughter. She was an easy baby. We were able to continue our social lives, unlike stories we had heard from other parents. I remember going out for a romantic dinner in a nice Italian restaurant, when our daughter was only one week old, and enjoying tasty lasagne, risotto and red wine, as she quietly slept in her buggy next to our table. When she woke for a feed, that was swiftly done without missing a beat in our conversation or disrupting the ambience. We were also both able to continue practising and performing with the Belfast Community Gospel Choir (BCGC), taking our little baby every-where. She grew accustomed to the sound and often slept through the loud singing, hand-clapping and foot-stomping that were naturally part of a gospel choir's rehearsals and concerts. The choir was our community away from home and we had the benefits of gifts, advice and frequent offers for babysitting.

I learned a lesson in humility by having my mother-in-law come stay with us and help us cope with our kids in a way that avoided the strain that babies can often place on relationships. Relate.org.uk[2] estimate that parents argue 40% more after having a new baby, due to lack of sleep, less sex, less money and additional duties with uncertain distribution. We had all the above but having the extra pair of hands gave us space to still invest time in our relationship with the assurance that our newborn was in good hands. Once my mother-in-law left, we were determined to maintain the rhythm and flow we had established as parents, with some obvious adjustments. This would mean having people we could trust with more intimate aspects of our lives and insight to our struggles. We learned along the way to invest and withhold trust with the same mindset as time and money, and to treat advice, recommendations and offers to help with careful scrutiny.

The 'Normal-Abnormal' Persuasion

Finding a community and establishing a circle away from home is a wonderful thing, even though it could not possibly replace the comfort and solace of a

---

2 https://www.relate.org.uk/relationship-help/help-family-life-and-parenting/new-parents/top-4-reasons-couples-argue-after-having-baby

tight-knit family you knew all your life. We wanted to persuade ourselves that living away from family was a perfectly normal thing to do and that we could recreate the same social support and network we had back in Barbados. Yet we encountered the reality of being obviously foreign in Northern Ireland daily, which is still not as ethnically diverse as other regions in the United Kingdom. The 2011 census recorded 0.2% black people[3] of Caribbean and African origin, which is consistent with the infrequent encounters we had with black people on the streets of Belfast. In fact, once I had become the Public Relations Officer for the African and Caribbean Support Organisation Northern Ireland (ACSONI), it felt as though I knew every black person in the province. Even if that was not the case, when two black people came face-to-face in the city centre, we greeted each other as though our paths stretched far before that moment. Having the sense that here before me was yet another person who could probably understand and share my experience is an inexplicable injection of hope.

We tried our hardest not to fall into an exclusive circle of blackness, which would isolate us from the majority of people around us and experiencing the native culture of the place we lived. That said, getting together with other Caribbean nationals have been some of our best times away from Barbados. Still, we refuse to give our kids the impression that skin colour should be a social filter and factor for determining their likes, dislikes and aspirations for life. There will always be events that place a spotlight on difference, no matter how hard you try to blend into the environment, but these are anomalies unless you are in a hostile environment or position where you have to encounter matters of difference as a profession.

I'll share one scenario where our difference seemed placed or misplaced in the spotlight. When my daughter was six months old, she had an extreme form of eczema, which left flakes of dead skin scattered in her bed every morning. We tried every form of baby-friendly ointment on the market and bathed her in the richest emollient prescribed, but the condition grew worse. On top of that, our daughter kept repeating her milk like a severe form of acid reflux, which meant that she had to be changed after every feed and was an unhappy, unsmiling baby, even though she had the rounded appearance of a miniature sumo wrestler. We took her to our local GP, who just advised us to keep on doing what we were doing and that reflux was a common issue

3 http://www.ninis2.nisra.gov.uk/public/Theme.aspx?themeNumber=74&themeName=Population

with tiny babies. Furthermore, the eczema was possibly an abnormality with her type of skin in the cold, wet Irish climate. While the GP meant well, all we heard was: 'You are not from here and you are suffering as a result.' Even with that interpretation, we took comfort that abnormality was sufficient explanation for her extreme skin condition, such that we should treat it as a normal phase of her development. After all, many of the medical statistics published by the NHS, such as hypertension[4], diabetes[5] and death on the transplant waiting list[6], often show black and Asian populations to be the major group affected. For example, according to diabetes.org.uk, 'People of Black African origin are up to three times more likely to develop Type 2 diabetes than people of White European origin.'

Then came a morning that is etched on our memories as parents. Our daughter had been looking pale and puffy as her skin peeled, she was losing her hair and the post-feed reflux worsened. On that day, her eyes started to swell and eventually protruded, startling us to a point of inert panic. We finally decided to go directly to the Accident and Emergency area of the Children's Hospital, which turned out to be the absolute right thing to do. There in the waiting room, holding our sickly baby, we felt alone, as there were no parents or relatives nearby, who would be compelled by blood to rush to our side. Once a consultant doctor on call saw our daughter, she immediately went about setting up urgent blood tests and got her attached to a saline drip. The upfront diagnosis was that our daughter was malnourished and had not been consuming sufficient nutrients from her feeding. Yes, one of those moments when you feel like a complete failure in parenting, as we had even joked that our daughter's chubby appearance and vomiting of milk was due to her appetite and overfeeding. It was revealed to us that her chubby appearance was swelling and retention of water in her body, and her iron, calcium, protein and zinc levels were desperately low.

Had we kept on believing that eczema and vomiting were normal infant experiences, we would have probably returned to the pharmacy to get treatment for her eyes. After further tests, the consultant doctor rushed into our ward and said to stop feeding our daughter! The tests showed that she had an allergy to milk protein including her own mother's milk. The

---

4 https://www.bhf.org.uk/informationsupport/risk-factors/ethnicity

5 https://www.diabetes.org.uk/research/our-research-projects/london/black-african-ethnicity-and-type-2-diabetes-risk

6 https://www.organdonation.nhs.uk/helping-you-to-decide/organ-donation-and-ethnicity/

allergy was the root cause of her eczema, vomiting, bloating and malnour-ishment. Our blinkered feeding regime was poisoning our daughter and we had no clue. My wife felt especially discouraged and judged as a mother, as these first few months of feeding and bonding are meant to be precious, intimate moments with her baby. As a result of the milk allergy, we had to shift our daughter to a non-dairy formula or she would have to be continu-ously tube fed in order to get her nutrient levels up to a healthy state. The formula smelt and tasted rotten, such that my daughter refused to drink it. To make things worse, my wife was not allowed to feed her the formula, as she would seek out the alternative. I then had to take on the role of feeding for the next few weeks, starting by getting her to actually take the bottle. Once she did finally drink and seemingly enjoy the formula, we noted changes in her alertness. Within one week we had a totally different baby. She smiled for the first time and her nature became more apparent. Yet she rapidly lost weight and roundness as the water retention that puffed out her skin had now gone. The eczema too had lessened, but the damage to her skin meant that we had to keep her wrapped in wet bandages for weeks to hyper-moisturise her body. On top of that, being the only infant of Afro-Caribbean descent with a severe eczema that they had seen in person, we were constantly being seen by student doctors eager to record and research this exotic phenomenon.

We spent two weeks in hospital with our daughter and had many visitors bringing meals and support, again reinforcing the need for community wherever you settle. Within another few weeks, our daughter was well enough to travel and she and my wife went to Barbados for a bit of relief. Once my wife's family saw this pale, balding baby wrapped up like an Egyptian mummy in bandages and drinking the potato-smelling formula, they immediately sprang into action and brought the Bajan remedies and recipes out of the cupboard. She spent six weeks being rubbed with cocoa butter and being anointed with castor oil, while her new diet consisted of barley, linseed and plenty of sunshine. Within days she started to thrive, her hair started to grow, her skin glowed and tanned and she was putting on weight healthily, defying the expectations of the medical staff back in the UK.

Up to three years after my daughter's miraculous recovery, we had appoint-ments with the dermatologist asking for hair samples and taking pictures of her skin for use in medical journals. The doctors seemed convinced that there was something extraordinarily healing about Barbados, as they had never witnessed such a full recovery. This did make us wonder if we were doing the right thing taking ourselves and having our children away from the climate, culture and cuisine that made us. It seems like there are no right or wrong decisions to some extent, except the decision to quit and refuse to get up and try again and again.

Welcome to the Neighbourhood

Moving house and country is a sure way of introducing uncertainty into your life. Not having a base and place where you feel rooted blurs the concept of home. We have moved house as a couple and a family several times. It has been both exhausting and expensive, as furniture was dismantled, promises of clearing the shed were finally fulfilled and fragile possessions were carefully wrapped and placed in boxes. Ultimately, it was not the packing and cleaning that fed anxiety, it was not knowing what to expect from the new neighbourhood. Nicky Lidbetter, chief executive of the charity Anxiety UK points out that moving house is one of life's most stressful experiences, and it's because it involves having to cope with change. We coped best when we were organised. I remember one move where I flat-packed and colour-coded every item of furniture based on its destination room once we moved house. The movers were impressed and marvelled that we actually got everything done in three hours. On another occasion, packing was so hectic that we almost missed our ferry, trying to pack random necessities into our small car. However, with each move, we did our research online, paid visits during the day and night before committing to moving, which gave us greater confidence when moving.

My wife and I were married in my second year of living in Germany and stayed there for a further three years before moving to Northern Ireland. Although we both learned to speak German sufficiently well, we did not feel the timing was right for children (*Es war einfach nicht für uns der richtige Zeitpunkt, Kinder zu haben*). I have so much respect for anyone placing themselves in a country where they do not speak the language and having to figure out life while trying to just figure out what people are saying. I have even more admiration for those bold enough to bring children into that situation and go on to settle, integrate and raise them in confidence. We were surrounded by families with young children, especially when we became members of the *Freie evangelische Gemeinde* (FeG) (Free Evangelical Church) in Karlsruhe, where we still have many friends and fond memories. German parenting and education looked different to what we knew. They encouraged their children to be independent, adventurous and nature-loving from a very early age. There was a calmness when children explored, climbed and fell. They were encouraged and expected to be bilingual by the age of eight or nine, and at least able to understand the major languages surrounding the region – French, Spanish and Dutch – along with English. In Germany, we decided that whenever we had children, we would want to raise them with some of the principles of *selbstaendigkeit* (independence) we saw from our German friends. However, that was easier said than done, as we have certain behaviours and instincts so deeply entrenched in us that they drive our decisions, even without us noticing.

When kids come along, the decision about where to live becomes even harder. There is the consideration of living within the catchment area of good schools, while having amenities, green spaces and decent places to eat nearby. Above all else, no parent wants to raise their kids in a neighbourhood with a reputation for crime and antisocial behaviour. The chances of them being harmed or falling in with the wrong crowd are too high. This does raise some difficulties for migrant parents, as we often come to the UK as students (even if working part-time) or on salaries that are lower than the average UK native, unless arriving as a highly skilled worker. The Joseph Rowntree Foundation (JRF) published a report in 2016 on foreign-born people and poverty[7], which showed a 45% poverty rate for children with foreign-born parents, compared with 24% for children of UK-born parents. Secondly, as migrants, we lack the local knowledge and social stigmas associated with certain areas, such that we may easily make decisions based on affordable housing as opposed to reputation. Given disconnection from the social situation of an area locally known as unsafe, it is easy for migrants to find themselves committing to living in neighbourhoods they regret. Doing our initial research and being intentional about obtaining local knowledge and perspective beforehand, we have spared ourselves the agony of living in a place that we regretted. Yet we know various cases where people have had to endure the grief of being racially abused on the streets and feeling unsafe in their homes, even having their windows broken and walls defaced with unfriendly sentiments, as they were unaware of the social tensions and forces. Back in 2014, just before we left Belfast, there were a series of attacks[8] on African and Caribbean migrants living in social housing, generally followed by the slogans 'Blacks Out' and 'Local Homes 4 Local People'. After hearing

---

7 https://www.jrf.org.uk/report/foreign-born-people-and-poverty-uk
8 https://www.theguardian.com/uk-news/2014/jun/18 nigerian-family-gives-up-new-home-loyalist-racist-protest-belfast-northern-ireland

one of my friend's personal story and the effect it had on her sons, I wrote a
poem called 'Lullaby in A Minor':

> *Now rest from your jumping and skipping and running,*
> *Arms and legs grow tired from playing,*
> *Exercising your rights all day.*
> *You must be tired, son:*
> *Dexterity and skill in high demand,*
> *As those who playfully chased you home*
> *Encouraged you never to look behind –*
> *I'm so glad you are seldom alone.*
> *Have a bath, son:*
> *You are soaked in history,*
> *Water won't dilute your beauty,*
> *You are polished with a varnish that nature prizes.*
> *Don't worry, son,*
> *Soap won't tarnish the memories of today –*
> *The bubbles will burst and float away…*
>
> *Don't be startled by the drumming on the door,*
> *Ignore the crash of the cymbal that now makes our*
> *Living room openly, undeniably part of the neighbourhood;*
> *Beads and shards of glass*
> *Lay like a pirate's bounty gifted and emptied*
> *At the front of our house, the street light causing them to glow –*
> *At some angles you can see the tiniest of rainbows.*
> *This stone, obedient to the attraction*
> *Of our dwelling's floor, is an invitation:*
> *Be strong by day and resilient by night.*
> *Sleep, my son.*
> *Sleep.*

There is very little sleep in the first week of moving. It takes time to feel
settled in a new space but there is also loads of work to do to make settling
in as smooth as possible. Whenever we move, once the essential dishes are
unpacked and the beds assembled, the next task is always to check out the
neighbours – the potential childcarers and sharers of news over the fence.
We've had some excellent neighbours in the different places we have lived,
but this is not the experience of all migrants and ethnic minorities. While

we have been able to live in quiet, reasonably middle-class neighbourhoods, we were aware of friends living in more socially deprived locations and having serious challenges with the neighbours and the neighbourhood. In the neighbourhoods we lived, meeting the neighbours was a task. You could spend your entire life in a place and only occasionally see your neighbours taking out the bins or rushing off to work. I've had occasions where I sat next to someone in silence for an entire bus journey, got off at the same stop, proceeded to walk in the same direction, still in silence, and never realised we lived in the same street. While it is good to have the assurance of privacy and quietness in these neighbourhoods, it can be a lonely place to raise children. Some years ago, a study on community spirit in the UK[9], based on a three-year research project by Sheffield Hallam University (2009–2011) concluded that stronger community spirit thrived in more deprived areas in Britain. This is ironic, as, in another study from Civitas.org.uk[10], highest criminality and victims of violent crime are from deprived areas in the UK. It seems that high interactivity and interdependency in neighbourhoods with less space and individual wealth can lead to both a heightened sense of community but a greater risk of violent contention, which are difficult prospects to reconcile as a parent.

Involve.org.uk[11] identify public participation as a major contributor to community cohesion but emphasise that this is not the only means by which this is achieved. Given that a strong sense of community is good for my children, I take it upon myself to find ways of encouraging community-mindedness. This involves simple things such as intentionally walking over to the neighbours and introducing myself, before they can scuttle back indoors. This is risky, as not all neighbours are open to needing to know others beyond a face and a door number. Otherwise, I extend gestures such as bringing in the bins, sweeping leaves and alerting them of things we should be aware of in the neighbourhood. It is by no means the form of open community spirit that we knew growing up in Barbados, but it is better than being isolated and disconnected. The benefits of being relational always outweigh the risks, once sound principles guide the process of choosing and losing relationships.

---

9 https://www.jrf.org.uk/report/low-income-neighbourhoods-britain

10 https://www.civitas.org.uk/content/files/povertyandcrime.pdf

11 https://www.involve.org.uk/sites/default/files/field/attachemnt/Everybody-Needs-Good-Neighbours-a-study-of-the-link-between-public-participation-and-community-cohesion.pdf

Friends Are the Family We Choose

Not only is a strong sense of community good for children, it is good for us as adults and parents. In the mid-1990s, Barbados' leader of the opposition, the late, Hon. David Thompson, created a campaign called 'Families First', as his answer to dealing with issues of rising crime and economic disparity on the island. Thompson, himself a father of three, was heckled by his political opposers, economic pundits and members of the public, who saw the focus on families as a fanciful proposition that had no place on a political stage. Certainly, we shouldn't be sorting out family problems when the economy is in such a desperate state. Thompson was unsuccessful in that particular general election, but did become Prime Minister in a subsequent campaign. Since his unfortunate illness and death in 2010, many have remembered his politics that stretched beyond economics into the reality of community, family and relationships.

As dads, it is often natural for us to think about the well-being of our partner and children ahead of our own and even beyond economic welfare. Looking back at our hospital episode with our daughter, we instinctively demoted work commitments and finances as major concerns, as our focus became regaining a healthy child. Personal sacrifice seems reasonable, when considering the longer-term investment in children, who will go on to represent our image, ideas and ideals when we are gone, hopefully passing these on for generations. Yet we end up wrestling with the two equally reasonable drivers of being selfless versus being satisfied. If we pursue personal satisfaction at the expense of our families, we will fail them. If we selflessly seek the well-being of our families and neglect ourselves, we will still fail our families in the long run. The only way I have found to create this balance is by having a good circle of friends – people that I could turn to beyond the family with whom I share every other aspect of life.

During high school I played volleyball for the school's team. We were rather successful and always made the finals of the volleyball league, often coming out as champions. Our coach was the school's librarian and as strict on sporting discipline as she was on education. She helped to nurture discipline, cooperation and determination in us during our teenage years, a time when it is difficult for young boys and girls to remain resilient against negative peer pressure that leads to antisocial behaviour. The friends I made during that time are still like brothers some two decades later. However, once I left Barbados, even with social media and the ease of keeping contact over the Internet, it became less realistic to maintain close, informed friendships without frequent gatherings, which normally included good food, and a steady flow of unguarded conversation, interrupted only by uproarious laughter. Looking back, I benefited from these friendships more than I can measure.

Moving to Germany on my own was much more daunting than I had anticipated. It was cold and, as I travelled further away from the main city, the signage and people stopped being bilingual. I was fortunate to have an intensive German course planned for my first two weeks, which was a great way of realising the challenges of learning the language. I looked forward to Mondays and dreaded Friday evenings, as my only proper encounter with people who knew me by name was in the workplace. I felt homesick and alone but managed to survive my first few months by working long hours and exploring the surrounding region by bike. I grew a lot on my own and in hindsight I am very thankful for those two years of lonely weekends and having to learn more about my character, strengths and limitations. Germans were also very private people and not ones for small talk and superficial chatter. It took a long time to make friends but once those friends were made, they were meaningful and significant. These friendships made a difference in learning to speak the language, become more integrated in the culture and maintain my mental well-being.

One other challenge I had while in Germany was being away from my girlfriend, now wife, for two years. We were together when I left Barbados and managed to survive a long-distance relationship through consistent contact (even before Facebook), making promises, keeping most of them and forgiving the ones that were broken. Before we were married and a couple, older people in Barbados would ask, 'So, when you two plan to get married now?' Once we were married, the next question was, 'So you married now, when are the babies coming?' You would probably need some immersion in Bajan society to feel comfortable with this personal, lovingly intrusive inqui-sition. Leaving Barbados spared us from these questions on a daily basis, but we had already resolved to spend time getting to know each other and our new world a bit better before introducing new people. I recall being back in Barbados on holiday and one senior member of our family circle stating in jest that we were not intent on obeying God's creation commandment to be 'fruitful and multiply'. My response was, in an uncharacteristic moment of quick thinking, 'we are being fruitful, multiplication will come later.'

Multiplication came in the second year of leaving Germany and moving to Northern Ireland when our daughter was born. Having kids creates a context for different types of friendships and conversations and again widens the friendship circle. Yet you can alienate your non-parent friends by switching conversations to nappies, milk and potty training. Another thing: friendships can easily become hand-picked based on childcare potential, for every young neighbour with the ability to keep their own kids alive is a potential babysitter. These types of parenting friendships continued to grow through casual meetings in the playground, after-school pickups and activities, birthday parties and Saturday morning football in the rain. As necessary as this mode of child-centred friendship forming is, making this the main point of friendship is not sustainable. Without authentic friendships that were not just based on our shared circumstance of parenting, I felt as though something was missing, even with a growing circle, including my 996 Facebook friends. Anthropologist Robin Dunbar proposes a theory that humans generally have the capacity to maintain up to 150 stable relationships, due to our cognitive limitations. Beyond 150 the bonds are more superficial, less reliant on assumed cultural norms and require rules, legislation and formal code of conduct in order to maintain functional cohesion. The way we discipline our children is based on cultural norms, our memories of how we were disciplined as children and the boundaries established by the legislation of the place we live in. Our approach to discipline is a continuous process of trying, falling, recovering and climbing.

West-Indian Discipline Is Not Everyone's Cup of Tea

If you grew up in the Caribbean or were raised by West Indian parents, you will be familiar with sayings such as, 'hard ears you won't hear, by and by you will feel.' The term 'hard ears' means disobedient or one who has difficulty hearing and translating instruction into practice. 'Hard ears children' were the source of torment for their parents and there was only one recourse – inflict pain in the form of a smack until their ears softened and their ways changed. I myself was dubbed a 'hard ears boy' for a brief period of my early years, but the feelings that I felt (usually from the snap of a belt or rod) during those years, led to some quick re-evaluation of my choices, such that I became the well-mannered, courteous man that I am today. When discussing with my friends and peers who grew up under a similar regime, we never felt abused or unloved and, moreover, we praised our parents for being so hands-on with their discipline. When we consider the alternatives, many of our peers who hardly experienced a 'good licking' from their parents as children were now, as adults, either unemployable, drug-addicted, incarcerated or dead. Still, if we are honest with ourselves, those of us brought up under strict, fear-led discipline struggled in other areas such as confidence, assertiveness and pushing the boundaries, which are all attributes required for roles in leadership and creativity.

The debate about corporal punishment and smacking being used as effective means of discipline has been ongoing for many years. Recent reports state that it is now scientifically proven that there are strong links between corporal punishment in children and problems they experience with mental health, learning and social interaction as adults. It is only recently that legal bans against smacking kids have been established in the UK, where it is completely banned only in Scotland. In other UK territories corporal punishment is banned in schools but allowed by parents as 'reasonable chastisement', if there are no cuts, bruises or marks left on the skin. Growing up in the Caribbean I can only recall few cases of children being smacked until they endured injury, but for each of these cases the parents had a history of aggression, mental health struggles (including depression and low self-esteem), substance abuse and neglect. However, I still contend that both ends of the discipline spectrum are responsible for aggressive, antisocial behaviour: constantly smack a child and they will believe that lashing out is the only way to respond when unhappy with someone's behaviour. Conversely, let a child do as they please and they will have no boundaries or respect for others. We need a measured approach to discipline, that protects and nurtures children in the right way, but also enables parents and teachers to be in control. If parents and teachers are not on the same page when it comes to discipline, there will always be children that are extremely difficult to manage. We need to have conversations together that honestly explore ways of improving the concept of discipline (reprimand, reinforcement and reward), unpacking the cultural baggage with which we all travel.

'Sparing the rod' has little to do with whipping children with wooden sticks and more to do with establishing boundaries. Establishing boundaries can be done through conversation, demonstration, incentive/reward or deterrents/punishment. Traditional Caribbean culture (partly from the remnants of British, Victorian culture) tended to rely heavily on physical punishment such that many opportunities to build confident, gentle character were possibly missed. Making work and labour into punishments rather than acts of service feels like an embrace of our historical narrative, which we need to rise above and beyond. Discipline should be periods of exclusion, reflection and vision setting. For those who still believe in a need for more physical intervention, they should make sure that does not become the centrepiece of discipline, meted out in anger, rather with love and desire for our kids to thrive. Though I still question if that is entirely achievable, as self-control and reason often refrain from any form of lashing out. Childhood discipline is not a 'one size fits all' approach – that's not what is required or should be pursued. It requires us to constantly evaluate and even change our principles of discipline, and only then discover new methods over time. When we hear the quotation from Proverbs 13:24 'Spare the rod and spoil the child', we no longer think of someone withdrawing their correction stick but understand this as a need to create measured boundaries within which children can flourish and not turn rotten. The way those boundaries are established, reinforced, tightened and extended will vary from child to child, but the principles of remove violence, increase reason, emphasise psychological safety and demonstrate respect can apply across the board. It is hard to stop what we've seen, done and known all our lives without humble acceptance that there are shortfalls, relationships that positively challenge us and the determination to change.

When Race Is In Your Face

One of the issues I often worry about, as a parent of ethnic minority children, is my kids being limited, pigeon-holed or bullied as a result of their race. Stereotyping and bullying are worldwide social phenomena that seem to correlate with the increasing levels of diversity and insecurity. The likelihood of bullying increases as a society becomes more diverse and differences are obvious and contentious. We can choose to find beauty in difference or be threatened by its existence.

P(BULLYING) ∝ DIVERSITY X INSECURITY

The Education Policy Institute (EPI)[12] found in a study that ethnic minority kids experienced more bullying than their majority group peers. The Anti-Bullying Alliance[13] revealed figures about the prevalence of bullying among young people in the UK, including that 40% of young people experienced online or in-person bullying within the last twelve months at the time of the study and that the most common form of bullying was name-calling. They borrow the following definition of bullying from the 1999 Stephen Lawrence Inquiry:

---

12 https://epi.org.uk/publications-and-research/bullying-a-review-of-the-evidence/

13 https://www.anti-bullyingalliance.org.uk/tools-information/all-about-bullying/prevalence-and-impact/prevalence-bullying

'The repetitive, intentional hurting of one person or group by another person or group, where the relationship involves an imbalance of power. It can happen face to face or online.' (Based on the definition of racism from the Stephen Lawrence Inquiry in 1999 by MacPherson.)

The above-mentioned study goes on to report on the effects of bullying such as truancy, parental or institutional exclusion (based on the victims' visible, behavioural response and not necessarily the bullies), raised aggression, physical violence and harm, and ongoing mental health problems. What seems like playful acts of name-calling can hence escalate into bullying and aggression when unchecked.

When we lived in Northern Ireland, our daughter started primary school. She was the only black child in her class and one of five in the entire school. We knew that at some point in time we would have a conversation about race and difference but it came sooner than expected. My daughter was always very socially confident and liked to make friends, before she could even walk. Everyday there would be someone new inviting her or themselves to a sleepover after school, to the point that we ran out of excuses. Children have a way of wearing you down. As she was fitting in so perfectly, we almost forgot that she still stood out until that day she came home visibly annoyed: 'Daddy, a boy at school keeps calling me "poo-poo face".' I rose up, put on my camouflaged overalls, used two fingers to apply black combat paint beneath my eyes and grabbed my machine gun from the cupboard. 'Where is he now?' I asked in my deepest, gruffest voice. Well, that is the scene that played out in my head, probably as a result of watching far too many late-night action movies. I hugged my daughter and said, 'He just doesn't understand the beauty of your lovely brown face.' She seemed consoled with that response and I felt like a top dad, who had been parachuted into Belfast to fight racism with an arsenal of music, love and reason.

Some days later, I was retelling the scenario to one of my dear friends of Jamaican origin, who also lived in Northern Ireland. I explained how I framed my response and did not dwell on the racial insult this victim of his environment had hurled at my daughter. My friend sighed and said, 'You obviously forget what little boys are like at that age. For them, every girl is a "poo-poo face".' It has nothing to do with race! Kids at that age hardly have issues with race and ethnicity, but they do recognise difference in gender, for reasons that are beyond my knowledge or space to explore. I had addressed the wrong issue, based on my own social conditioning. I was in fact rein-forcing racial difference as opposed to having a more general conversation about kindness, respect and relationships.

It was around this time I had an idea to write a kids' book, which I eventu-ally published in 2017, called *Nia and the Kingdoms of Celebration*. I wrote this book after being dismayed by the lack of kids' books featuring black characters but, moreover, the absence of characters described as beautiful. Unlike the classical Euro-centric fairy and princess stories that weighed down my daughter's bookshelf at that time, black characters were hardly referred to as beautiful. Snow White, Cinderella and Belle from Beauty and the Beast were all renowned for their physical beauty, which was established upfront and often overlaid inner beauty. The fair maidens are always kind, caring and loved even by birds, chipmunks and talking fish. Most kids' books with black characters tend to talk about struggles with poverty, identity and hair, where the acceptance of beauty comes at the end of the journey, rather than a clear reality at the start of the story. In *Nia and the Kingdoms of Celebration*, Nia, the protagonist, is introduced as follows on the second page of the story:

'Princess Nia was very beautiful. Her skin was dark like the bark of the cassia tree and glowed as though the sun's rays lived in her cheeks.'

Before I was a dad and bedtime-story reader, I would not have realised the significance of the above statement. As I promoted the book and received feed-back, I became more convinced that this missing affirmation of beauty in kids' books has had adverse effects on self-image and culture. The skin-bleaching market continues to grow to a multibillion industry, as the perception that people with lighter skin tones are more beautiful and even more intelligent prevails. This results in a social disparity between degrees of darkness, where darker-skinned people are often hired, paid and progressed less than their lighter-skinned counterparts. Lighter-skinned people are hence often more confident and assertive, while darker-skinned people with strong, dominant personalities can be misunderstood and labelled as 'aggressive'. As a father, I don't want race and ethnicity to be major topics of discussion with my kids, as this takes away from time spent developing social skill and expanding their broader knowledge of the world. Yet I need to ensure that they are confident in their skin and know without a doubt that beauty does not have a race, colour or ethnicity. It is not exclusive to a specific physique, hair type or style. Every child needs to be told they are beautiful and see themselves in the stories they read. We cannot be too hard on ourselves when we continue to expose them to the same literature and repeat the same mistakes over and over again, but we have to be actively aware that living and moving within the confines of cultural stereotypes and behaviours is detrimental to our children achieving their greatest potential. None of us are perfect. None of our cultures are perfect and it is almost impossible to change from what we have seen, known and done all our lives.

Roots, Rituals, Relationships and Restrictions

It is the things that we have seen, known and done all our lives that set us up or set us back. I often get welcoming questions about my accent, as it tells a story of my journey over the last twenty years. It is at its roots a Bajan accent, but it now comes with an extra layer of intent, from my time in Germany, where I had to focus on being understood, and meanders into a recognisable Northern Irish lilt whenever I make jokes or recall experiences from our ten years in Belfast. I can no longer claim to be 100% Bajan, even though I still hold the passport, memories, ties and vernacular of the nation and culture. I notice it when I go back for a visit, even though my wife and I often exchange thoughts about what life would be like should we choose to return. Nevertheless, having children not born and raised in Barbados becomes the overruling factor that brings those conversations to a graceful end. Our children do not have the same experience and affiliations as us, such that any judgements we make about their well-being have to take this into account.

In her talks and writing, Taive Selasi[14] talks about having multiple identities and coins the term 'multi-local', emphasising that our current locality is more relevant to discussion at the point in time than the place we were born. Selasi states that our locality is where we carry out our *rituals* and *relationships*, but how we experience our locality depends in part on our *restrictions*. This perspective of multi-locality helps to shape the way we raise our children to commit to the place they are living in but recognise that as a result of their cultural connections, they may have different opportunities to pursue but also different constraints and barriers to tackle.

Every time we take our kids back to Barbados, within the first week they tend to stick out. While they are black and have Barbadian features, their mannerisms, posture, style, speech and expectations are very British. This works to their advantage, as the impression of *going up north to better yourself*

---

14   https://www.ted.com/speakers/taiye_selasi

still exists in Barbados, and they would be treated, ironically, like royalty. Within one week, once they socialise with their cousins, relatives and other neighbourhood children in the sun, their demeanour and speech change, as well as the depth of darkness and glow of sweat and oils on their skin. They become Bajan and seem to enjoy it, until a plate of rice and peas, cou cou (a mixture of boiled cornmeal or polenta with okra) or pudding (a steamed, spicy, sweet potato-based black pudding) and souse (pickled pigs' feet) is placed in front of them. Children are experts at assimilating culture and we enjoy seeing them embrace some of our native traits and experience some of the joys we had as kids. However, bearing in mind that their time on the island is only short, we consciously remind them that 'tek dis from muh' is better said as 'please take this from me'. I love that they understand and enjoy speaking our native dialect but, by not practising the 'Queen's English', this puts them at a disadvantage when back at school in the UK. It may seem like we are snubbing the rhythm and tone of our native home, but that is not the case. We try to ensure that our kids are familiar with and appreciate our cultural context, but it is more important that they remain relevant and equipped for the one where they are being raised. That said, there are things we want to keep and reinforce from our upbringing and others that we are happy to leave behind.

One of the things we wanted to leave behind is fear of deep water. There are very few people in my family and friendship circle from Barbados who are able to swim, and fewer who can do so competently. This was not what I experienced in Germany or the UK. Most of my friends and colleagues swam as naturally as they walked and were shocked to learn that a person from a small, tropical island could not even manage to stay afloat. Swimming was not a feature of our curriculum when we were children and our parents protected us from drowning by insisting that we not venture too far out. I can still remember going to the beach and my mother shouting at my brother and me for going neck deep into the water. Both of our kids have been learning to swim since they were four years old and are now competent and confident in deep water. In fact, last holiday, we enjoyed watching them boldly dive off a catamaran into the deep, perilous, fish-infested Caribbean sea, snorkelling to see an old shipwreck and feed turtles. We could never imagine doing that at their age. We are still intent on going to swimming classes so that we can join them on our next trip.

The greatest joy of returning to Barbados with the kids for holidays is meeting up with their grandparents, aunts, uncles, cousins and other relatives. Not having close relatives nearby to meet up for birthdays, Christmas and random Sunday meals is a setback. This is the experience we grew up with but our children only get to play in person with their cousins every few years, by which time they have changed significantly. Otherwise they depend on the wonders of social media, which is by no means a sufficient substitute. Witnessing the pleasure on my parents' faces as they get to know their grandchildren is timeless. Knowing that they are ageing and our distance makes it impossible to visit with them every weekend, as my brother and his kids are able to do, makes our choice to reside in the UK bittersweet. We do have a number of relatives across the UK and friends with whom we spend Christmas and special occasions, but we openly acknowledge that this life we live and choice we have made for our children is at the expense of many precious relationships and moments. Aspects of our cultural heritage mixed with our experience of redefining and adapting to changing contexts continues to bring us many social advantages, but these are mixed with many trials, some of which I have shared in this piece. That said, every parent's journey comes with challenges of managing uncertainty and responding to situations they have not previously encountered, even if they do not involve changing continents, languages and demographics.

Finitude

The year 2020 was one of those years that drew on our reserves of resilience. It disrupted our rituals, routines and relationships. It introduced tough restrictions with social consequences. Even though we as a family often choose to be at home rather than having a packed social calendar, 2020 removed the freedom of preference. I furthermore missed my cycle into work, a daily routine of functional exercise and reflection, and the morning coffees with colleagues, as we sought to fix the problems of our workplace and the world with each sip. But the hardest lesson of 2020 was coming to grips with the sickness, death and grief that seemed very close to home. I lost three men who had an impact on my life. They were friends, dads and still young. They died under different circumstances and left gaping holes that could only be filled with tears and memories. I reflect on them below but I have made a choice to withhold their names.

At the beginning of the year, one of my dearest and loved work colleagues ended his ongoing struggle with depression. I met him about five years prior to writing this chapter. We started our roles in the same team back then and even though he was a few years younger than me, we instantly took a liking for each other's company. He was one of the funniest guys I knew and a loving husband and father to his wife and young daughters. He was a good listener and as insightful as he was inappropriate with his commentary. When I received the news of his death, it was on the same day we had planned to meet up for lunch. I can still remember the moment when my phone alerted me of the lunchtime appointment that was never to be. I stared at it as though keeping it open would alter the reality. I remember calling his wife, expecting to console her with words and then not having anything to offer. I was angry, grieved and in disbelief, an unhealthy concoction of emotion but real and raw. Instead, it was his wife's words that comforted me – 'You were so loved, but there is nothing that you could have said or done.'

About two years ago I met a man at church who always had a smile on his face and good words. He was older and well respected in the community. He invited my family over for lunch one Sunday after church, without hesitation or ceremony. We felt at home. I took a lot from our conversations and observations. He was becoming a mentor, without signing up to a programme. He was generous with his finances, hospitality and heart. He presented the gospel of Jesus without preaching. He was the sort of person who people looked up to but he never held himself in high esteem. He was wealthy, a building contractor, owned businesses and properties, including a set of care homes for people who were less able to live on their own due to dementia or age. I remember approaching him one Christmas to ask about the possibility of carolling in one of his care homes and the immediate, enthusiastic support he gave to the idea. It fit his vision of living, loving and serving. He was a husband, father and grandfather. He cared well for his elderly mum. In April 2020, we heard the dreadful news that he had had a heart attack and was hospitalised. Being in intensive care during the growing pandemic was cause for greater concern. Visitation was restricted. After a few days, he sadly passed away. There were no words, explanations or consolations other than this was a heartbreaking loss and a time to grieve.

One of my big plans for 2020, cancelled as a result of the Covid-19 pandemic, was to visit Kenya on invitation from a friend I met at a wedding a few years earlier. He was full of energy and ideas. He was the director of a charity dedicated to working with children and young people, especially those living in poverty and disability. Some of his social media feed would show him venturing at times for many days into the bushes, following tips that there were children in a remote village needing assistance. He would go, full of Jesus, full of faith and full of love. He would bring words of hope, sometimes new wheelchairs but always a set of puppets to entertain and bring smiles to the children's faces, while landing messages home that they needed to hear. He was also the full-time youth pastor at his local church in Kimilili and would often include his entire family, wife and four kids, in presenting Sunday School. He made intentional time for his kids, as he was often away, and they would be off on adventures by the rivers and through the thickets, being fully aware of wildlife. The way he lived reminded me that freedom is not living without boundaries or limitations, it is living aware and fully within boundaries, limitations and dangers of the environment we cannot control. It is accepting the things we cannot change and changing the things we cannot accept. The last few messages I have from him are looking forward to my visit, hopefully the following year, but informing me of his health situation. He had contracted malaria, recovered, but then came down with typhoid fever that seemed to acutely affect him, as he was still weak from his prior illness. He was still hopeful of recovery, even as his strength deteriorated and the test results of his vitals came back with discouraging reports. He stopped responding to messages for a few days but then we received the news that our meeting in Kenya would never be. A few Sundays later, I watched his kids online presenting Sunday School without the physical presence and guidance of their dad. I saw his face in each of them, his antics in their movement and heard his humour and words in their voices.

Yes, death is inevitable and the older we get the more acquainted we become with its inevitability. The space between lament and hope seems empty, until love turns up. Comfort never comes from a place of dismissal or denial. It requires honesty, vulnerability and acceptance that our time and paths are infinitely finite, as chapters, pages, verses, sentences and phrases, even characters and spaces, in an ongoing story. A story that started long before we were here and will continue long after we are gone. It was written by our ancestors and their ancestors through time, and in time we will pass the pen to generations still to come. Being a dad has made me more conscious of my finitude. This awareness can bring panic or peace, as we go to bed at night or leave home for the day, with no guarantees about what the next day or moment holds. May you find peace in being humble, relational and determined in your ongoing parenthood practice.

Chapter 10:

Your Children Are Your Friends: Across the Episodes of Life

Peter Kawalek

My role as a father has changed as my daughters have grown from babies to teenagers. As I look back across the still short span of our lives together, I observe that there have been three broad phases. Here, I've called them 'The Time Team', 'Building the Core' and 'Coach'. Within each I had to adapt myself to a new reality of my children growing around me. Then again, above and beyond all this, the very flux of life, and all of its deepest challenges, also required a special kind of dynamism and an ability to respond to whatever arose.

These days I am an academic, a professor in a business school. I grew up in Manchester in a place called Whalley Range. It lies between Moss Side and Chorlton, around Alexandra Park. It was a phenomenal place to grow up. On the first street where we lived there were lots of transient tenants and their kids. My dad would organise big football games for them in our garden and on a summer's evening with my brothers and sisters and a group of neighbours it felt like we were at the centre of the world. Sometimes it was also a scary place to grow up and that is probably why we left our first house there. There were some kids who knew a soft touch when they saw one. I was that soft touch. I was on the receiving end of some fists, kicking, spitting, that kind of thing. So, when I was twelve, we moved to a really beautiful road with a clock tower at the end. The area was changing and over time a lot of our neighbours moved out and a lot of Muslim families moved in. I am really glad of that now – they were fantastic families and our street was always peaceful.

My wife grew up over in Parrs Wood, on a big, flat estate full of gardens and trees – a little Letchworth with coin meters for the electricity. I had some friends there and we would sometimes go out on bikes, so I actually first set eyes on my wife when she was in her early teens. That moment flashed by but there were quite a few Sundays with my friends or nights spent walking down to Didsbury where obliging landlords would let us in pubs. So, it was somehow ordained that I had to run into her again and by the time we were in our early twenties we were properly together. I mean properly, like no one else mattered, and like that grey Manchester pavement had moved a dozen feet closer to the moon.

The Time Team

Our first was born at five pounds something, five weeks early, after a tortuous birth in which a rapidly escalating set of conditions brought midwives and obstetricians in from the corridors in such a hurry that they left open the doors to the delivery room. Our mite was all right, born to the howl of her mother and in the full glare of any passer-by. For the seven days that my wife and baby daughter were in hospital, I felt that heaven had commissioned me, and each evening as I drove the A46 home, the road seemed flat and smooth and orderly, with a beautiful spring light. There were foxes in the fields, deer in the woods, owls awakening – you get the idea...

It was not that it was an easy time. Our daughter was jaundiced and separated from us for phototherapy. My wife was agitated by the staff whom she thought too protective of our 'prem' baby, too eager to prise her from her mother, and too keen to insist that mother had rest. She could not breastfeed, and one nurse in particular seemed keen that she should not try.

When we finally drove her home, we fastened our baby in so tightly and so warmly, and with such a pretty hat, that we had to pull into a shaded car park to unfasten her and to cool her. Her face was reddening and her arms were outstretched in crying exclamation. We had a lot to learn.

One thing I understood from those early days, just from observing her, was that my daughter was as clever as me, pretty much, as clever as any of us. Babies wash in potential; the early days of life are a voracious moment of curiosity and learning. What differentiates us as adults from our very youngest is not really any kind of raw intelligence, babies have that rawness in abundance, it is just experience and all that experience implies.

That gift of being able to lift her, to take her from her basket, to dab her teardrops, to button up the sleepsuit, to laugh with her, to do all the chores, to help my wife (the nappy stuff is easy – just do it), to warm a bottle, to fall into exhaustion, to sleep beside her, to slightly recover and to feel daunted all the time, all the days. To be a part of the weather. The dad is the butt of jokes, there with prissy baby carriers (I never had one), and fussing over their womenfolk, but inside the bubble of child-rearing is a territory and a landscape that the outsider does not see. You are a family now, a cosmo-illogical team, leaving the good sense of Planet Rational Lifestyle, for the labour and joy and worry of Planet Meaningful Madness. There was the bad luck of my wife being unable to breastfeed but the good luck to me of being a part of the bottle-feed timetable. I cannot remember how many nights I woke at 1 a.m. to lift our baby on to my knee and to feed her: to hell with tiredness, why would it matter?

The earliest stage of child-rearing is all about being a team. You are a time team, in compression, through the bends, and you will never work so hard.

Building the Core

I have two daughters. They are teenagers now and are my best friends. Well, let me be precise about that, for we all have many 'best friends': they are *my best friends who also happen to be my daughters* as *my wife is my best friend who also happens to be my wife*. There is something under-observed here: all good relationships head towards friendship, some friendships more special, more symbolic and more historic than others. But, ultimately, that's the game that you are playing – to build a special friendship with your child.

Let me dignify my wife by calling her M, her middle initial.

Over their childhood, I've had fifty or a hundred nicknames for my daughters, and I'm still at it, so here I'll refer to them as Kite, the elder, and Kid, her younger sister. They make me laugh and it will always be good, but it has been hard as well and I've made many mistakes. I've also been lucky many times.

One time I got lucky was maybe four months after Kite was born and I drove out to the local shop around the corner from our house. I turned on

the radio in my car and there was the psychologist Oliver James talking –
I don't know what station or what show – but he was saying that he sort
of understood all the rules and the conditioning that parents give to their
children, but for him it was definitely possible to have too much of all that.
He then drew a distinction between a child that is spoilt and one that is
indulged. To be spoilt is bad but to be indulged, to feel indulged, well, that
is good for a child and her feeling of place in this world. I heard that loudly.
I had never fancied my chances of being much of a disciplinarian, I wasn't
much into setting rules, so James helped confirm what I already suspected
was true. I did not have to be good at the discipline thing. I could follow
my own instincts. I could indulge my daughter, my daughters. I could let
them know their immeasurability. Also, M talked a lot about the attachment
theory of Rutter, 'the purpose of attachment is detachment', or hold them
close and true and then they will grow. I became into all that, right through
to the research that says care and love are positive for brain development.
Love. At the centre. At the core. Theory of love. I found my way.

Kid is three and a half years the junior of her sister. She too was born
prematurely, but this time only three weeks short of full term, and she was
a couple of pounds heavier than her sister. She was delivered by C-section
by a team of doctors and nurses who were so skilled and so caring that they
made me feel very humble. The breastfeeding went well. M was buoyant and
brilliant, and 'the time team' was in good form.

So, there is this spell of a father's life that lasts from somewhere close to
your child's third birthday and extends to somewhere just before or just after
the teens. Let's call this 'Building the Core'. Within it, your child settles further
into the rhythms and moods of the household. School arrives. Friendships
arrive – the cycle of birthday parties and events. The family organises weekends
and holidays in order to be itself and to grow. Sometimes there is sunshine.
Sometimes there is not. There is the park, the beach, the ice cream, the farm;
that kind of thing. The local shop and the familiar walk. Your child lives in
the warmth of big time – each new month is a new ocean, but Mum and
Dad, we are desperately trying to make this time special because one thing
we know is that it is transient. It will pass. We try not to think about it too
much, but packing away the picnic, or starting the car on the way back from
holiday, well, maybe I sometimes saw it in M's face and sometimes she saw
it in mine. These seasons are racing. They race. A child lives on the meadow,
but her parents are on the running track. Meanwhile, another week is closing
down and we need to ready the things for school tomorrow. There are clothes
to dry, kit to find, homework to be finished. Always, there is school.

Your work life will eat at your time. It did for me. Future generations will pity us for how much time we spend at work. We all are living through a difficult era with working life expanded on the back of the Key Performance Indicator, email, the mobile phone, and the dissolution of traditional protections and expectations. Dads are cheated by this. Mums are cheated by this. Children are cheated by this. The UK is by no means the worst place in this regard, but it is far, far from the best. There are better places. The rules in this country are set by the nannied, but ordinary mums and dads have a different equation to solve. We all need quite a lot of cash to deliver a lifestyle to our children, but that cash asks us for a huge amount of time. M and I were just kids from inner Manchester. We also had no parents of our own to call upon, not after M's mum became sick a little while after Kid was born. So, we were a kind of hyper-nuclear set-up, feeling our way. It always felt precarious, time always felt tight, and whenever a new demand arose at work, as it always did, time had to be sequestered from the night, or the early morning, and from every single weekend.

But it was a magnificent time.

Something I figured when my daughters were very young is that a lot of parenting is done on bended knee. There's a dignity to that, and a kindness. I would bend or crouch down to their level, face to face, and be tactile, holding hands, or shoulders, that kind of thing. Words are important, but not that important; I'd always try to set the emotional tone first. I wanted that tone to be calm and warm and reassuring. The mood at home was usually good or great but, of course, there were times when the house became frazzled. Those times I understood my job as to act as a kind of earth wire, to encourage the storm to pass, and for us all to return to our happier keel. I never thought that I needed to find out who was right or who was wrong, who said what or who started what. I did not want to put myself in the role of a judge, I just had to help the family come back to itself. I always felt good when I did this well but I went to bed frustrated with myself when I did not.

When I talk of 'Building the Core', I am speaking mainly of an emotional core. I'm not sure that much else matters, nor should matter.

Flux

As parents, typically, all of us, we feel this great will to shelter our children from the world. I did. I'd have turned it into Disneyland if I could. I'd have made it like a colouring book, like a chapter from one of those early-stage reads where kids run with dogs and have an endless afternoons in the park:

'The dog wags its tail … Jane throws the ball.' We want life to be beautiful, we want to make it beautiful. There's something noble in that, sure, really noble, but the real world keeps intruding and sometimes it rips up the trees and tears up the lawn.

So, A was as handsome a boy as you could ever wish to see. *He too was beautiful*; born ten weeks after Kite to my sister-in-law and my brother. A was Kite and Kid's cousin, they played together and were part of the world together. He was a big part of their earliest knowledge. They lit up just to speak of each other, as children so honestly do. A had a big sister and it was great every little time that the four children played together.

So, the world vaulted when A died of leukaemia at the age of ten. We all lost something beyond calibration, something deeper than we could ever express. My sister-in-law and my brother, their daughter, Kite and Kid, all his cousins, all our family, and a collection of neighbours and friends as well: something was severed from all of us.

That was a moment of departure. Many other parents have been through it too, that point, when your children are still children but can no longer wholly believe in the world in a child's way. M and I, Kite and Kid, all of us, together, we had to find another way of explaining the world, another way of journeying, and another way of taking comfort in what was around us.

We still talk about A. We always will. In life, there are many trivial things that pass quickly to the past tense. But we notice that love for those we have left behind, well, that is always in the present.

Coach

Few words are as loaded as 'teenager'. The concept is probably the most charged in our culture. I cannot recall how many times we were told to expect trouble. Parents more experienced than us told us of seasons of difficulty, of conflict and of a shuddering end to normal family life.

I do not doubt that the teenage years are a tremendous crossing: a white beach, a wind, a collection of sudden storms. We know this anthropologically, as well as biologically. But I also felt that there could be an unhelpful expectation around it, and a lot of negative labelling could be suffered by the child. Maybe, sometimes, the trope 'teenager' is so powerful, so bound into movies and TV, so ironically bound to the parents' expectations, that it is easy to lose sight of the individual child, who will actually fit no pattern but her own.

There are cultural differences, after all. A teenager in the UK is not the same as one in Spain, or in Germany, or France, or South Africa, or Turkey, or China, or Australia, or Brazil and so on. If it was all preordained, a potent genetic algorithm wriggling its course, then we'd expect no cultural differences. Correct?

In the circles in which I live now, there is a danger that we metricate teenagers – that we reduce the years of flowering to a system of performance measures. The grades, the tables, the sets, the weight, the shape, the number of friends, the price of the clothes, the count of party invites and the 'like' score. Where once there was time to watch the day unfold, as there was for me as a skinny youth in Whalley Range, today there is a timetable, a programme and a software program. I believe that there should be something inherently heroic and idealistic about the teenage crossing, something romantic in the creation of self, but I also think that the potential is easily diverted. Modern society productises everything, even our children, and it makes everything fit into a spreadsheet. The adult world is so dumb sometimes. It's not the kids, it's us.

A big part of a parent-teen relationship is the ceding of power. I did not want to negotiate boundaries with my daughters, I wanted to step back, to cede territory voluntarily before much negotiation ever took place. I knew that they would develop aspects of life that were their own, beyond our door, beyond my knowledge, and I did not want them to have to fight for that. I hoped to observe and to know the moment when I had to loosen the ties. I remembered that when I was a teenager, my own parents trusted me, and that they told me so, and that I carried the consciousness of that through all of it.

Anyway, there is another role I can play, that of coach. I have a lot of experience and a lot of ideas. I can share a lot. We can talk over all that happens in the educational world, say, or how best to keep some confidence about you when the season of life is difficult. I can talk on how to be resilient but, then again, how to laugh and seize the moment when it lies down in front of you. There are a million things I am interested in and I will talk to Kite and to Kid about any of them. I do not patronise them. I talk to them as I do with M, say, or to an adult friend, and they talk back about things they are discovering, the things they know. In fact, as I write, I am thinking about how much they inform me of things, and how much I have learned from them. As I reflect upon it now, I realise also that they coach me sometimes. It works, as I have never claimed to have all the answers nor the equipment to cope with every situation.

There was this time when we joined a correfoc in a steep, Spanish village. The term means 'fire-run' and it is one of the great experiences of this planet (but take an old jacket). Kite was fourteen and there among all the lights and the bangs of the *festes*, I remember her fizzing with excitement and that she felt handsomely at home among the mystical, creative and adventurous Spanish. How else could I respond to this enthusiasm, such connectedness, this youthful embrace of the fibre of living, except to, perhaps, help nurture the path, to help fan the flame, to coach, but also to step back and to see her grow? That teenage crossing – it is brim-full of great episodes.

Outro

Kid is fifteen now. Recently we sat at a sheltered table outside a sunny cafe in Matlock. We watched the passers-by and the waitress working the tables. We did not talk much, we do not always, but Kid is always alive with observations. She sees everything and is utterly unfooled by all the accoutrements of the adult world. She is funny, like Kite is, and wise, like Kite is, but they are different too. A little later that day we ambled among a few shops, not doing very much. We bought some incense sticks from some hippy place. I'm not sure why. She has them in her room.

Kite is away at university in London. When I am also in town, I drop by to see her and buy her dinner. There is always news to catch up on and things to discuss. She is a bar worker and a hospital volunteer – she has really embedded herself in her community. It is nice to hear how things are coming on and between all that, and whatever she is reading, I am always learning from her.

The transition to university was hard, to be honest. I will never forget the sunny day we took Kite down to her halls. I will also never forget the low swell of emptiness that occupied me those first weeks she was gone. I am writing this here, but actually it is the first time I've admitted it. Those first weeks were a strain for everyone and I realised my best place and role was just to be positive and optimistic – no matter what doubts I held inside. Some weeks later, I remember sitting with Kite in Mabel's Tavern beside Euston Road and thinking *I have missed you in my bones*. Again, I did not tell her but should I have done so, she would have kicked me from under the table.

There is a lot that is very positive about this transition, and at the end of Kite's first year we had an idyllic summer together. M and the girls had an especially special time and I joined in when I was home. Meanwhile, I am conscious that my role continues to change. I am a coach still but with Kite in particular, I am a coach who will quite often be ignored. That's fine. In fact, it is really important. What is a family anyway, but a series of serious and mutually affecting connections? We all win. We do not have to be in the same room all the time or even the same house. It is just to know that someone is there for you, that someone is concerned. It is friendship, yes, definitely friendship, but what else did I call it? I think I called it a theory of love.

Chapter 11:

Just Man Up:
Being Bullied at Work as a New Dad

William Nicholson

It's 6.30 a.m. The lights are on in our bedroom as they have been since I got home from work just five hours ago. My wife is asleep with our four-month-old son on her chest, where he has been all night. As I stand at the door, I feel sick in my stomach. My phone vibrates and a message pops up to indicate I've already got ten unread emails. A text comes through from **him**: *'Where the hell are you? This report is total garbage. Get to my office as soon as you get in.'* The lump in my throat gets bigger, pushing against my tie as I picture **his** face. I dread the day ahead of me.

I take a deep breath and think to myself: *'For goodness' sake, just man up and go to work. You're a grown man and a dad now. Being bullied is just not something that happens to dads or a guy in his thirties.'*

My eyes well up – these should be the happiest moments of my life. The last thing my wife needs is to have to worry about this on top of everything else. I turn and leave before I start crying…

Who Am I?

My name is William Nicholson. I'm forty-two years old and have been married

148

to my wife Aisléan for eleven years. We have three wonderful kids – Liam (ten), Saorla (five) and Órán (two).

My passions in life are supporting health and well-being and enabling thriving communities – making connections, building relationships, facilitating partnerships and creating networks. Discovering the things we have in common and celebrating our differences and individual quirks. I love collaborating and finding ways to do things together.

Two main things have had a huge impact on my life and defined who I am and what I care about.

Firstly, I was born and raised in Hong Kong in 1978 to a Scottish dad and a Chinese mum. Being mixed race has had a huge influence on me. Initially, I struggled with my sense of identity (and sometimes I still do if I'm honest). I always wanted to belong to each race but I felt like an outsider of both. In Scotland I looked Chinese but I spoke English (worst of all with an English accent!). In Hong Kong it was the other way round. To the locals I was considered a *Gwai-Lo* (the Chinese term for a white man) and I couldn't speak Chinese. I didn't really fit in either camp.

But, at the same time, I also really thrived and enjoyed being the best of both. An 'exotic blend of Chinese and Scottish' as I like to describe myself! Bruce Lee in Tartan. I love being a bit of both and being able to be the connector. I love celebrating each culture, both the differences and what they have in common.

Secondly, I went to boarding school in Scotland in 1988 when I was nine years old. My parents were 6,000 miles away in Hong Kong meaning I would be away from home without seeing them for three months at a time. I learned what it was like to be on your own, to be afraid and lonely and to feel like you've been abandoned with no one to turn to. On the positive side, I learned character, independence and resilience. I had a lot of fun and some of the best times at boarding school. I made an amazing group of friends for life, a bunch of mates who have been through thick and thin together. Pals that would go into battle for each other no matter what.

Being Bullied

I want to share my story of being bullied at work at the time of becoming a new dad. Before I do that, I also want to share my experience of being bullied as a kid. For me, this has had such an impact on how I struggled to deal with being bullied in later life and there are so many similarities between the two.

In my first year at boarding school, I was bullied a lot for looking different.

Back in the late 1980s there wasn't much diversity in Scotland and I was singled out for being the only Chinese-looking kid at school. The other kids called me 'Chinky' (it still hurts) and regularly made fun of me for having slanty eyes, yellow skin and being small.

I even remember one of my teachers in a biology class asking me to stand up and show the rest of the class my 'oriental eyelids'. Not only was this humiliating, but having someone who was in a position of authority high-light my differences like this reinforced to everyone that it was normal and acceptable behaviour. This made me realise that no matter how much the bullying hurt, there wasn't much I could do about it.

I couldn't complain to anyone as the whole 'system' was against me, so I had no choice but to accept that this was the way it was going to be and if I didn't like it, tough. With my parents in Hong Kong, I knew I would have to dig deep and find a way to get through this on my own. Alongside the academic benefits of private schooling, this was one of the main reasons they sent me to boarding school – to learn how to be strong and fend for myself.

Going to boarding school was a family tradition and an extremely impor-tant part of my upbringing to my parents. It was like a rite of passage. I was the third generation in my family to go to the same boarding school after my grandpa and dad. Without it ever being spoken out loud, I felt that there was an expectation on me to tough it out and succeed and uphold the family name. After all, my grandpa and dad got through it without complaining and from what I had heard, boarding school was a lot tougher back in their day. What I was going through was 'character building'.

I made a big mistake in my first few weeks at school which resulted in me being bullied every day by two of the older lads. Back in the day, I was pretty decent at squash and I was Hong Kong under-ten champion (sadly it is still my greatest sporting achievement!). I was asked to try out for the team and during the trials I beat the top two players in the school. This turned out to be a huge mistake – they were both thirteen and in the top year of the junior school and did not take kindly to being beaten by a small, nine-year-old Chinese-looking kid.

In a world that expects boys to win and to be strong and successful, I hadn't realised how much beating them damaged their status and made them feel vulnerable. Their anxiety from losing resulted in me being bullied relentlessly for the rest of the year to restore their pride and put me back in my place. I was made to do whatever they wanted, whenever they wanted. I had to clean their shoes, make their beds, get them food or drink, get up at 6 a.m. for military-style 'knacker sessions' in the freezing cold. These sessions lasted about an hour and were a hideous continuous cycle of sprinting, planking, press-ups, sit-ups, burpees, leopard crawling in the mud all while having abuse screamed at you. I was made to stand up in front of the other kids each night during homework and would have stuff thrown at me – shoes, pens, rubbers, squash balls, whatever they could get hold of. I was verbally abused at every opportunity, almost entirely racist. I can't repeat what they said as it was extremely unpleasant.

Strangely, I didn't blame them for what they did. The expectations placed on them by the other kids, the school and our society meant that it was either them or me. I actually blamed myself. It was my fault, my poor judgement. If I hadn't beaten them, I wouldn't have put them in a position of weakness and they wouldn't have had to react as they did.

So I just sucked it up, took the bullying on the chin as my punishment and never said anything to anyone about it. It wasn't the done thing and would have been a sign of weakness if I showed that it bothered me. If I had 'grassed up' one of those boys it would have made things worse as I would have been labelled a snitch or a troublemaker. On top of the mistake I made, the last thing I wanted to do was rock the boat even more. I wasn't the only one who was bullied and the abuse I received wasn't out of the ordinary. Knowing I was not alone and that others had it worse than me, helped me get through this.

I also realised that the only way that I was going to get some reprieve from this was to let them beat me at squash in a way that restored their pride. I wanted and needed them to look good from winning. I didn't just throw in the towel but I made it close to let them and others in the school think that they had beaten me through their superior talent and strength. This had the desired effect and slowly over time they lost interest in bullying me as I was no longer a threat. They left to join the senior school at the end of the year and I was free to move on.

It seems strange looking back at it now. I blamed myself for what happened and I had to sacrifice my squash abilities to fix it and get respite from the bullying. But what choice did I have?

Overall, my experience of boarding school was amazing. I was very lucky. As time went on I adapted and learned to survive and then thrive. I learned how to fit in; using my differences as strengths and recognising the importance of good friends you can trust who will have your back. I worked out how to play the game and avoid trouble (for example, never beating either of the bullies at squash again!). I learned who the big boys were, what made them tick, how to stay out of their way and, importantly, how not to upset them.

I've never forgotten the experience of being bullied at school and how I felt at the time. I keep the bits that hurt deep in the back of my mind, I focus on the good times I had and it hasn't really bothered me since. Time is a great healer and I don't hold a grudge against any of those that bullied me. They bullied me because they felt threatened by me and in a strange way that made it easier to deal with. They were just kids and didn't know any better. A lot of the bullying behaviour wasn't their fault and is down to the unhelpful societal expectations placed on boys that were ingrained in the way the school operated.

Fast forward twenty years to 2011 and life was great. Having moved to London in 2002, I was now happily married to my wife, Aisléan. We had just bought a nice house together and I had a good job working at a large, well-respected City accountancy firm.

Above all else, in January 2011 I became a dad for the first time. A father to a newborn son and probably the most exciting and rewarding moment of my life. I had dreamt of this ever since I was young; having a son and naming him William Nicholson! Just like me, my dad, my grandfather, my great grandfather. In fact, Liam (we shortened his name to Liam to avoid confusion with all the other William Nicholsons and because my wife is Irish and she wanted all our children to have Irish names) became the seventh in a long line of William Nicholsons dating back to the early 1800s.

Work was also going well and I was being considered for promotion to Senior Manager. To provide a bit of context, the company I worked for employed approximately 150,000 people worldwide with over 5,000 people in the fancy City of London headquarters where I was based. Although the firm provided consultancy and accountancy services to some of the biggest organisations in the world, I wasn't particularly interested in working on the big deals with the big companies. I much preferred working with smaller, innovative, growing companies. So I worked in a small team of around twenty that provided financial and business advice to midsized clients who were raising investment money or were buying and selling companies. My team was like a family. We all enjoyed working together and helping each other out. We weren't the most glamourous as we didn't work on the big deals but we worked hard, had a lot of fun and did well.

Having talked to my line manager, we agreed that although I was doing well in our team, the best thing for me to secure promotion was to gain some experience outside our team in the Private Equity department. It was by far the biggest department and where the big money was being made in the firm. More importantly, it was where all the power was. It was like a rite of passage – if anyone did well working on one of their deals and impressed the big wigs in that team, promotion was all but guaranteed.

However, I was really anxious about joining Private Equity for two reasons. Firstly, it had a reputation. An aggressive, money-making culture like you see in films such as *The Wolf of Wall Street* or *Boiler Room* – big deals, big money, guys in expensive pinstripe suits puffing their chests out and shouting at their teams, working late nights and long hours – you get the picture. It was just accepted that was the way it was. Everyone else just went along with it. No one challenged it. The deal was simple – if you wanted to get promoted you needed to prove that you could handle it in this world.

Secondly, of real concern was that as a new dad I was exhausted. Liam was proving to be a very challenging baby. Breastfeeding was not going to plan. Aisléan had serious mastitis and Liam didn't sleep for more than two hours at a time. He slept on Aisléan's chest with the lights on in our room pretty much all day and night for almost three months. I was desperate to help out and I was getting about five hours of broken sleep a night. It was starting to take its toll.

During the first six weeks or so of becoming a new dad, my team had been fantastic; extremely understanding and flexible. I was able to make the most of my two weeks' paid paternity leave and allowed to combine it with some overtime I had built up and my annual leave. My team boss also ensured I was given a relatively light-touch project to work on during this challenging time. This meant I was able to work from home or flex my hours to help Aisléan out at home and at the hospital or breastfeeding clinics when needed.

This was everything I would have hoped for from an employer. I can't stress how important it is that you are supported by your workplace at such a life-changing moment as becoming a dad. Work-life balance is already hard to achieve at the best of times but when you suddenly have such huge additional responsibilities at home (as well as no sleep), being made to feel supported by your colleagues and employer is vital. This is even more so when it is your first child and you have little to no idea what you are doing!

But I knew I wouldn't get the same understanding in Private Equity. In fact, I would get the opposite. In that team it was seen as a sign of weakness if you 'allowed' your home life to get in the way of your work.

Yet despite knowing all of this, I still agreed to do a four month project in the Private Equity department. It was a small project team of four led by the partner who had the worst reputation. He had a director on the team who was his 'yes man', there to back up everything he said and did and to carry out his dirty work. Then there was me and one junior team member. They had all worked together for many years and it was clear from day one that I was the outsider and that I was going to be given a rough time.

I clearly remember on the very first day that he gave me a job to do that was deliberately set up for me to fail. It was a new type of analysis that only someone in their team could do and they knew that I wouldn't be able to do it. He made me try, and ridiculed me when I couldn't do it. *'Why can't you do it? I've explained this to you five times now. It's embarrassing that someone at your level should be struggling like this. How the **** is someone like you up for promotion?'* To add the finishing touch he then got the junior team member to do it and show me how 'easy' it was.

Our firm's offices were exactly what you would expect for one of the top City firms. The building was impressive, modern, spacious, well-furnished and in a wonderful glass building with great views of the Thames and Tower Bridge. However, for the entire project we were located in a secure internal meeting room by the toilets. It had a glass door but no windows or glass walls. We were regularly working sixteen-hour days and I asked several times to move to a room with a view or at least one that wasn't by the loos. He turned it down every time, giving excuses like: *'There aren't any other rooms available,'* or: *'It's a confidential project so you need to be in a room with no windows.'* We all knew that neither was true. On its own this wasn't a big deal but it was another example of the suppression. It was so dejecting. That room was like a prison cell, just without the bed.

One of the worst moments was when we were nearing the late May bank holiday weekend. I remember it as Liam was just over four months old and we were starting to get on top of things with his feeding and sleeping. Summer was approaching, the weather was improving and everything just felt brighter. I was desperately looking forward to a long weekend where I could help out at home, give Aisléan a bit of a break and take my mind off things at work.

Friday came and I was counting down the clock. Just a few more hours and then I'd have three days away from this nightmare when all of a sudden I heard his voice shouting down the hall, *'Oi Nicholson! What the **** have you been doing these last few days? This report is utter rubbish, pathetic. My ten-year-old could do better than this.'* The shouting was deliberate to let everyone else in the office know exactly what was going on. I felt sick. He marched into the room. *'Give me your phone number – you are working this whole bank holiday weekend.'*

'But I've promised my wife I'd look after our son and give her some much-needed rest? He's only four months old. I've hardly seen him since he was born...'

'I couldn't give a ****! Be in the office and expect my call.'

My heart sank and I remember crying as I headed home, dreading telling

Aisléan that yet again I would be working at the weekend and wouldn't be able to help out. Worse still, I had to lie to her that it was because I was working on this really important deal that would get me promoted.

I was in the office all weekend but the call never came. Deep down, I knew it wouldn't. That wasn't the point. He knew I would be there and that was enough for him.

Incidents like this were hard but only told half the story. Almost worse were the little things that happened every day, including the weekends. Every morning I would dread looking at my phone. The moment I woke up at 6 a.m., I could see the red light flashing to say that there were unread messages and emails. There was always one from him, just to remind me of something I hadn't done or to tell me I had done yet another thing wrong. I had that sick feeling in my stomach every morning. In fact, every time a message popped up on the screen.

Then there were the regular emails to senior colleagues about me and how I was underperforming. He always added a leading question like, *'I'm sure William will agree with me that he could have done better and tried harder?'* There was never really anything of substance, just repeated criticism of me. The face-to-face conversations he had with people about me were always done in a way that made sure I knew it was happening. *'Just to let you know I've got a meeting lined up with X later to talk about you.'* Or, *'Come to my desk at 12 p.m., I'm meeting with your line manager and I want you to know what we have been talking about...'*

He had it in for me. He constantly wanted me to feel small and to know that I didn't belong in his team, that I was inadequate. I kept asking myself, why? Why me? Why am I in this situation? Why am I putting up with this? Why don't I tell anyone about it? Why don't I just leave and get another job?

It seems really strange telling this story now. Why didn't I do something about it? It seems completely ridiculous that I let it happen, that I didn't just walk out or stand up for myself. Surely I should have just said that this behaviour was unacceptable. That I didn't want to work for someone who was going to treat me like this, so I was off.

But I didn't. I couldn't. I had to stay, didn't I? What choice did I have if I wanted to get promoted? I didn't have the courage to stand up for myself and neither did anyone around me. I was also so tired and I really struggled to deal with it. Mentally and physically I was drained from struggling as a new parent on five hours of broken sleep, but also from the stress at work, from the sixteen-hour days and the constant bullying. I couldn't think straight and was overwhelmed. I just focused on surviving this four month project.

I told myself that I just needed to suck this up, get through it, get back to my team and put it behind me.

I also couldn't talk to anyone about it. I definitely couldn't tell Aisléan. She had enough on her plate with Liam and dealing with her mastitis. The last thing she needed was this problem on top of everything else.

I couldn't tell any of my friends or family that I was being bullied at work. It was like being back at the start of boarding school all over again being bullied by those two older boys. But this time I was thirty-two years old and I was a dad and this was at work. I denied it was happening as it seemed so ridiculous. Bullying happens to kids in the playground, not to grown men in an office! I felt so embarrassed at the time that I couldn't tell anyone. Even writing the words now I feel deeply embarrassed to admit it, almost ashamed. I find I still hesitate to say it out loud as it sounds weak, that there was something wrong with me for not being able to stand up for myself.

I never really raised this with anyone at work. I was too worried about the consequences of doing so and it would just make things worse. I wanted to get promoted, so how could I admit I was struggling and having a hard time?

We all knew there were others who had been bullied but very few people ever complained. There was no point. Even though the bullying was in plain sight, the control was very subtle. In hindsight I now realise everything was set up to control it. The way the projects were set up. The power that the Private Equity team held in the firm from the money they made. Their control over the promotion process. No one stood up to it. No one could risk it.

The problem with so few complaints was that those in Private Equity would always be able to defend themselves by saying that they weren't aware of the impact of their behaviour. We were told that we should have raised these issues at the time. But how could you? It became a vicious circle.

Those that did complain ended up leaving the firm or were made out to be the cause of the problem. They were told that it was their fault for not fitting in with the culture of Private Equity, for not trying hard enough or not being good enough. It was always justified as part of 'doing big business' and that any upset caused was unintentional, as if this made it OK. It basically sent a message that you could treat others how you wanted as long as you made good money for the firm. The results justified the behaviour and if you couldn't hack it, you should leave.

The Final Straw

I had convinced myself that once I had completed this project, I would still get promoted. That somehow, despite all of the bad feedback, my team and the firm would see that I was doing well and this was just a one-off blip.

I was kidding myself – what chance would I have of that with this guy?

Sure enough, when promotion time came, he absolutely made sure I wasn't successful. For three weeks before the annual promotion meeting, I asked him for formal feedback from the project. I wanted to see what he would say on paper so that I could explain things from my perspective and build my promotion case around the other work I had done.

I got nothing. He waited until five minutes before the promotion meeting started and sent a short email to all the line managers in the meeting saying simply, *'I do not believe William Nicholson has any of the required attributes to justify promotion to Senior Manager. At best, his performance over the last four months has been poor.'* No evidence, no time to discuss it, no time for me to respond. It was delivered as a *fait accompli* and that was that. I wouldn't get promoted.

At the time he sent the email, I was sitting three metres away from him. He didn't say anything to my face. He just looked and smiled at me as he did it.

By then I was without fight. There was literally nothing I could do. It was done. I had a strange mixture of utter dejection, anger, exhaustion but oddly, relief. The relief came as I knew this was the lowest point possible and that there was nothing more he could do to hurt me. He had no more interest in me. I was stripped to the bare bones but I was now free from his control.

I did talk to my line manager and a few members of my team and asked what I should do. It was a strange conversation. We all knew that unless I was going to go all out and try to take on the whole firm in a big HR battle, there was nothing I could do. There was no point in fighting. It was time to rebuild and move on.

Moving On

The bullying turned out to be one of the best things that has ever happened to me. It made me rethink everything and gave me a sense of urgency to act. I had always wanted to do something more with the skills and experiences I had and this was the kick I needed. I didn't dwell on the bullying. I couldn't. It was way too painful. I dealt with it by getting busy and moving on, more or less denying it had ever happened.

Within a month I joined the Prince's Trust on a one-year secondment from my team to support them with their merger with Fairbridge. Both charities do amazing work supporting disadvantaged young people in the UK and I had such an enjoyable time helping them come together.

The most ironic thing happened while I was on secondment – I got promoted! My firm *'appreciated the leadership skills I demonstrated in positively moving on from the experience of the previous year'* and I had done a good job for the Prince's Trust that was worthy of Senior Manager. Even more ironic was that no sooner had I made Senior Manager, I left the company as I wanted to dedicate my time and energy to what I care about most – supporting health and well-being and enabling thriving communities.

After all that!

Everyone Has a Story

Leaving the City was one of the best decisions I've ever made. When people asked me why I left, I had a great story to tell. After ten years developing my skills in the City, I had a wonderful experience at the Prince's Trust that helped me discover my purpose and passion in life. I'm now applying those skills and experiences to a greater social cause.

I put the whole bullying experience behind me and, like the bullying at school, buried it deep in the back of my mind. It was such an embarrassing and painful part of my life that I didn't want to relive. I had good things in front of me to focus on.

It wasn't until seven years later that I finally talked about it, and it was only as a result of pure serendipity.

I attended an event in the City of London put on by a fantastic workplace mental health charity Minds@Work. They have mobilised a network of over 2,000 community members united by a mission to create a healthier working world and to end the stigma of mental illness in the workplace.

There were over seventy people in the audience at a swanky City office and I was due to talk to the network about a workplace mental health project I was leading. I was listening to Geoff McDonald, one of the founders of Minds@Work and an incredibly inspiring speaker. The whole essence of Minds@Work is storytelling and Geoff was challenging everyone in the room to tell their story. His message was simple: *We all have a story. If we can all tell our stories about our mental health struggles and recovery, we can create healthy workplaces and end the stigma associated with mental ill health. When we speak openly about our own vulnerability, everyone else feels safer and empowered to ask for help when they need it.*

As Geoff was speaking, my mind was racing. What was my story? I was due on stage later on in the event and I didn't have one. I felt like a fraud. How could I stand up in front of everyone and talk about workplace mental health without a story?

At the break, I was networking and telling someone about how I used to work in the City, but I had left and was now working on a number of interesting health and well-being projects, one of which I was going to talk about later. He asked me what made me leave the City.

I burst into tears.

It all came flooding back. It was the first time I had thought about the bullying for seven years. That whole time I pretended it had never happened. At that moment, I realised that I was finally ready to talk about it, it was my story.

This poor guy didn't know what was going on. He became the first person that I ever talked to about it and to this day I don't know who he is! If you're reading this, I'd love to meet you and thank you. You have transformed my life and are the reason why I'm writing in this book. I never planned to tell my story that night but, shortly after, I went on stage and ended up telling seventy people. I guess it was meant to be.

Some Thoughts for the Future

In a perfect world, no one would ever be bullied and have to go through experiences like I have. Realistically though, bullying and bullies will always exist. My dream for my kids and for future generations is that if it ever happens to them, they feel that they are able to talk about it, that they are supported to do so by those around them and that our society views this as a strength and not a weakness.

There are three main hopes and dreams that I have got from my experience of being bullied. I want to highlight these three factors as I believe that if we are to try and tackle bullying in our society, we need to address the role each one plays.

First, I think about what I could have done differently as the person being bullied. How I wish I could have opened up and talked to my friends and family. I think about how I can encourage others to do this. At the time, I felt so embarrassed and weak that I couldn't tell anyone – not my wife, friends or family. I realise now that a lot of this was down to my own misguided view that bullying was only something that happens to children and that as a man and a dad I just needed to 'man up' and deal with it. Since I have started telling my story, I know that this just isn't true and that you're not alone in experiencing bullying as a dad. My dream is for other dads to be able to speak up and be proud to be vulnerable. That not only is it OK to speak up about things that are really difficult but that it is good for you and good for those around you.

My second hope is that employers and schools realise what a huge role they can play in supporting people to positively tackle bullying. I have shown in my story how much the culture of an organisation can encourage or justify bullying. I wonder what my story would have been if my employer had adopted a different culture where employees felt comfortable, supported and encouraged to raise any concerns about bullying and where bullying behaviour was actively discouraged. My guess is the person who bullied me would have left.

Lastly, my dream is to change the narrative around bullying. There is a real stigma associated with being bullied as a sign of weakness. This isn't helped by a culture of 'toxic masculinity' which creates an expectation from a young age that men need to be tough and strong. That life is about competing, winning and being the best. Being vulnerable is seen as being weak.

The way we are taught about bullying reinforces this narrative. As I was writing this chapter, I looked up the definition of bullying in a very well-known American dictionary. Bullying is defined as 'abuse and mistreatment of someone vulnerable by someone stronger, more powerful'. A bully is 'one who is habitually cruel, insulting, or threatening to others who are weaker, smaller, or in some way vulnerable'.

I find this definition really troublesome. Just because you are bullied doesn't mean that you are weaker or smaller. Describing it like this elevates the status of a bully and suggests that bullying is a sign of strength. My dream is that we should think of it the other way round; that being a bully is viewed as being weak. I would rewrite the definition of a bully as 'someone weak who, by being unable to deal with their own vulnerabilities, is habitually cruel, insulting, or threatening to others'.

When I think about the bullying I went through, it still feels like it was yesterday. That sick feeling in my stomach and the lump in my throat returns. There is tension in my neck and my heart rate increases. I can still hear his voice, picture his face. The swearing and shouting and that look in his eyes. The smug glare that says *I own you and we both know it*. It comes back. A bit like how an old scar hurts on a cold day.

But now it is different. Now that I've been able to share my story, I don't feel weak or embarrassed about my vulnerabilities. I feel strong being vulnerable.

Chapter 12:

Stillborn:
Life After Premature Death

Jamie Cowen

Sam, my firstborn son, died after seven months in the womb.

The first trip to the hospital is etched in my memory. As Kath lay on the bed, I remember feeling the certainty that something life-changingly awful had happened mixed with desperate hope that it wasn't what I thought it was. Meanwhile midwives, nurses and doctors used increasingly complicated pieces of equipment to search for a heartbeat that wasn't there any more.

It was the single worst moment of my life.

***

I grew up in Hackney amongst a loving, fairly normal white middle-class family. The eldest of two children, we had loads of family friends and went on holiday most years. I wouldn't say we were wealthy, but it was definitely a privileged start to life.

I don't remember having any real ambitions when I was younger except for one: I really wanted to be a dad. I wanted loads of kids. At least four, ideally. It's definitely possible that in my (at that point probably teenage) mind this purely equated to having loads of sex, but I like to think there was more to it than that. Many of the families I grew up around had lots of children, in particular an uncle and aunt whose four kids (my cousins) had been very much like siblings before my sister was born. I guess I decided at some point that I wanted something like this for my future – a relaxed family environment where children could be themselves. I wasn't really worried about what job I would end up doing (this changed over time, particularly when I eventually found a job that I loved and was passably good at), but the adults who I really looked up to were amazing parents first and foremost.

This desire for numerous children might also have been partly a reaction against my own family situation. An only child until I was nine, I was pretty envious of other children who had big families and plenty of siblings. The irony is, of course, they may well have been equally envious of me getting all my parents' attention, but I guess that's how it goes.

***

Sam was our first pregnancy. He was conceived when we were both twenty-nine, so not the youngest parents but not the oldest either. Up until the point he died, the pregnancy had been completely normal. Ours wasn't considered a risky situation, so we just had the regular number of tests, and aside from the physical complications that come with being pregnant, Kath had been fine.

We had been away for the weekend, seeing friends in Devon, when Kath realised something wasn't right. The baby (we didn't know he was a boy at that point) had stopped moving around as much, and she gradually became more and more certain that there was a problem. A midwife we saw after the birth said – with extraordinary insensitivity – that she didn't understand how parents didn't immediately leap into action when a baby stopped kicking in the womb, but this was our first time. We weren't given an instruction manual as to what to do and how to respond to every situation. Regardless, we went to the hospital first thing on the Monday, by which time it was too late.

The initial realisation that Sam had died was a huge shock, and I remember falling to the floor when the news was finally given to us after all the tests had run their course. But I found the period of time that followed that initial moment of horror to be disturbing and awful in a very different way.

We were told by the doctors that Kath would have to be induced; this meant her being given various drugs to kick an early labour into action, so after the drugs were administered we would go home and wait a day or two then return to hospital so that Kath could give birth to a dead baby.

**

Those days passed in a blur. Close friends and family came from all over the country to keep us company and try to help us pass the time until this dreadful thing in our future became the present. I don't remember sleeping or eating much, if at all.

The process of the birth itself was a horrific reversal of what we had hoped and expected the birth of our first baby to be. In order for Kath to have the best possible chance of having natural births in the future, we agreed to not have a caesarean section, meaning that she would have to push the baby out.

They recommended an epidural, which Kath agreed to, but she hates drugs that mess with her head and was pretty sick as a result. I think it did take away some of the physical pain, but she was spaced out and confused during the birth. I remember holding her hand during labour and realising that all the jokes I'd heard female stand-ups do about men having no clue about pain thresholds, were absolutely 100% true: what she was doing was beyond anything I have known or experienced either before or since, both in terms of physical pain and psychological trauma. I have no idea if anything I did was in any way helpful, but I tried.

When the baby was born, he was small and had a pointy head but otherwise looked fairly normal. The midwife took Sam away briefly to clean him and wrap him in blankets, and we were given a short time alone with him. I remember being told that he was a boy, and that moment being particularly awful – I had said all through the pregnancy that I didn't mind what gender the baby was, but it turned out that wasn't true. I had really wanted a boy, and I had got one.

Kath was then taken to the operating theatre as the placenta had not delivered properly and had to be surgically removed. I remember thinking very clearly at that point that there was a definite possibility that both my baby and my wife were going to die on the same day, but I smiled and squeezed Kath's hand as they wheeled the bed away.

She came back an hour or so later, the placenta having been safely and successfully removed. I must have been incredibly relieved to see her again, but I don't recall feeling anything much at that point other than grief.

We were given a couple of hours, and our families both came to spend some time with us and with Sam. I cried a lot. We all did. We gave him cuddles, and got to know him as far as that was possible.

He was very tiny, and he was my son, and he was dead.

***

Sam's funeral came soon after. We opted to have an autopsy carried out; the choice wasn't too difficult for us as we knew we wanted him to be cremated, but we also both felt that one of the few positives to come out of his death could be some greater understanding of any medical problems that he suffered from and which caused him to be stillborn.

In the end, we didn't go to the cremation. I know our bereavement midwife did, but I don't think any of the rest of our family went with her. For Kath and me it was just too much; crematoria are soulless, strangely industrial places at the best of times, and the idea of watching that process given the context was just too grim to bear.

I felt really guilty about this decision though. The most powerful feeling I can recall from the time after Sam's death was a sense that I had failed in my job as his dad; I hadn't been able to look after my son – to prevent anything bad happening to him, or to make it better when it did. I still carry this emotion with me now, and I think it probably influences me in ways that I don't even realise. This feeling was very strong around the time of the cremation; I remember feeling totally conflicted about the need for someone to be there to look after him, but not being able to bring myself to be there.

Out of a long list of pretty awful days, that one was right up there.

***

The news from the autopsy, when it arrived, was that Sam had a bunch of stuff wrong with him. The doctors couldn't be sure, but suspected he had Down's Syndrome – a genetic disorder which affects one child in every 1000 in the UK[1], purely occurring by chance as opposed to any inherited predisposition. They also found that he had multiple problems with his heart. All in all, had he made it out of the womb alive then he would have been very sick indeed for his whole life.

---

1 From the Down's Syndrome Association website, 2020: https://www.downs-syndrome.org.uk/about/general/

It was difficult to work out how I felt about this. Our son was dead, so the dominant emotion was grief, but the knowledge that he had some serious health defects that had resulted in him being stillborn changed things. Had he been born alive I would have taken care of him and done whatever he needed to be as happy as he could be – that's the job, and I would have done it gladly – but it would have been hard, for us as his parents but primarily for him. I feel guilty about this emotion all the same; the idea that it was perhaps better that he didn't make it, both for him and for us. Even having considered it for the last eleven years, I still don't have an answer to this. It's just a question that has been with me since he died, and which I assume will be with me forever.

After the birth, Kath stayed in hospital for another night and was then discharged. She should probably have stayed in longer, as she was physically in a pretty bad way after the surgical procedure to remove the placenta. I remember coming home to my parents' house, where we stayed for a bit, and her having to be carried up the front steps on a chair as she couldn't manage on her own.

I remember finding it really difficult to get going and actually do anything useful for a long time after he died. I went back to work after the standard (for the time) two weeks' paternity leave, but I was not even nearly ready to do so. My boss told me during a very tough phone call that I 'had to come back some time', so I did. There was a lot of staring at the wall.

It's difficult to describe my immediate grief, and it was a confusing thing to go through. You often hear words to the effect that 'no parent should outlive their children'; obviously, that's referring to the crushing sadness that a parent feels if their child dies before they do, but was I entitled to be *that* sad? After all, Sam was dead when he was born. He hadn't lived a life and built relationships, hadn't had siblings, known the rest of his family, had friends or anything else. He'd never even seen us, his parents. Did that mean he was somehow less of a person, less relevant somehow? I remember thinking about conversations I had been involved in previously about the abortion debate. Did my strong views on women's right to choose make me a hypocrite for feeling as I did about Sam?

One decision I took very early on, however, has stayed with me: I resolved to actually talk about the fact that Sam had died to anyone who asked. I'm not really sure how I came to this decision; it was definitely out of character at the time for someone who tended very strongly, as I did and probably still do, to bottle stuff up and try and just get on with it. This never actually worked, by the way, as I think I was quite often depressed, but that was definitely how I existed.

This decision was liberating but also scary. I was having conversations with people at work that I kind of knew but kind of didn't, in that colleague-you-see-every-day kind of way, about how I felt about my son's death: the single most awful experience I had ever been through. To be honest, quite a few people didn't know how to deal with it and would politely move the subject on in a typically British way. But a surprising (to me, at least) number of people responded with stories of their own, with love and with support. I was – and still am – blown away by this: people who I would have felt slightly awkward with, had I ended up sitting next to on the tube on the way home, offered their support and a listening ear. Most importantly, they also told me their own stories.

What these stories told me was invaluable: Kath and I were not alone, and our experience was by no means a rarity. Many of the people I spoke to had been through miscarriage or stillbirth, or had experienced serious and traumatic complications around childbirth more generally. Others were having persistent problems even conceiving a baby; again this was something I had taken for granted, but which I became much more aware of.

I don't want to paint an inaccurate picture here. I wasn't marching around the world bending the ear of everyone who would listen about my terrible fatherhood experience (even though I think I felt like I was at times). I was just talking openly about what had happened to us, when I felt like the situation allowed for it. I still feel to this day that this was not necessarily a good or bad decision, but that it was the *only* choice I had at the time. There was no way I could have bottled up and internalised the grief and sadness I was feeling: it would have been disastrous. On some level I think I knew that I had to do something about my grief, for my own good if nothing else. With that said, it still definitely felt like a selfish decision – I knew there would be people I spoke to who couldn't cope with hearing my story – but I felt I had to do it regardless.

I also remember talking to people from my parents' generation: mums and dads of friends, who had been through similar things, but in a different era and with very different responses from society to what they had been through. One woman, the mum of a family of five children, one of whom was one of my closest friends at the time, told me that their first child had been stillborn. The baby had been whisked away immediately after delivery, and she never saw him again. Her husband never saw him at all. I'm not

100% on this, but I think she even said that there was no mention of her stillbirth in her medical records; it was treated as something that had never even happened, swept under the carpet never to be seen or thought about again. There was no support – no counselling, no bereavement midwife, nothing whatsoever. She was sent home shortly afterwards and left to deal with her loss alone.

Whilst I wasn't hugely surprised by this Victorian-era attitude towards stillbirth in the recent past, it was still shocking to imagine parents having to go through the death of a child with no outside support whatsoever. Awful though that is, it did make me reflect on the care we had received, and feel very grateful for it.

***

There are very few positives to come out of losing your child. But one thing both Kath and I felt was that the care that she was offered by all the NHS staff we encountered (with the single exception of Weird Judgy Midwife mentioned earlier) was nothing short of extraordinary.

Sam was delivered by a trainee midwife under supervision from a superior. I think her name was Joanne. She couldn't have been older than twenty, and she was professional, warm and unbelievably caring towards two strangers that she would never be seeing again once we left the hospital. I remember feeling totally awestruck by midwives in general actually; I'm not a spiritual person by nature, but these women (they were all women, in our case) seemed to me to be part doctor, part counsellor and part Stone Age shaman. They were just *wise*; dealing with the beginning, and sometimes the end, of new lives on a daily basis.

We were also very lucky with the consultant Kath was treated by during Sam's birth. His name was Mr Wai Yoong, and he became such a pivotal figure in our lives. I think about him often, how sensitive he was to how we would both be feeling whilst delivering life-changing diagnoses and medical news.

There were dozens of others. An extraordinary bereavement midwife called Marilyn who visited us at home on numerous occasions, helping without judgement and great patience with all the procedural stuff we had to organise, and just being there to listen. She went to Sam's cremation in our place; something I still can't quite believe she was prepared to do. She even came to visit when we eventually had our next baby (more on that later) and gave us a blanket as a present. Like I said, extraordinary.

There were nurses and registrars too. Every one of them was remarkable;

working in a system where they are overworked and underpaid, without the basic resources necessary to do their jobs, but still doing so with a hug and a smile and giving love and care to their patients.

A few years after Sam's death I watched, live on TV, the opening ceremony for the Olympic Games in 2012. When the celebration of the NHS came around I was standing on the sofa, cheering and weeping simultaneously (I may have had a couple of ales). Given the current political climate, I'm terrified that my children will grow up in an era where the NHS as I know it will no longer exist: it's an extraordinary institution which should be supported and able to provide equal care to anyone, regardless of their financial situation.

***

The decision to try for another baby after Sam died took a lot of soul-searching.

Kath was not in a good place psychologically, and we both felt a lot of guilt over his death. Even though we had been reassured that his stillbirth had been a total accident, and there was nothing we could have done to prevent or predict it, I had a feeling that I have never been able to shift that I failed at my first responsibility to Sam as his father – to look after him and prevent anything bad happening to him. Ultimately what we decided was that the reasons for us wanting to start a family in the first place hadn't gone away, so we decided to try again. This was no easy decision though, and we both took it knowing full well what we were getting ourselves into.

We had some tough times as a couple during the year or so immediately following Sam's death. I remember one holiday in particular which was supposed to be our first with him as a family; my parents rented a house in Italy and we all went – uncles and aunts, Kath's mum and stepdad, my sister and her boyfriend. It was the strangest thing to be in one of the most beautiful places I'd ever been to but almost completely unable to enjoy the experience of being there.

Sure, on the outside I was drinking nice wine and eating and possibly even laughing occasionally. But it was frankly pretty hollow. *I* was hollow.

Beyond that holiday I really don't remember a great deal of that time. One of the things I have realised over the years since Sam's death is that our minds are very good at innately protecting us from trauma. I have found that my toughest memories tend to come back to me in periods where I am able to deal with processing them; when I'm grounded and happy enough to be able to cope with remembering. This makes perfect sense, of course – our mind is protecting us from painful memories at times when we are not able to deal with them. I've learned to trust this arrangement I have with my brain: at first I felt bad that I wasn't thinking about Sam every day, but I gradually realised what was happening, and that I would think about him when I was able, and not when I wasn't. I guess this might come across as quite a calculated means of dealing with grief, but I don't know any other way. That's what I've got, and it's what got me through.

***

Ten months after Sam's death, Kath got pregnant again. I was of course thrilled and immediately terrified at the same time, but not in that way that you feel the first time around. I was heart-in-my-boots dreading nine months of a pregnancy that both Kath and I were convinced was going to fail at any time.

We had been reassured by our consultant that there was no medical reason for us to not try again straight away should we want to; Sam was just the unlucky one in every 225 babies in the UK who, on average, are stillborn[2]. Regardless, when we went in for our first prenatal appointment he told us they would be treating the pregnancy as 'high risk', meaning that Kath would be given more frequent scans and other tests to ensure we collectively knew as much as possible about the baby and the pregnancy more widely. This was simply because Sam had died – regardless of the causes, stillbirths tend statistically to be followed by complicated pregnancies.

As if the world was trying to prove this point, we discovered from one of the early scans that Kath had placenta praevia. This is a condition where the placenta covers the exit from the womb into the cervix and can result in the placenta rupturing, causing bleeds which can be fatal for both baby and mother. The probability of these bleeds occurring also increases as the baby grows. We were informed that in the vast majority of cases, the placenta moves up around the back of the womb, where it is eventually meant to fix, and that this was likely to happen for us too.

You can probably guess this next bit: it didn't. The placenta stayed firmly wedged underneath the baby, preventing it from safely emerging from the womb as part a natural birth. We were at twenty weeks, and there were now increased risks to both baby and mother now from potential bleeds.

I remember this news being a serious psychological blow for both of us. For obvious reasons, we had spent the first twenty weeks or so of this second

---

2 NCT website, 2020: https:www.nct.org.uk/labour-birth losing-baby stillbirth-what-it-means-and-what-causes-it/

pregnancy convinced every day that something awful was going to happen. It was very much a grind in a mental sense, in that we were living one day to the next and doing what we could to try and get through and remain level-headed. Both of us were working full-time too, so attempting at the same time to give what we could to our careers.

At around twenty-four weeks Kath had a bleed. We rushed her to hospital, both terrified that the worst was about to happen. Heart monitors for the baby were strapped on and Kath was kept under observation for a few hours. Eventually the doctors were satisfied that it had been a small bleed and therefore not much to worry about, and given that the baby was not in distress, we were sent home.

Three weeks later, however, at twenty-seven weeks into the pregnancy, Kath had a much bigger bleed. In a glass-half-empty way I had been kind of expecting this to happen, but nevertheless it was another terrifying moment that resulted in a rush to hospital with a hastily packed bag. Kath was admitted to the prenatal ward, where she was told she would have to stay – being monitored constantly – until the baby was developed enough to be born safely. We were now in a weird Mexican standoff with the placenta; wanting to leave the baby in the womb for as long as possible in order for it to stand the best possible chance of survival, but knowing that every day it stayed there increased the probability of Kath having another bleed.

In the end, Kath was flat on her back in the prenatal ward at the North Middlesex University Hospital in London for seven weeks. Seven whole, entire weeks of the baby heart monitor strapped to her stomach, listening to that heartbeat and being convinced that – at any time – something awful was going to happen. I'll be honest, if that had been me, I would have been stark raving mental within six hours. She did seven weeks.

By the end, Kath knew literally everyone on the ward. The security guard (who wasn't supposed to let her off the ward) was befriended, and occasional sneaks down to the canteen were allowed. Let's just say she can be persuasive when she needs to be. Everyone, of course, came to visit, bringing food and things to do. She watched every episode of *Dial M for Murder*, and I remain surprised that neither of our kids ended up being named Dick as a result. She knew the woman in the next-door room, who also had placenta praevia. Toward the end of our stay there that lady had a huge bleed and was rushed to surgery for a caesarean section; mother and baby only just survived.

For my part, I was working nine to five, leaving on the dot to commute home (Hammersmith to Tottenham, around seventy-five minutes), jumping straight in the car and going to the hospital via a stop-off to pick food up for both of us. I'd stay on the ward until around nine then drive home, go to bed, then get up and do it all again.

As before, I really don't remember much about this time other than a pervading feeling of dread at a time in my life which should have been filled with hope and optimism. I should have been painting nurseries, building cots and stroking my partner's bump, just like the guy in the adverts.

I guess the first three weeks were the worst, but that whole time when Kath was on the ward is heavily blurred in my memory. We had been told by the doctors that thirty weeks was a big milestone, as babies born before this point are statistically much less likely to survive than those which come later. It was really just another grind though; living day to day and attempting to get through to a notional point in time that someone who supposedly knew what they were talking about had told us was in some way important. I'm not saying this to suggest that I was cynical about what we were being told or the doctors' expertise, just that we had been the victim of so many statistics by this point that it had all started to feel totally arbitrary: either the baby would survive or it wouldn't. The future of our lives together was hanging on a coin-flip.

**

Jacob was born by planned caesarean section at thirty-five weeks. He weighed six and a bit pounds, which is quite healthy for that length of time in the womb, and he looked weirdly just like my dad who – at the time – was seventy and bald. He's still bald. He was just seventy at that point in time.

The operation was performed by the same consultant who had looked after us during Sam's stillbirth, and it went very well. Kath was kept in for a night and had a pretty tough recovery from the operation in a physical sense, but we were home quickly and had a baby. He was fine. No Down's Syndrome, ten digits of each variety, breastfeeding quickly and doing everything he should. He didn't sleep much for the first day or two, so Kath's sister Vic (who is also one of my oldest friends) and I took turns looking after him in the rocking chair in our old house.

As I write this, sitting at my kitchen table, Jacob (now nearly ten) is upstairs getting ready for school. Ella (six, also born by planned C-section after an otherwise-normal-but-still-terrifying pregnancy at thirty-seven weeks, under the watchful eye of the same extraordinary consultant) is already in her uniform and is watching the telly.

They, along with Kath, are my everything.

***

Kath and I realised soon after Sam's death that the pain and loss would never go away, but that it would gradually become more possible for us to live with it.

In my mind this looks like a tree's roots growing around a rock; the rock remains in place, the tree just slowly grows around it and gets on with its life. We were certainly right in this – eleven years later my grief feels the same now as it did then, and hasn't dimmed or shrunk at all.

I cry a lot more than I did before he died, and my grief can catch me out at unexpected moments. My kids walking down the street in front of me, a tear-jerky moment in a TV show about a father, certain pieces of music (*Re: Stacks* by Bon Iver is one of the most beautiful songs ever written, but I now cannot listen to it at all), all of these and plenty more can reduce me to tears.

There are more direct ways of remembering Sam too. There is a tree planted at Kath's mum's house in his memory; when we go up to visit we will often, either together or alone, go and sit under it and say hello to him. We also have a rose planted in our garden that was grown from a cutting taken from Myddelton House in Enfield. Kath and my dad took it the day they went to pick up Sam's ashes from the crematorium, when the rose there was flowering. It has survived being dug up when we moved house, and a rogue builder (who was hired to extend our loft and kitchen) deciding arbitrarily to demolish our entire garden. 'I thought the architect told me to,' he said. The architect didn't.

Sam's birthday is always a difficult time to get through each year. I remember on one of the early anniversaries of his death, Kath and I – searching for something to distract us – binge-watched the entirety of a bizarre TV show called *Iron Chef UK* whilst drinking heavily. It wasn't pretty. Our approach these days is that it's simply a time we have to get through; we're getting better at seeing it coming, and planning our lives so we can just hole up and come out the other side.

All of this – our grief, and how we cope with it – was something we knew that even those closest to us could never truly understand. Our families shared our loss (after all, they lost a grandson or a nephew too) but it was less direct for them. And as a result it was obviously going to be different. If there is one positive thing to come from this though, our shared understanding and experience has without question made us and our relationship stronger.

***

My hope is that someone somewhere who is going through any of the stuff that happened to us might read my fatherhood story and realise that they are not alone; that there are others who have been through the same experiences and have come out the other side still in one piece, and that this might help them get through what they are experiencing.

This all goes back to that decision I took when Sam died to talk to people about it. It would have been far easier to bottle up my feelings and not talk about them, as I would have avoided those awkward moments where you tell someone that your son has died and they just can't deal with it and in that awful British way, they change the subject. For every one of those moments, nonetheless, there were ten people who astonished me with their openness, warmth and love, and who responded with stories of their own – either about themselves or those close to them – which demonstrated to me that what I was going through was, albeit awful, not unusual or weird. The act of sharing built connections between me and how I was feeling and the people in my world, and by doing so prevented those emotions festering inside my head.

It was through this that I learned the importance of being more open about my emotions and my mental state, as by doing so I could see that there was a direct benefit to me and my psychological well-being. I also realised how terrible I had been at doing this for the first part of my life, and how bad this had been for me. Bottling up anger, sadness and other negative feelings had just made them worse over time, and led to some bad decisions along with long periods of depression.

I get the sense that men, in this country at least, are getting a bit better at opening up and talking about how they are feeling. I certainly hope that's the case, and if by writing this I can play a tiny part in helping to keep that change rolling, then it will definitely have been worthwhile.

Chapter 13:

Balancing Patience and Childhood Trauma: The Trials and Tribulations of Becoming a Stepdad

Saffa Kallon

My name is Saffa and I had my first biological child at forty years old, so I guess that would make me an older father, at least in comparison to my friends who have teenage children. I had always wanted to be a father from a very young age but, looking back on my life, I am happy things happened as they did. I was quite immature back then (I'm still quite immature now) but I think I have grown enough to be able to make the sacrifices necessary to be the father that I want to be, without having any regrets.

When I was a bit younger, with a lot more time on my hands, I used to be out quite a lot. Not out boozing (all the time) but I enjoyed open mic nights. I love live music and used to write and perform poetry. This slowed down as I got older and I found it harder to get out of bed and function with reduced sleeping hours. And it stopped completely as I became a father. I still write poetry, sometimes about my daughter, sometimes about doughnuts. It really just depends on how I feel and what I'm in love with more at that moment in time. My other hobbies included five-a-side football, boxing and badminton. But breaking both of my wrists in a freak accident while playing football curtailed my football, boxing and badminton careers. I still go to the gym and have recently taken up running, yoga and golf; the latter two are my current obsessions.

I'm also a stepdad. I initially didn't want to be one; it was never in my plans. I guess the main reason for that is that I had, and still have, a very poor relationship with my own stepfather and I didn't want a child to have to suffer and experience what I went through. In retrospect, my stepfather and I couldn't be more different.

I used to always say that if I met a woman who had a child, or (shudder) children, it would never be serious as I had always wanted to start a family from fresh with someone, rather than be with someone who had been there and done it all before. I wanted everything to be new to us and for us to experience things together for the first time.

Funnily enough when I met Claudia, my partner, I quickly discovered that she was someone that I had met many years before when we were both teenagers, but it must have been prior to the mobile phone era as we never kept in contact. She was a 'cousin' of a 'cousin' and when I first met her, I assumed I would see her again at a gathering somewhere. I had no idea that it would be about twenty years later at my 'cousin's' wedding. I was a groomsman and she was a bridesmaid. As soon as she walked into the church hall (she was late and I have come to expect nothing less from her) I remembered her. Not her name or anything like that, but something let me know that I knew her, or had known her.

I don't think anyone grows up thinking that they want to be a stepfather – I certainly didn't. But Micah, Claudia's son, made me want to be a stepdad. When I first met him, he was such a good, polite boy, very playful and a little devious, as most young boys are. I used to see him and his mother only on weekends, sometimes only every other weekend. As time went by, living by myself became less and less fun. I actually missed both of them and wanted to spend more with them. After a year or so I moved in with them, and watching him grow has been an absolute pleasure.

My Uncle, My Father and My Stepfather

Growing up I only had one real father figure: my uncle. He's a loving, patient, intelligent, jovial, fair-minded person, who always had time for a talk, a laugh and basically kept me sane throughout adolescence and my early adulthood. I always admired his temperament and I have learned so much from him.

As my relationship with my own stepfather wasn't a good one and my interaction with my biological father was quite limited, I had poor experience of a close positive father figure. So, it was tough for me, but I promised to somehow get it right and not emotionally scar, or damage, my stepchild.

My stepfather was always irritated, irrational, impatient, angry, distant and non-communicative. In the end, we probably didn't pass more than two words to each other between me hitting the ages of maybe eleven and twenty-five, when I left home. I feel as though I have been tarnished and emotionally stained by my experience with him.

I feel that he bred a lot of anger in me that I found hard to control, even up until my mid-twenties. I have tried to quell that fire, although from time to time my temper can be short and I do hate myself for it. I have since discovered through therapy how not to hate myself for anything and to begin forgiving myself for things that I have done in my past that I wouldn't do today. It is very important for me to acknowledge things that weren't great in my past, forgive myself and move forward, rather than carry that negativity into my present, which affects my future. I speak to a therapist a couple times a month and it has helped me to deal with my lapses.

My first memory of my biological father was when I was around six years old. He came to our house for my birthday (I'm not sure it was on the actual day) and he had a card. I remember hugging him really tightly and feeling so incredibly glad to finally see him. Up to that point I had virtually waited my whole life to do just that. My next memory of him was right before my GCSEs, so I was about fourteen or fifteen. He said that he wanted me to be properly prepared for my exams, so I would go to his place on the weekends and he would buy me exercise books and I'd study at his before going back home.

My relationship with my dad always left me longing to be with him. He seemed like a very focused person, who knew what he wanted. He was very calm, knowledgeable, self-assured and confident. It was a nice feeling being around him.

I wish I could have spent a lot more time with my father as I believe my true essence is the wholeness of his character.

My experiences with my biological father and stepfather gave me an insight in to what kind of dad I didn't want to be. I didn't want to be absent – either physically or emotionally, while being physically present.

I wanted to be a great dad who had a deep relationship with his children.

Someone who listened and learned and earned their respect rather than expecting or demanding it.

Challenges – Highs and Lows

The very first challenge I faced as a stepdad was trying to understand where and how to set the boundaries. When I first got into Micah's life he was five years old and saw only his mother as a figure of authority. He obviously had respect and love for his father, but he was only seeing him every other weekend and I can only assume that in his younger years they had spent most of their time together enjoying each other's company. His mother used to say often that she always had to play bad cop.

With Micah, I didn't want to come across as a miserable disciplinarian, but I wasn't about to be a doormat either. As I mentioned earlier, I had always wanted to be a father and since neither I nor many of my closest friends grew up with our biological fathers, I was determined to be a positive influence in his life.

One story that comes to mind is when Claudia was out for the evening and asked me to shower Micah and make sure he was in bed by 8 p.m. No problem. At 7.40 p.m., I took him upstairs, I got him in the shower and took the sponge to wash him. He then said that his mum allowed him to wash himself. I thought to myself that he was maybe a little too young to do this but I thought I would see for myself what he would do. He then took his sponge and near enough squeezed a third of the shower gel onto it. I was in complete shock. This was obviously the first time he had been allowed to have the shower gel in his own hands and he was fully prepared to make the most of it. It was at that point that I said to myself that the Mr Nice Guy approach wouldn't work.

All children need boundaries and they need a parent to set them. I told him there and then in no uncertain terms that I knew that he had lied and that I wasn't happy about it and that I would never allow him to deceive me again. I made it clear that whether his mother had permitted him to do something or not, when he was in my care, if I said no, it meant no. He's eleven now and we're still working on that. I would say that children are always looking for ways to push the boundaries and as a father of a four-year-old now, I can see that they start from very young. All weaknesses will be exposed and used again and again. Humans are creatures of habit and will do all that they can to get their own way.

Emotions and Events

Emotionally, for me, being a step dad has been a bit of a rollercoaster. The thing is, Micah and I are very close and there have been times (or, more accurately, there are times) where I wish that he was my biological son. I'm very fond and so very proud of him. We spend a lot of time together, laughing, joking, debating, watching football, chilling and, to be quite honest, if I were blessed with a son in the future, and it was another Micah, I would be more than happy.

The reason it's been a rollercoaster is because at certain times reality has come out of the blue and hit me where it hurts. Due to our close bond and because we are a family, I have at times forgotten the fact that we aren't actually father and son. For example, one time I had taken him for training at football and once the session was over and all the kids came out, one of the other kids said to Micah, 'There's your dad', to which Micah replied, 'No, he's my stepdad'. The bottom line is he was correct, but it really hit me hard in my chest and left me reeling for a few minutes.

I felt as though in him saying that, he was making it clear to everyone that he didn't see me as a father and that I was only a stepdad. I know now that the reason I felt that way was due to the relationship that I had with my own stepdad and how he, as the emotionally numb man he is, made me feel that being a stepfather was almost like a sneer. Micah, though, was only being factually correct and didn't see my role as stepdad in his life as a lesser part to play.

Another instance was on his sixth birthday. His mother organised a picnic in the park for all of his family and friends and invited Micah's dad along with his friends and family. Near enough the whole day I just felt out of place and didn't know what to say or what to do.

When it came to Micah cutting his cake in front of everyone, his mum invited me to take a picture with her and Micah but I refused. I just didn't feel comfortable taking a picture as a family with Micah's dad watching. His dad really tried to make an effort with me but every time he approached me I just froze. I was as polite as I could be, but was unable to shake that feeling that day. I confided in my friend that I was experiencing an emotional response that I had never felt before. One that I did not know what to do with or how to react to, but I knew that Micah's dad being there was the reason. She asked me if the emotion was jealousy and I said to her that I didn't have a reason to be jealous; if anyone should be jealous it should be him as I was the one who was living with his son.

She then said to me that in order for me to stop feeling like that I would need to make peace with the fact that Micah's dad was now in my life and him being in my life didn't make my role in Micah's life any less important. Since then, Micah's dad and I have developed a really healthy relationship and I know for a fact that Micah enjoys the two important men in his life being 'friends'.

Stepdad vs Biological Dad

I would say the difference between being a stepdad and a biological dad is all in the mind of the parent, but also the child. I guess it's a similar mentality that a school class would have with their regular teacher versus a supply teacher. Obviously, I have spent more time with Micah than his dad, but his dad is his dad. The love and respect that he has for him is just innate, whereas I had to work to build a rapport, then a relationship, all the while trying to earn, demand and deserve his respect.

Initially, Micah would second guess everything that I would say and would run any request I made of him by his mum. It ended up really getting to me, so we both had to talk to him to make him understand that I was a parent as well and that whatever I asked of him he had to do. I can understand where he was coming from, as the only figure of authority that he consistently knew was his mother. But it was obviously an unworkable situation to have, where Micah thought he had to run everything I said by his mum. That phase only lasted a few months, but ever since then, we've been fine.

From my own experience, I would say that there shouldn't be a difference between being a dad and a stepdad. A child needs love, guidance, boundaries and discipline and any parent should be willing to give that to their child, or their partner's child. Micah now has a younger sister – my biological child with Micah's mum – and I do my best to not treat, or raise them differently. In my mind, Micah is my child so I will do for him whatever I think is in his best interests.

However, there are some things that I think should be between a father and his son. For example, Micah's mother asked me to help him learn to ride a bike, but I told her that that was a task for his father. It wasn't that I didn't want to teach him, but because if the boot was on the other foot, I would want to help my child achieve certain significant landmarks in their life. I think that it is really good that Micah's father takes an active role in his life and I will encourage them to spend as much time together doing things as possible, even if I do get a little jealous sometimes. I always miss him when he is with his dad for the weekend.

My Relationship with Micah's Dad

As I mentioned before, my relationship with Micah's dad started off quite badly, but mainly because of me more than anything else. The issues I had were all created in my mind and he didn't actually give me any reason to dislike him, although I didn't actually dislike him, I just didn't know how to feel around him. Maybe there was a tinge of jealousy. I mean, not only had this person known my partner, he had obviously slept with her and she had given him a child. I don't put too much importance into what someone says about why their relationship ended with their ex, so I have never held what he may, or may not have done to her against him.

As time has gone by, I guess I have realised that we have one thing in common and that one thing is very important to both of us. That one thing is Micah and we both only want what is best for him.

Over the years, Micah's dad and I have spent quite a lot of time together and I have to admit, I enjoy his company. He's quite an easy-going guy and I admire his maturity about the situation we have found ourselves in. I admire his calmness because I don't think that I would have been the same or, if I had appeared calm in public, privately I would have been seething.

Especially now that I have a four-year-old girl, the thought of another man bathing my daughter before bed, reading her a bedtime story, tucking her in and giving her a goodnight kiss would boil my blood.

He has trusted Micah's mother's judgement and given me the benefit of the doubt. You hear about baby-father drama, but I have had none of that and have to give him a lot of credit. Micah enjoys the fact that when his dad comes to pick him up, while he is getting ready, his dad and I have a little chinwag about whatever – football, Micah, my daughter. He's a really cool guy, even though he is a Manchester United fan.

Making Sure I Don't Have Favourites

When Elliott first suggested this segment to explain why I don't have favourites, I wanted to write that I do have a favourite and my favourite is my daughter.

The reason I wanted to write this is because she is my biological daughter and, as her father, my love for her would and could never be paralleled. I was going to write that I wasn't ashamed of that fact and for me, my aim was for Micah to feel that he was wasn't loved any less.

The more I think about it, though, the truth of the matter is I may very well love my daughter in a different way to Micah, but I don't think I love him any less. For the past six years I have treated this young boy in the same way I would have treated my own son. I ensure that Niyari, my daughter, respects Micah as her older brother. I would never allow her, or anyone, to refer to them as stepsiblings. I don't refer to my siblings that way and I don't think of them in that way. My siblings are my siblings, end of, and I want Micah and Niyari to have the same kind of relationship.

So, I don't have a favourite because my role is to raise both of these children to be good people. I wouldn't want either to be seen as a better person in comparison to the other. That wouldn't benefit me or them. I am equally proud of both of my children and my mother is happy that she now has two grandchildren. She spoils them both equally and showers them both with as much love as she can whenever she sees them. With Niyari being the youngest she may get indulged more than Micah by me, but I hope that Micah feels equally loved, because he is.

To summarise, Micah is my favourite son and Niyari is my favourite daughter.

What I Have Learned

The last six years being a father to Micah has taught me a lot.

I have a good friend called Kwab and one of his famous quotes is, *'I'm not here to be my children's friend!'* I thought that was quite harsh at first, but now I realise that sometimes you can't be your child's friend. Tough love is needed in order for children to learn and we need to teach them lessons that will help them develop as they grow older.

With Micah, this particular area has been a journey and a learning curve. When I first came into Micah's life, I felt as though I needed to be his friend first to build that trust and rapport and love before showing him my stern side. He has since shown me that that isn't the correct way to do things. Balance is the key. Discipline and boundaries need to be set from early on, as *'give them an inch and they will take a mile'* is a very apt saying, especially when applied to children.

He has definitely helped me to grow. I thought I was an adult when I turned sixteen, again when I turned eighteen, twenty-one, twenty-five and thirty, but I feel as though one of the most important chapters in adulthood is when you first become a parent.

I have mastered properly curbing my temper. I didn't realise how my voice impacted those around me, but seeing his reaction to my disappointment, even when I wasn't really angry, made me reevaluate myself. I gave up my PS3 as I didn't want to be a bad influence on him. I wanted to be able to say to him without being a hypocrite that he couldn't spend all day playing computer games. I tried to keep the fact that I smoked away from him and eventually gave up for the benefit of him and his sister, and I try to do as much as possible around the house in the way of cooking and cleaning as I don't think traditional gender roles should be encouraged by our generation.

Times are changing and the way we give information to our boys and our girls should be different to how the information was given to us. I want him to be a better man than me and I'm sure his father wants the same, so I have learned to focus on the positives and try to instill into him all the things I lack. We spend a lot of time together and I genuinely love passing on my experience and words of advice to him.

When I was younger, I didn't think I had the capability to love someone else's child as though they were my own, but I have happily proven myself wrong. I honestly couldn't imagine my life without Micah in it.

Chapter 14:

Why We Need to Better Support New Dads:
A Tale of Postnatal Depression

Mark Williams

Some of you may remember a TV series, *Life on Mars* (still available on Netflix). It's a police procedural with a twist. As the protagonist, played by John Simm, says at the start of each episode: 'My name is Sam Tyler. I had an accident and I woke up in 1973. Am I mad, in a coma, or back in time? Whatever's happened, it's like I've landed on a different planet.'

Life in the seventies was very different. The standard of living was way down on what we take for granted today. After all, the seventies were closer to the war than to us today – and remember, wartime rationing went on long after VE day. The UK's cities still showed signs of the war damage; vast numbers of people still lived in very poor housing.

And where I was born, in the Welsh valleys, the majority of people depended on coal mining for their livelihoods, whether they went below ground to the coalface or not. My dad did, and his father before him, and his before that. They were like a local militia, marching to their shifts and then back again, their faces blackened with coal dust, masked with wafts of cigarette smoke, through which the usual banter flew, sharp as a pick. They might have looked intimidating to outsiders, but they were our dads and our uncles and their mates, and we kids worshipped them.

They clattered home in their heavy boots straight to the bath, which by then, at least, had hot running water. Dad emerged, in his clean clothes, his still-damp hair brushed back, his face glowing and split by a big smile. He'd ruffle my hair and ask what I'd been doing all day. If it was term time I'd mutter something about school and he'd say he hoped I'd done my homework.

During the holidays, all the kids had the run of the place. We played in the streets, which were perfectly safe in those days when there were far fewer cars around; or we'd go up into the woods and chase each other around in packs until someone fell over, cut their knee open and had to be escorted home to be patched up.

Quite often that was me. And not surprisingly, given my daredevil disdain for danger. I was inspired by a stuntman on a TV show called *The Fall Guy* – and indeed aspired to follow him into the stunt business when I grew up. One of my stunts was climbing telephone masts which could reach 130 feet into the sky. One wrong move and they would have been shovelling my broken bones into a bag. It makes me shudder to think of it.

I obviously didn't make that wrong move; but I made a lot of other ones, quite often involving new ways to catapult myself off my bike. I had more broken bones, stitches and cuts before I was ten years of age than most people have in a lifetime, and to this day am ashamed at the amount of worry and inconvenience I must have caused my parents. But nothing could stop me. I was just a ball of energy. I needed to let off steam and took no heed of danger, running wild in the woods with my mates, daring each other to do the next silly thing.

We didn't have watches, so judged time by the light. My mum would tell us to come back when the street lights went on. In summer, all the mums would stand on their doorsteps and shout up into the woods for those still playing to come in for their tea.

Of course, I'd be ravenous, and my dad would have worked up a decent appetite working his shift, so the meal didn't last long. But no one went to bed hungry. There was always enough food, and to be honest, we had a pretty good life. Dad was on a good wage because he was a skilled man, one of whose jobs was shoeing the pit ponies. My mum had trained as a mental health nurse, but didn't go back to that after she'd had me. Instead, she became part-time as a manager in the local garage. Because she went out to work as well as my dad, our family was different to a lot of our neighbours.

You could say it was more modern. I certainly remember Dad doing a lot of housework, which was great for my mum.

Traditionally, the miners had always fought hard for recognition of what they contributed to the country's economy. They were generally seen as the most militant group of workers, whether they mined in Yorkshire, Durham, Derbyshire, South Wales – or even Kent. Before the Labour government nationalised the pits after the war, the coal mines had been owned by private companies and there was a long history of disputes, resulting in strikes and lockouts. It was hoped that nationalisation would bring an end to such conflicts, but it didn't change the fact that you had one group of people who spent their working lives underground in dark, cramped and potentially dangerous conditions, and another group of people in suits and ties sitting in offices telling them what to do.

Generally, the miners, led by the National Union of Mineworkers (NUM), got what they wanted. After all, without them, the power stations wouldn't work because they were fired by coal. And no government, Tory or Labour, wanted to have tell the electorate the bad news that they wouldn't have the electricity they expected. There was trouble all through the seventies, with a miners' strike in 1972. That didn't last long as the demand for a pay rise was granted. But a year later there was another stand-off, with the Tory Prime Minister, Ted Heath calling for a Three Day Week. I'm not old enough to remember it, but I imagine it must have been like our Covid lockdowns, with shops and businesses under strict rules about opening, and even the pubs shut, but with much less to watch on television. A year later, Heath called an election, asking the question: Who governs Britain?

It turned out not to be him, but the Labour governments of Wilson and Callaghan that replaced the Tories had continuing trouble with the unions, culminating in the Winter of Discontent in 1978–79. It was a very cold year and the whole country was brought to its knees, allowing Margaret Thatcher to win the General Election for the Tories. Thatcher hated the unions, calling them 'The Enemy Within', and it wasn't long before she locked horns with the NUM, led by Arthur Scargill.

The Miners' Strike of 1984 was an epic confrontation, which divided the country and saw confrontations on the picket lines between police and miners which sometimes flared up into violence. Dad, of course, joined the rest of his mates on the picket line, spending long days trying to keep warm around an old oil drum smouldering with waste from the slag heaps. The longer the strike went on, the more depressing life became. Money was tight, but thankfully we had Mum's pay from the garage to fall back on. Though even with that, there was a lot of belt-tightening. The strike lasted for months and caused untold hardship and bitterness in mining areas.

You'll know which side won, and you'll know which side I was on. Mining communities all over Britain were crushed by a government that simply would not give in. The scars are there to this day, testimony to Mrs Thatcher's determination that the country would never again be dependent on home-sourced coal. The programme of mine closures which followed decimated whole communities. The heart of their local economies was torn out; the future stripped of hope.

From a personal perspective, it became clear I was not going to follow in the footsteps of my dad, his dad, and my great-grandfather. There'd be no mining for me. What to do instead? I suppose the obvious answer was to do well at school and get some qualifications that would open a range of options as I grew older.

But schooling didn't really work for me. At primary school I was put in a special class for those who were behind with their reading, but no one realised I was dyslexic. It wasn't really a thing in those days. They just assumed you were a bit slow, a bit stupid, and very bad at concentrating.

That last bit was true, and it carried on being true when I moved up to big school. Though I wasn't put in a special class for slow learners, there was no doubting that teachers' expectations for me were not high. Which, of course, meant that my own expectations were low too. If enough people treat you as though you're thick, you'll come to accept that you are.

But the fact is, school wasn't designed for me – or I for it.

What I now know is that, in addition to being dyslexic, I am hypersensitive and suffer from audio overload, which means that sitting in a class with thirty other kids was not a good learning environment for me. I found it impossible to focus: just too many distractions. I simply couldn't sit still and listen for forty minutes or an hour at a time. It was torture. I felt like a wild animal in a cage, restless with frustrated energy, depressed at the imposition of this cruel imprisonment.

I wasn't a bad kid. You could even say I was respectful. That was the way I was brought up – respect your elders. But sometimes the boredom became too much to bear and I'd end up doing one of those pranks which the other kids loved but which teachers hated.

And so I turned into the dog given a bad name. I bet I was namechecked more than most in the staffroom. And, of course, my reputation just got worse and worse. I can see it from their point of view – with the benefit of hindsight. There you are trying to teach a class about equilateral triangles or whatever it is, and there's some boy messing around in the back row with his mates. Frankly, if he doesn't want to learn and get any qualifications, that's fine by you; but the trouble is, that sort of behaviour puts everybody else off. And let's face it, it's easy to be distracted from equilateral triangles under the best conditions.

It seems unthinkable today, when children's rights are given the acknowledgement they deserve, but back in early eighties we suffered the final stage of the tradition of physical punishment that trailed back through the centuries to Shakespeare and beyond into the mists of time. Thousands upon thousands of teachers had lived by the biblical injunction 'Spare the rod and spoil the child', and we were the last generation of school kids who feared and suffered regular corporal punishment.

In primary school we'd be slapped on the back of our legs or have our hair pulled. In those days of blackboards and squeaky scribbles in chalk that you were meant to copy down in your exercise book, teachers also had a habit of throwing board rubbers at us. These were made of felt set in a piece of wood about the size of a shoe brush. Imagine getting one of those on the head as you were swapping a football cigarette card with a mate under your desks. It damn well hurt!

In primary school there was the cane, which rested along the top of the windowsill in full view as a constant reminder of what we'd be in for if we misbehaved. I and my first-year friends worried ourselves sick thinking of how much pain a stroke of the cane across the open palm would cause. When we were summoned to face our fate, we'd often be lined up for as long as an hour before our punishment was administered. The waiting was almost worse than the caning. For all the stinging pain, it was at least over quickly.

As was corporal punishment itself. It was finally banned early in my secondary career. Despite traditionalists' doom-laden prophecies of pupils roaming school corridors in feral mobs without the threat of physical retribution to restrain them, schools carried on as they had before – but in a more civilised way.

I can't claim my behaviour improved though. I just couldn't keep still at my desk and would often shout out something without even thinking about it – just to break the boredom. So into the corridor I would go, and then I'd get put into detention and glare at the work I'd been set, and stare out of the window, and wonder why the clock on the wall had stopped, and whether this was going to be the year Manchester United finally knocked Liverpool off their perch.

Because, by the time I got to secondary school I was completely hooked on sport. Football first. I was always kicking a ball around with my mates – up and down the street outside our houses, or, at school, in the yard at break time. And as soon as I was old enough, I got picked for school teams. I was decent. Tried hard, ran hard, shot hard, tackled hard. And there was some skill in the mix too, so it wasn't long before I was pushed up above my year group and started competing with boys who were older than me. Which, of course, I relished.

Wales isn't renowned as a footballing nation – not compared to rugby (and boy were we good at rugby in the seventies!). But I didn't play rugby, so wasn't that interested in it. And although there were good football teams in South Wales, as a kid you really had to support one of the big First Division teams. This was decades before anyone thought of the Premier League, Sky Sports and sky-high salaries making even quite run-of-the-mill players millionaires in their twenties. Imagine what George Best would be worth these days! Instead he plied his unique skills on waterlogged pitches, getting hacked to bits, week after week for a wage that wouldn't buy you a mediocre Conference League player these days. The seventies really were a different planet.

But it was our planet, and you could turn up at a ground, queue for the turnstiles and get in to see a match for a scrumpled-up ten-bob note. It didn't take me long to persuade someone to take me to the big matches, and once my mum had been persuaded that no one was going to make me drink beer or smoke cigarettes, I was allowed to go on the supporters' coach and off we'd go to wherever Man Utd were playing. We'd set off early and come back late, the coach rocking with an endless singalong whether we'd won or lost. For me it was boy heaven.

The other love of my life from an early age was music. I watched *Top of the Pops* and stuck posters of my favourite bands on my bedroom wall. People growing up in the sixties always claim to have had it the best – imagine buying the new Beatles hits, brand new, as they came out! Not to mention the Stones and the Kinks and Pink Floyd etc. But we didn't have it bad in the seventies, with glam rock setting new outrageous fashion standards. And then, as the seventies segued into the eighties and Margaret Thatcher's Britain became more and more divided, there was the working-class backlash of punk rock, with the leading anti-establishment band, the Sex Pistols expressing a lot of the rage and resentment that was floating around at the time.

ACDC were slightly more musically accomplished, but no less rebellious – witness their early hit 'Highway to Hell'. But the first record I ever bought was 'Our House' by Madness. I guess I loved the way they took something very ordinary and familiar – a terraced house and its occupants – and turned it into something totally zany. I still love it to this day.

As I got into my teens, I guess things were in the balance. I was failing at school – no ifs, no buts – and the family career path that led down the pit was off the menu. The mid-teens are a dangerous period, a time when young lads can lose the plot a bit, blown away by the new freedoms of being on the cusp of manhood.

For me the saving grace was the local youth club. It didn't look much from the outside, but once inside, thirty-odd boys like me found entertainment, fun, focus, friendship and real encouragement to make something of our lives. Stan Norris was the main man, and I owe him plenty. He's gone now, sadly, but he was a true friend and mentor to me. He volunteered at the club for fifty years and deservedly was awarded an MBE for his services to our community. (And it makes me proud to be coaching boys there – including my own son – following in his footsteps.)

Unlike my teachers (except the PE staff), Stan saw something in me. Of course, the obvious thing was my sporting ability. But however naturally gifted you are, you need character and persistence to succeed in sport. And Stan saw that I had it. He told me I could do anything and prophesied that I would represent my country and win a British title.

I did pretty well as a footballer, just missing out on a Welsh U-14s cap. But given the opportunities the club offered, I was soon into everything. Table tennis just came naturally, and being a non-physical sport, I could play against people much older than me – and beat them. Great. From being the youngest member of the club, I soon gained confidence simply through my sporting prowess. For once, grown-ups were praising me, supporting me and believing in me.

In addition to football and table tennis (at which I was runner-up in the Welsh championship), I also went quite far in judo and then, in my mid-teens, started to excel at pool. Stan's prophecy came true when my partner and I won the British pool title, travelling over to Leicester to take part in the finals. Coming back in triumph with the trophy was one of the proudest moments of my life – and, of course, a wonderful way of repaying Stan for his faith in me. The youth club – and Stan – really helped me on my way. I can't imagine what my life would have been like without that wonderful, warm, welcoming, supportive place that gave me so much pleasure, success and stability.

But for all that security and companionship and all the sporting trophies I won, I was still only a kid who left school at fifteen with no qualifications.

However, I didn't have any problem with work. I always wanted to earn my own money. I'd had a paper round, which is quite a challenge as you have to get up so early. And more recently I'd gone in with some older friends to start a little window-cleaning business. (At least I had a head for heights!)

What I really needed, though, was something that would produce a proper wage. Fortunately, I benefited from the local YTS schemes and trained as a bricklayer. Bricklaying pays well, but by definition involves working outdoors in pretty much all weathers. I decided it wasn't for me, and got a job on the production line at a local factory turning out television sets.

It wasn't the most stimulating work, but I enjoyed being part of a team and made lots of friends over the six years I was there. What I didn't like was the way the managers seemed to have a down on me. It was a bit like teachers at school. Perhaps I talked too much, or spoke out when told to do something that was obviously daft, challenging their authority. After I'd been there for a few years I started noticing that people who had come in after me were being promoted above me. I didn't like that. It wasn't fair. So I gave in my notice and left.

The great thing about regular work with steady wages was the freedom it gave. You could do what you liked; and as I went through my teens, I started to spread my wings. In the late eighties and early nineties, music and the way people enjoyed it changed. The rave scene was massive, and I loved going to raves or clubbing with my mates: whole nights blown away on a tide of elation, all cares forgotten, your whole being focused on the beat as you ran through your moves or just bobbed up and down with a bottle waving above your head. Unfortunately, but unsurprisingly, given the prevailing culture, that elation was increasingly fuelled by alcohol and drugs. Not something I'm proud of, but facts are facts.

With the money I was earning, I could go clubbing every weekend. With a bit of saving, I even got out to Ibiza which was just building its reputation as the party capital of Europe. I was a member of a vast community of like-minded people, who lived for their nights out, and who spent all their money on clothes, music and entrance fees.

Then, what you might call proper pop made a welcome return with bands like Oasis and Pulp, and I found new heroes to worship. I loved Stone Roses. With bands coming back into fashion after the domination of the DJs, we were soon heading for huge arenas to listen to our favourite groups. I think I must have been to more than seventy concerts over the years.

I was living the life. But it was taking its toll. I got drunk every weekend. Devoting my time to playing football was a thing of the past. But my lifestyle was now impacting my work. In 1997 I was arrested three times for being drunk and disorderly, and causing affray – though I was only trying to break up a domestic altercation that was getting nasty. The trouble is, it's difficult persuading a policeman that your intentions were good when you're obviously under the influence. Predictably, I ended up in a cell trying to get to sleep on a very hard bench. And shortly after that, I found myself in court, facing fines and the threat of prison.

I was physically a shadow of my former self. I no longer made any attempt at keeping fit; my weight had fallen to nine and a half stone and I looked terrible. My excesses had made me ill. With the experience I have had working in mental health over the last few years, I can easily diagnose my condition. I suffered from anxiety, and like so many people, I turned to alcohol to numb my fears. The trouble was, drinking heavily at weekends and then turning to the bottle when I got stressed in the week, was only going to make matters worse. Of course, I recognised that, but then the next wave of anxiety would sweep over me and I'd be reaching for the bottle again and the downward spiral continued unchecked.

What saved me was meeting Michelle that same year, 1997. It wasn't love at first sight, but I developed a growing appreciation of her as we went to the cinema or had meals out. You're not going to get very far with a woman if you're drinking too much, so I cut back drastically, and thankfully I began to clear some headspace so I could start taking back control of my life.

I decided I needed a bit of time on my own, so left the factory and got a European railcard so I could travel round Europe for a while seeing a bigger world than I'd been used to. And it was during that sightseeing tour that I realised I would be enjoying things a great deal more if I had Michelle by my side to share the experience.

I returned home to a woman I knew I loved and who, happily, loved me. I looked around for a new kind of work and got a job in sales, earning more money and working fewer hours than in the TV factory. I turned out to be good at the job and soon had a company car. Michelle and I celebrated our new life together by going on a more ambitious tour, backpacking around Australia together and taking in beautiful places like Bali and Thailand on the way back.

After living with my parents at the beginning of our relationship, we obviously felt the need to take the next step: buying our own home. And this led to the next step after that. We got married and chose to tie the knot in another exotic location: Cyprus.

It wasn't hard to anticipate the next step after that. I had done so much in my life and weathered a really bad patch which I assumed was completely behind me, that I felt ready to become a dad. But like so many fathers with a past history of anxiety, depression and traumas, I would find I had far greater battles to fight in the future.

***

Michelle agreed about starting a family, and in due course she became pregnant. We were both excited, if a little apprehensive. The pregnancy was fine, and all the tests and check-ups were good, so we were really looking forward to becoming parents. When the time to go into hospital came, we were ready – bag packed, baby clothes neatly folded. We drove over in good spirits, feeling well prepared, our heads filled with what we could remember from the antenatal sessions we'd attended, both of us hoping for an easy delivery, but full of confidence that the medical staff would see us – and the baby – through any difficulties or setbacks.

It turned out to be a nightmare. Michelle was in labour for twenty-two hours, with the midwives and doctors getting increasingly concerned. I was sitting by her side throughout but felt helpless. I don't know how many cups of tea the midwives must have brought me. They were only trying to help, but the truth was I was becoming overwhelmed with anxiety – fear that I would lose both my lovely wife and our baby. Eventually three doctors came and told us that Michelle needed an emergency C-section. Michelle sighed in resignation; but if that was the only way, then that was what would have to happen. She was almost too tired to care.

I, on the other hand, was wired. I'd had no sleep except for the odd snatched snooze in an uncomfortable hospital chair, and now I went straight into what I later realised was a panic attack. I was full of gloom; our baby wasn't going to make it into life. Maybe Michelle herself wasn't going to make it through. The thought of leaving the hospital doubly bereft made me collapse – not physically – I could stumble after Michelle as she was wheeled away to theatre – but mentally. I had lost control; I had no input to make. I just had to witness what happened and somehow cope with it.

I don't know how long we were in theatre. I didn't know why I was there – except that Michelle wanted me by her side. There was certainly nothing I could do. Her life and that of the baby was in the hands of the surgeons. It was without question the worst experience of my life and I'll never be able to unsee the things I saw while the team of surgeons worked so hard to deliver our wonderful son.

Which, thankfully, they did. Both mother and child were rescued from a perilous situation. Michelle wanted – and needed – to sleep for as long as possible, and I was handed our newborn son and told to take him down the corridor to get him weighed.

It was fantastic to hold him in my arms, but I was in such a state that I really thought I might drop him. I was hugely relieved to hand him over to the nurse to put on the scales: 8 lb 9 oz.

Job done! Thanks to the incredible skills and focus of the doctors, midwives and nurses, we'd made it through our ordeal. Obviously, Michelle would need time to get over the physical trauma, but then we could sail off into the glowing future we'd been looking forward to over the previous months.

What no one knew at the time was how much of a hard slog awaited us up the road ahead.

***

Michelle had survived her ordeal physically, but not, as it soon became apparent, mentally. The trauma had been too much for her and she was not the person she had been going into hospital excited at the prospect of becoming a mum. She was lethargic, tearful, seemingly indifferent to everything around her, including me and our boy. It was obvious she wasn't right, and it wasn't long before she was diagnosed with severe postnatal depression. So started the worst – and yet, in many ways, the best – twelve months I have ever lived through.

One thing I learned was that you can never take anything for granted. The plan was: have the baby, enjoy a fortnight at home getting acclimatised to this wonderful new addition to our lives, and then I'd go back to work while Michelle would stay at home showing the baby off to all her friends, and we'd be the perfect example of the perfect couple.

But it wasn't like that at all.

Depression's a monster. To those who have never experienced it, it may seem a question of people simply not having the moral strength to pull themselves together and get on with it. But it's not the case that you can beat depression by willpower. It's a disease, like a giant tapeworm, sucking everything out of you from within, leaving you a hollow ghost of your real self. Postnatal depression is one of the worst forms of the illness because the most amazing and beautiful thing has just happened: you have brought a new life into the world, the focal point of all your emotions, the bond between you and your partner. And you can't respond. The best you can do is listlessly go through the motions.

Michelle was so bad there was no way I could leave her to go back to work. I had to stay at home for six months caring for both of them. But while I did this to the best of my ability, I myself was shattered. I was taken completely unawares. I was adrift. I couldn't cope. And I couldn't feel the love, the tsunami of warming, all-enveloping love, that I had been expecting. My wife was the ghost of her former self, and our son – well, put it this way, babies demand a lot, and if they don't get what they want when they want it, they let you know in no uncertain terms. I found myself under huge pressure, and my own previous difficulties started to creep back, sapping my energy, my will, my general ability to cope with the challenges I was facing.

Although I was physically very fit, due to my latest sport, kick-boxing, at which I won a national competition and was on the way to winning my black belt, sadly my personality began to change. I started feeling angry, but obviously I couldn't be angry with a seriously depressed woman and a newly born baby. The only way I could keep the onslaught at bay was to resort to my old standby, alcohol. Of course, I was suffering from depression, and as previously, relying on alcohol was the worst option. But that didn't stop me. It became the crutch I relied on every day. There was no one I could talk to about my predicament. I was the carer, the loving father. I had to be strong. I wasn't allowed to be weak, to be ill. So I pretended. Every day, I lied, if not in word, then in deed, smiling, putting the brave face on, never even thinking of asking for help.

The person I was closest to was Michelle, the love of my life. But I wasn't communicating with her, thinking that she shouldn't be bothered with my problems. She had enough to do trying to combat her own. I was alone and isolating myself from my family and friends. I could always force a smile, wave away enquiries as to how I was from those I loved the most. I put myself beyond help and turned in on myself. The self I now loathed and despised.

There was a night when I was so torn apart, so fuelled by self-hatred that I smashed my fist against the sofa and broke my hand. It hurt, but I needed to inflict pain on myself. I came up with some sort of half-convincing lie to explain the damage away. I would rather suffer in silence than put myself at someone else's mercy by opening up to them.

Dinosaur thinking, as we now know all too well, but very much typical of the time. And it was certainly the case that the world in which I was brought up did not encourage sharing feelings. Life was as it was; stuff happened; if you got knocked down, you got yourself up again and carried on – like a man. End of.

And ending it all did come into my mind as a solution. I wouldn't even have to make it look like suicide. I knew the local roads well enough to choose a suitable bend. What a tragedy; poor man, worn out looking after his wife like that. He must have been tired. The script would write itself. As it does in so many cases. The statistics show that the biggest killer for men under fifty in the UK is suicide. The World Health Organisation reports that there are over half a million male suicides a year around the world. Now that is tragic, and we must do everything we can to stop it.

What held me back? My son. I had to be there for him. I couldn't bear the thought of Michelle finding someone else to take my place and for him to be my replacement as a dad as well as a husband. And as Michelle slowly and painfully recovered from her postnatal depression, so I stepped back from the abyss that I had almost chosen as the easy get-out through the most difficult times.

We got through and found ourselves and each other once more. But after the lengthy struggle to survive I was no longer the man I had been. I realised that I wouldn't be capable of dealing with the stress of selling, even assuming I could muster the confidence to push on to clinch the deal. I needed a completely different way of living, with different goals. I wanted to help people, to use my experiences of the depths to help others out of the situations I had been in.

So in 2006 I moved into the voluntary sector as a youth worker, like my old friend and mentor, Stan. I started in the local town where we lived, but then moved back to my own home village where it all began for me as a child.

***

To describe the intervening years as a roller-coaster ride would be an understatement. If they prove anything, it is that you can never be complacent about your mental health. You may think you have seen off depression or any other harmful conditions, but they have roots in your past and always have the potential to return. I have spent the last fifteen years living with mental health issues, studying them and applying the knowledge I have acquired to the service of others. I know what I'm talking about.

So strap yourselves in and off we go once again.

Being back in my own local youth club was great. I enjoyed coaching the boys and even better, talking to them about their lives and their futures. I had a fair amount of experience to draw on and I also got a fair bit of respect because of the trophies with my name on that they could see in the cabinets on the walls.

But although I was happy working with local kids, I was aware of a dark cloud covering the wider locality. There was a spate of suicides among teens and young men and women in the Bridgend area. They were just finding the stresses of life too hard to bear. Beneath the bravado of going out on the town with mates, making a bit of noise at a football game, going clubbing, there was a seeping despair, an undermining of confidence, and emptiness and loneliness that they couldn't live with. There was a real lack of non-judgemental support available to them in the area.

It didn't help that the world was in the process of committing financial suicide and the follies of greedy bankers were throwing the world into the worst recession since the Great Depression, which meant that those at the bottom of the heap had the prospect of long-term unemployment stirred into the mix as well.

There was nothing we in the Welsh valleys could do about that. But that didn't mean we shouldn't try to address the local suicide spike which was way above the national average. With my own suicidal urges not far behind me and my own mental state hardly stable, I started to study the problem and took courses on mental health and especially suicide.

This is not the place to go into details of how people can be rescued from the tailspin of suicide. But the one guiding principle is that we need early intervention to give those at risk of taking their own lives the help they so desperately need. There is help out there, from many organisations and individuals – but you have to open yourself to it; you have to ask for it. And the sooner you do that, the sooner you can get the help that will pull you out of the hole you're in.

As part of my quest to understand mental health issues better, I worked for a while in a psychiatric ward where I witnessed so much human misery, but also so much professional kindness and support. It was an eye – and mind – opening experience and made me very humble about my own condition and needs.

Then ten years ago, in a six-month period over the winter of 2009/10, I suffered two hammer blows which sent me reeling back into the deepest depression. First my grandfather died of dementia. He was a special figure in my life, always supportive, always there for me when perhaps my dad was too busy working and living his life. I would have seen him pretty much every day through my childhood and never missed a chance to go round to his in later years – cup of tea, catch-up on what I was doing, congratulations on the latest sporting achievement. And even when the fresh-faced teenager gave way to the ridiculously dressed, arrogant party-going raver, he still saw the real me in there somewhere. He was a pillar for me and seeing him dwindle into a shadow of himself as the disease invaded his brain, brutally pulling the plugs out of their sockets, trashing his memory, ripping away his words and compromising his sanity was an agony for me.

You can say death comes as a relief when a loved one is suffering like that; but death still leaves a gaping shell-hole when it finally strikes. And then, a few weeks later, in the new year, my mum phoned me one day and calmly told me she had cancer. I didn't believe it at first. I didn't want to believe it. But when I took her into hospital it all hit home. I thought it would prove terminal, and I was terrified about having to face another death. (As it turned out, the cancer wasn't terminal and she is alive and well today – but I didn't know that she would survive at the time, and the dread of her dying was a pile-driver blow to me.)

I was coming apart at the seams once more. Work was becoming difficult – and so was stopping drifting back into dependence on alcohol. To be honest, I didn't fight that terribly hard. Booze threw his old bruiser's arm around my shoulder, and I was too weak to shrug it off. My personality was slipping back to where it was during Michelle's postnatal depression.

She was over that now and proved the rock on which I could rely; but I still couldn't front up and tell her what was really going on inside me. She saw me focused on our son, playing with him, teaching him new skills. If I looked out of it at times, then, she must have reasoned, I had a lot on my plate.

I was in a seriously bad place, driving off in the morning 'to work' and then not being able to face it, and instead parking up and sleeping all day in a lay-by till it was time to go home. Living a lie makes you antisocial: the fewer people you mix with, the fewer lies you have to tell. I guess those close to me just assumed I needed my privacy to cope with my losses. But the reality was I desperately needed help.

And I found it. By chance I got chatting to another dad in the gym I went to. One thing led to another and suddenly we were talking about real issues and how someone in my situation could get themselves out of it. He'd been in the same position, having to cope with a wife suffering from postnatal depression, and as we talked on, it struck home that there must be a great many fellow dads in the same boat.

It was a lightbulb moment. I could not only help myself, but I could help other people going through the same problems. I went on to set up a support group for dads with postnatal depressive partners, and once we started meeting up, we realised none of us had to carry on suffering in silence. The relief of it was a huge boost to morale in itself, but of course we were soon reading up on the literature of postnatal depression – and much wider in my case.

Once I get onto something, I stick to it like a dog digging up an old bone. I wanted to find out more about my own mental state and started seeing specialists who could help me make sense of my chequered past. One of them even led to me getting an official diagnosis of ADHD – at forty! No wonder my school days had been so barren.

ADHD is under diagnosed in people of my generation, and it didn't help having the diagnosis so late in my life. But I now know what to look out for: stress, restlessness, edginess. I have a quick temper, can be irritable and suffer from extreme impatience. I over-talk things, fidget and mislay stuff, just as I did at school. But at least I understand the reasons for this and so don't beat myself up about it.

On I went, finding out more and more – and then developing ways of sharing what I had learned and helping people to deal with their problems. On postnatal depression the facts are clear: it's a huge issue, which has been kept under wraps for far too long. Take a look at this:

- Dads can suffer anxiety and depression in the perinatal period
- PTSD is an anxiety disorder which can affect dads who witness a traumatic birth
- Reports suggest up to 39% of new dads are concerned about their mental health
- Paternal OCD is rarely talked about among health professionals
- Up to 50% of dads will become depressed themselves while looking after a partner with postnatal depression
- Behaviour changes in the perinatal period to look out for include avoiding social situations, substance abuse and feelings of anger
- Dads struggle to bond with their babies and feel they're not good enough to.

It took a long while and a lot of work, but, with the enormous help of my mentor, Dr Jane Hanley, I fulfilled my ambition to become an expert on and spokesman for dads' mental health issues. I founded International Fathers' Mental Health Day and have taken my campaign for awareness and support around the world, talking to audiences in universities, on radio and television; and I have been the key speaker at 200 conferences.

I have also written many articles on aspects of the subjects and collaborated with doctors and academics, like Jane Hanley, on a range of projects, culminating in my first book, *Daddy Blues*, which was published in 2018. This has been made into a film of the same name, released in March 2021.

On top of the book, I have produced the Fathers Reaching Out Report, based on research and interviews I conducted with hundreds of parents. On the evidence of these interviews, it recommends screening for dads going into fatherhood and mental health support for the whole family where necessary. Individuals suffering in silence causes lasting damage and simply isn't necessary.

I became a pioneer in this sadly neglected field through my own experiences, and now take huge satisfaction from being able to help fellow sufferers around the world. There's still more to find out, and much, much more to do. But it is the most worthwhile thing I could be doing with my life.

Of course, I wouldn't have got through to this stage without the help and support of many people, chief among them being my wonderful wife, Michelle. And then there's our son, Ethan. I won't embarrass him by saying how much I love him in public (oops, I just have!), but he has been a constant focus for all that's best in me since the day I first held him in my arms. I'm proud to be his football coach these days; but in years to come as he grows into manhood and maybe takes the huge step into fatherhood, I'll hopefully be there to help him if he needs me. I know if he does, he won't shy away from the conversation about his own mental health.

Hopefully, the days of suffering on our own are over, and I welcome and applaud the wider interest in mental health issues encouraged by the younger members of the Royal Family. We must and we will do better. And that, I hope, will be my legacy. I have seen a lot of misery when working in the secure unit, but the most terrifying thing I have experienced is fearing that my loved ones were going to die.

Life is the great gift and depression will always be a threat to it. But however bad it gets, there is help, there is support, there is knowledge. If I have helped make the light at the end of the tunnel that bit brighter, I am satisfied.

And for anyone reading this who is currently suffering from anything I have touched on, my advice is absolutely clear: Please talk to someone today.

Chapter 15:

From Cultural Collision to
Celebrated Identity:
Parenting in an interracial relationship

Arion Lawrence

As children, we often imagine what our futures will look like. We often think our lives might look like those of adults around us, we see a story that we are part of and another that we will go on to create. We presume we will live in houses like the one we were raised in and that we might, if our parents are married, marry people that look like our parents. Through our limited perspective we imagine this is the way of things. But as we get older our parents become people. People with likes and dislikes, who make mistakes and have flaws and whose lives are formed through a series of decisions in context.

As a child, I was an overthinker, but even so I did not spend much time thinking about who I would marry. Although, had I been asked what the race of my wife might be when I was older, I imagine I would have said she'd be black. Specifically, black British and of West Indian descent, just like me. Just like my mum and my dad.

From Windrush to Queen's Park

My mother was born in Barbados and my father in Jamaica. Both emigrated to the UK, where they met, in their teens. They joined their respective parents, who years before them had travelled across the Atlantic Ocean to what they saw as the mother country.

Like most West Indian immigrants at the time, my grandparents came to the UK as British subjects in response to a post-war labour shortage and rebuilding effort in the UK and a lack of employment in their home countries. It was a similar story throughout the former British colonies in the region and beyond as an unravelling British Empire became a financial responsibility that post-war Britain was unable to sustain. Attracting labour from the British West Indies was deemed mutually beneficial to the labour challenges both Britain and her colonies were facing.

Both my parents came to the UK at a time in their lives that meant their formative years would have been spread across life here and in the land of their birth. This made for a British West Indian experience that for them was nevertheless weighted in favour of the latter and that experience influenced how they chose to raise me, their British-born first child.

Growing up, my world was black. I've always had mixed-race cousins, and therefore non-black uncles and aunts. Generally, anyone else around me was black. Interracial relationships weren't as visible as they are today and they typically comprised of a black and white partner. Other combinations of ethnicities weren't unheard of but they were arguably rarer than they are now. At the time, the demographic of the area of London I grew up in was predominately black and Irish with a few other ethnic minority groups.

I grew up in Queen's Park, an area that straddles both west and north-west London, a few streets away from the Mozart Estate where my mother's family lived shortly after arriving in the UK. Now featuring an increasing number of pockets of gentrification, back then it was a solidly working-class community where the vibrant cultures of its residents were highly visible. It was populated with Irish pubs alongside black barbershops and hairdressers, where lively debates voiced in heavy patois could be heard over the din of bashment and reggae blaring through shopfronts. Patties could be bought from takeaways that were only a stone's throw from local fish and chip shops, providing a juxtaposition of traditional British food and the cuisine of new arrivals.

Walking home from Church on a Sunday afternoon with my family, the unmistakable aroma of rice and peas and chicken wafted from homes as radio stations like Unique FM and Choice FM would provide a soundtrack to dinner being prepared. There was always a sense that others in the area lived a similar life to me, and that we shared a black British experience that was essentially all I knew. In my class at primary school, I could count on one hand the number of non-black students.

I assumed any children I might have would share the experience I had growing up. They too would be black and their upbringing would be like mine. That meant rice and peas on a Sunday, with leftovers on a Monday. It meant being raised on a diet of soca, bashment and reggae and being familiar with the dialect of my parents. It meant christening and confirmation parties that, despite the non-secular reason for the celebration, were more like raves with my parents, uncles, aunts and extended family skanking until the wee hours of the morning.

It turns out I was wrong.

I'm now married, to my British-born, Kenyan Gujarati wife. And we have a mixed-race son with a background that spans four continents. He's a Nigel Farage, Jean-Marie Le Pen and Donald Trump nightmare, which makes him even more impressive in my eyes.

Where I once thought I would be a black dad to black children, I'm instead a black dad to my mixed-race son. That makes no difference to how much I love him. Yet in acknowledging he's mixed race, it's important to me and my wife that we mirror that in his upbringing. As a black dad, at times that comes with a parenting experience that I didn't anticipate, and one that has admittedly come with its own challenges on account of my early experiences of being in an interracial relationship. Nevertheless, my son is the best thing that has ever happened to me and sharing in his identity has made my parenting experience so much richer.

Kenyan Gujarati History and Cultural Taboos

I attended Queen Mary University of London, where I studied History and Politics. There was a significant South Asian student community at my university and that broadened my awareness of a culture of which I was broadly ignorant. One of these students, a newly gained friend at the time, is now my wife.

I learned much about Asian culture from my peers during this time. When it came to relationships, it was clear that marriage was a pretty big deal in their community. They all anticipated weddings on a grand scale by Western standards, with children to follow within a couple of years of their nuptials.

After graduation, their lives would eventually resemble those of their parents. That also meant marrying someone from their community. Indeed, as I came to learn, interracial and interreligious relationships were, and for many still are, considered taboo and a big no-no amongst the parents' generation of my Asian peers. Some of my own generation still share those views too.

For my wife, this was an irrelevant detail. We were platonic friends during university and it was a predicament she imagined would never concern her. She too believed she'd marry a fellow Indian, probably Gujarati, and someone who her parents strongly approved of. Had someone told her back then that she would marry a black West Indian man, she probably would have laughed them out of the room.

Within her own family, she had seen how a relationship with a non-Gujarati, let alone a black person, was received. Her uncle had married an Indian from Guyana, rather than a Gujarati. That was enough for her grandparents' disapproval. For years, his siblings had to visit him and his new wife in secret so as not to provoke the ire of their parents who had prohibited any contact with them.

My wife's parents' response to relationships with partners outside of the community had softened from that of her grandparents'. As long as her partner was Indian, it was fine. But a black man would cross a line that was not to be crossed.

This probably seems highly prejudiced and, if we're calling a spade a spade, it is. Although to understand this perspective, specifically for Asians from East Africa, a brief history lesson is required.

The history of East African Asians is one that has included a frosty relationship with the black diaspora. Albeit not as pronounced as in Uganda, where black President Idi Amin expelled the Asians, in Kenya, many Kenyan Asians felt compelled to leave as a result of President Jomo Kenyatta's policies of Africanisation. These policies exacerbated existing ethnic tensions between the Asians and black Africans that British colonialism had facilitated and embedded throughout the Empire. Many Asians had come to experience financial success which wasn't an experience shared by many black Africans. As a result, this merely highlighted the lack of egalitarianism in Kenyan society.

When Kenya achieved independence in 1963, Asians, who had previously held British passports as citizens of the British Empire, were given two years to take up Kenyan citizenship in the newly independent state. However, this was barely taken up which led to the Kenyan government, and many black Kenyans, perceiving this as Asians not viewing themselves as part of Kenyan society. This led to hostility from the black Kenyan government who were content to push the narrative of a successful Asian community that were only out for themselves, rather than the nation.

For my in-laws' generation, a black man wasn't just someone different. It was someone in the image of those who they felt had effected their departure from their birthplace. Understandably, that shaped the stance of a community and a generation.

A Coming Together of Cultures

Prior to and in the early stages of our relationship, I hadn't really considered any concerns about my wife and I having a mixed-race child. I didn't, and still don't, see it as taboo. In fact, it was something that I saw as increasingly commonplace in British society. Having a mixed-race child within an inter-racial relationship, where cultural principles might be at odds, can however make that more problematic. Thankfully, by the time my wife became pregnant, her family and I had moved past the stage where that could have been an issue several years beforehand.

Before my wife became pregnant, I did consider how my in-laws would play their role as grandparents. I knew they would love our son unconditionally but would they assume that he'd be raised as they had raised their children in a quintessentially Gujarati way? Would they recognise that he wasn't just Indian but was also black? Would my wife have cultural expectations that I didn't know about but might be opposed to? And how would my son be perceived in my wife's community, a community that would be his too once he was born?

Despite my concerns, I didn't feel unprepared to raise my son, at least not on account of him being mixed race (as far as the trepidation in being good enough as a father, a feeling that many new dads experience, that was still very much there). The challenges he might face as he was older, were no different to what I experience as a black man. In that regard, I knew I could parent him from a position of shared experience for much of what I would need to prepare him for in adulthood.

As far as growing up, there was somewhat of a question mark over that. I couldn't anticipate what challenges he might face being mixed race. Instead, I hoped his diverse heritage would be something he and others celebrated and that he would proudly champion.

After losing contact with each other after graduation, my wife and I had a chance encounter. And fast forward years later, we were married. When she eventually told her parents she was seeing a black man, they took the news as best as could be expected. Despite their disappointment and anxiety over her revelation, there wasn't any anger or animosity towards her or her choice of partner. Instead, in their eyes, she was making a mistake and embracing a cultural taboo. It was also a decision that they were not willing to proactively co-sign, even if they reluctantly accepted it was happening.

Given the perspective of many within their generation, they took it much better than my wife anticipated. Their reaction was still lukewarm, to say the least. For a while, before I met them, our relationship was somewhat the elephant in the room. It wasn't a secret but they would rarely initiate a conversation where I was the subject. My father-in-law, a very phlegmatic character, almost remained in denial. The vision of proudly seeing his daughter marry a fellow Gujarati in an Indian wedding, that he would no doubt have long envisaged since she was a child, was now in tatters. That wasn't about me. It was about the experience and the accompanying joy not being realised in the manner he had long assumed it would be.

Eventually that changed. With time, and with the encouragement of extended family, my wife's parents asked to meet me. That was a huge step on their part as they were now facing a reality they had never thought would be theirs. When I met them, they were warm and welcoming. I think the time that had passed since my wife told them she was in an interracial relationship perhaps also lessened the taboo for them.

As they got to know me, the reservations they had about my being of a different race and culture gradually melted away. And the concerns they had about characteristics they sought in their daughter's partner not being present in a non-Gujarati, proved to be unfounded. With their strong Stakhanovite work ethic, my own work ethic found much favour with them. As did my prudence, my view of the importance of family and above all how apparent it was that I cared for their daughter. I think there was still an unspoken disappointment that I wasn't Gujarati, or at least Indian. But otherwise, they were able to shed many qualms they once had. I also took a genuine interest in their culture. That was something they appreciated and it mitigated the concerns they had regarding my having a lack of appreciation or awareness of their community.

Thankfully, and with time to adjust, I now have a great relationship with my in-laws and my wife's family. They've accepted me on a par with their own children and they're the most supportive, involved and incredible grand-parents to my son.

While they aren't exactly asking if they can attend bashment raves with me or requesting I make them rice and peas, my in-laws do make an effort to be aware of my culture; more so now that they have a mixed-race grandson. We've also found much common ground in the British colonial and immigrant experience within our respective communities.

When we discuss institutionalised racism as a hangover from the British Empire, they get it. More so than me, they've lived it. There are also similarities in how my wife and I were raised with regard to discipline, high expectations and traditions that are consistent between ethnic minority communities. Some of those, such as smacking being a prevalent form of discipline and behaviour management, we haven't carried forward. But others, such as respect for elders and our expectations for manners, ethics and education, we wholeheartedly embrace. Where my wife's family once thought our cultures were a million miles apart, they're not actually that distant.

We'll introduce each other to fruits from our respective countries and every summer, my father-in-law and I will pit West Indian and Indian mangoes against each other once they're in season. Not to mention there's always banter over the cricket when India and the West Indies are playing.

Their generation will always be culturally insular and my wife will often give them a nudge to take more of an interest. Although given that context, they really do make an effort that I cannot bemoan. I still feel they subconsciously lament the opportunity of having a Gujarati son-in-law, and the Indian in-law experience that comes with it, but that doesn't affect our relationship and it's very much superseded by the experience of being grandparents. With time, that's meant the frustration and indignation I once held towards my wife's family and community for how they perceived me as a black man, has now also dissipated.

My parents don't live locally and therefore don't see our son as often as my in-laws do. As a result, they aren't as present in their roles as grandparents or in-laws. That means my son's and my wife's cultural education from my heritage largely comes from me. I don't give it much thought but it does mean I can't be complacent or rely upon others to balance the education being brought from my wife's side.

When we got married, our wedding brought our cultures together once again. With a bespoke menu of Kenyan-Gujarati and West Indian food, and a playlist of soca and bashment alongside Bollywood classics, it was a glorious mixing pot of our two ethnicities. Everything was planned to show who we are as a couple and more importantly what we value from our own and each other's cultures.

Curry goat and fish cakes alongside paneer and rotli and shak on the same menu might seem unthinkable but it worked. There wasn't anything forced about it, just as there isn't anything contrived about my son's identity. That's something we want him to realise as he's growing up in a way that many British-born, ethnic minorities of my age weren't able to achieve as children.

I'm British, but…

When I was younger, my response to anyone asking where I was from was a caveated reply of 'I was born here' or 'I'm British', followed by 'but my parents are from…'. It might seem a cack-handed phrase to anyone not used to it. But from a young age, I always felt the culture of my parents was such a significant feature of my identity that I absorbed it alongside that of the land of my birth.

For anyone mixed race, that response will also be familiar as a similar attempt to balance diverse cultures within their identity. For my son, those cultures can be traced back to India, East Africa, the West Indies and the UK. As he grows, I'm aware that he will have to navigate these respective cultures, that they will not always agree and that they will not always accept him, even though they should.

I'm not certain which parts of each culture will endure with my son, but I know that my son shouldn't need to hedge, explain or justify his own Britishness as I once did as a child. The experience of many first generation British-born children of immigrants is that our Britishness has been sidelined on account of our identity also comprising the country of our parents' birth. Conversely, a somewhat nomadic identity has been the result of the split between where our parents are from and the Britishness that we grew up with. In Jamaica and Barbados, despite the direct link via my parents, I'd be considered West Indian but also an 'English bwai'. To some in the UK, being black also still means I fall short of being able to claim complete Britishness.

I want my son to be part of a world where his ethnicity doesn't have to be justified. I want him to comfortably embrace what is a diverse, yet rich, heritage that reflects both sides of his family and the country of his, and his parents' birth.

But I know that by accident of his birth he will face challenges both within and outside the worlds he has come from. Being mixed race still isn't welcomed in some sections of society. For the black community, interracial relationships aren't an anomaly but there still exists some ignorance around the subject. There are also some who oppose interracial relationships. Their stance is on the basis that they reduce the odds of producing a 'strong black couple' that can showcase 'black excellence' in a world where positive black images of relationships are often downgraded or distorted by society. Those with that line of thinking can be similarly opposed to anyone mixed race claiming any blackness in their identity. It's as if they're deemed less entitled to 'blackness' on account of being only part black.

I also worry about how much the cultural nuances of my son's background will be understood by those on his black side. If they aren't familiar with the culture of his Gujarati side, how much will they embrace it and respect that he seeks it as part of who he is? If they aren't receptive to it, will that make him feel less comfortable with the part of his identity from his mum's side? And will my son encounter prejudice from his Indian side where interracial relationships, and mixed-race children, can still be seen as an aberration?

We will of course ensure that he knows and embraces his Gujarati side, but what if he's ignorantly told by someone within the community that he isn't *really* Gujarati because his dad is black? If anyone was audacious enough to utter such prejudice in front of my father-in-law especially, it would probably be followed by them swiftly finding themselves on their backside. I am acutely aware that my son is part Gujarati and am adamant that no one can take that away from him. With that mindset, I'm now ironically a bigger champion of his Gujarati side than my wife is. Still, I can't help but wonder how on earth my child will be able to juggle these cultures, and whether the various people in his life from these communities might try and push him towards 'this' or 'that'. As parents we discussed all this before our son was born, trying to work out ways that between us we could foster a strong sense of his identity in him as he grew up.

Culture and Compromise

Any relationship requires compromise as no two people will have identical experiences and expectations from a relationship. That can often be compounded within interracial relationships given the cultural differences each partner may bring. Before our son was born, it was also necessary for my wife and me to negotiate some of the cultural traditions that his dual heritage offered.

Some of the principles we set out in achieving this were:

• Actively wanting our son to speak, and be exposed to, Gujarati;
• Respecting that both cultures had equal weighting and therefore needed to be reflected equally;

- Acknowledging that some traditions wouldn't be compatible with others and would therefore need to be compromised over;
- Taking opportunities to attend events such as Panorama (the steel-band competition the night before Carnival) and Navaratri (a Hindu festival that includes traditional garba dancing that Gujaratis take part in) that would expose our son to both sides of his culture;
- Taking a united front if needing to reject cultural influences or expectations from either set of grandparents;
- Not attempting to replicate every aspect of our own upbringings in how we raise our son;
- Recognising that like us, our son is british-born and that too would comprise part of his cultural identity.

Language provides a strong connection to one's culture and I knew that was a link I wanted to foster, so before my son was born, we asked my in-laws to speak to him exclusively in Gujarati. While it wasn't something we discussed, I could see they were wary about speaking to him in their mother tongue (as they would do automatically if their daughter had married a fellow Gujarati) and it being an instance where their experience of being 'Indian' grandparents was being eroded. Being East African, their Gujarati dialect also includes a smattering of Swahili, again connecting back to their Kenyan beginnings. Despite my limited vocabulary and anglicised pronunciation, I too speak to him in Gujarati alongside English to ensure he recognises this as part of his identity.

On the sixth day after a baby has been born, Gujaratis have a 'chati', a traditional naming ceremony for the baby. We didn't actually give him a name him that day as we'd not yet decided on one. However, having the ceremony meant a lot to my in-laws and as something experienced by most Gujarati newborn babies, it was something we wanted to do as an early acknowledgement to the culture.

Whenever he's at Nana and Nani's (his maternal grandparents) house, he'll often have Gujarati food. If the television's on in the background, at some point during the day it's probably on an Indian channel. He calls his uncles and aunts on my wife's side by the correct Gujarati title and we've had to tell his nursery some Gujarati words because that's how he'll refer to things when asking for them. It's something my wife and I value but also a feature of our parenting that I know my in-laws greatly appreciate as they see their culture being passed down to yet another generation.

The opportunities for a diverse identity and experience growing up as a mixed-race child are undoubtedly abundant. That said, they can sometimes present competing aims in striking the balance between our respective cultures. For West Indians, many boys won't have their first haircut until after their fifth birthday; something I experienced and had always intended on doing with my son. Conversely, for boys of Gujarati descent, their first haircut takes place much earlier at a Balmura. It's a ceremony to coincide with an auspicious occasion in the family, such as a wedding, where their hair is completely shaved off. Had I been Gujarati, the same would probably happen for my son yet we've decided not to have one.

Compromise has been key in achieving the balance we've sought in how we raise our son, especially when it comes to respecting traditions on both sides. Sometimes, we just have to say no to something that may be at odds with what we want as parents. Despite our respective cultural backgrounds, we are parents first and foremost.

In many ethnic minority communities, including my wife's, after birth, a mum and newborn baby will stay with the maternal grandparents. Gujaratis do this for forty days but in a more modern context, today the grandparents usually move in with their daughter-in-law and their new grandchild. It would undoubtedly have been helpful but we – perhaps foolishly – relinquished the opportunity for on-call, live-in help and decided it wasn't something we wanted as we established our own new family unit. Without moving in with us, my in-laws still came round for most of that period. Particularly after I went back to work after my meagre two weeks of paternity leave, it gave my wife company and practical support and allowed my in-laws to continue the age-old tradition of nurturing a new mother in ways that were meaningful to them.

The same goes for the dynamic with grandparents and the influence they wield over how their grandchildren are raised. My wife's 'Ba', her maternal grandmother, was the family matriarch who exercised total control over how her children raised her grandchildren. That provided a precedent for my in-laws in signalling how much influence they probably expected. While we'll respect and acknowledge the views of both our sets of parents, how our son is raised is a sphere of control that my wife and I will never relinquish. My in-laws accept that, but I can see it's something that traditionally just isn't intuitive to them. Consequently, it's an area where they've had to adjust. When they were new parents themselves they wouldn't have dared question or oppose anything Ba told them to do. Yet they acknowledge and respect that while we'll listen to their views, as parents we have the last say on how we raise our son.

It's the same for my parents who will often preface their advice with 'We know you're his parents but…' as an overt acknowledgement that they have less influence than my grandparents may have had over them. Before I was born, my paternal grandfather attempted to foist a name he'd chosen for me upon my parents, with the expectation that they would accept it. My dad stood his ground and said no, but it's indicative of the 'grandparental entitlement' many ethnic minorities of my parents' generation have as a throwback of their own experience. With my wife's culture presenting those sentiments even more strongly than my own, that's something my in-laws have had to grapple with. Being a dad to a mixed-race child isn't just about managing the challenges of the child. You're also managing the expectations of your in-laws who bring a perspective completely different from your own.

Having a mixed-race child can make you acutely aware of the importance of preserving your heritage in the experiences you present to your child growing up. It isn't necessarily about replicating your own childhood, but rather the aspects and memories that you want to share with your child.

West Indians make a Christmas cake we call 'black cake'. As a child, I remember seeing the fruit being soaked annually and the cake being prepared and baked in advance of Christmas Day. The aroma of spices would flood our home and I'd be allowed to have the remnants of the cake batter from the bowl. It's one of my favourite sensory memories as a child. When he was barely a month old, I took my son in the kitchen as I prepared my black cake because I wanted him to share that sensory experience. A year later as a toddler, I had him in the kitchen again, but this time 'helping' prepare the cake with his own apron just like Daddy. When it was Easter, I gave him bun and cheese, a traditional Jamaican snack that's always eaten at that time of year. It might seem insignificant, but it was important to me that he experienced this feature of my childhood as a feature of his own. As a place of cultural significance, I even make sure he's acquainted with everyone at my barbershop (although he won't be getting a haircut himself for a while).

Our meals are routinely a carousel of British, West Indian and Gujarati cuisine and he is learning to enjoy and distinguish between different flavours and cooking styles. We'll typically have rice and peas on a Sunday and he devours plantain. I gave him macaroni pie and ham for the first time last Christmas, again West Indian cultural staples for me, and he absolutely loved them. He's even allowed a teaspoon of pineapple punch (for anyone not familiar with it, it's non-alcoholic but very sweet) and it'll be the same for soursop punch once they're in season.

The eclectic soundtrack to our wedding isn't dissimilar to what can be heard in our home. Only now, it's punctuated by nursery rhymes. Just as there was lovers rock for my parents, as their soundtrack to being black and British at the time, clean versions of grime and rap, featuring artists like Wretch 32, can also be heard as today's soundtrack of inner-city Britain.

Balance is key

Despite being mixed race, I know for many my son will nonetheless be considered a black man in society. And being intimate with the connotations that brings, it's my duty as a black dad to make him aware of this without foisting that identity onto him at the expense of recognising his mixed identity.

It's my duty to let him know the narrative of being a black man: the history, the challenges and what there is to celebrate. As a black man, I'm acutely aware of some of the negative stereotypes black men are faced with and just as I seek to refute these, I need to ensure he does the same. He might be mixed race, but should he be judged or stereotyped negatively, it's likely that the focus will be on the fact that he is part black.

As a black man and a black dad, my identity plays a role in how I'm perceived and I am concerned at how this will manifest itself for my son. I want him to feel proud of his mixed-race identity. Although I know that his black side may be used to perceive him negatively, I don't want him to take that negativity that can sometimes be projected by society. That needs to be countered by me celebrating the richness of being a black man.

The ethnicity of my son is undoubtedly secondary to the fact that he's my son and the most important person in the world to me. That doesn't change the fact as an ethnic minority in the UK, my culture is important to me as a connection to my past and the history of my culture. I want to share that with my son while he receives a similar narrative from the culture of my wife.

Ultimately, I believe maintaining that balance is key and while I might be a black dad, it's a mixed-heritage experience and identity that I reflect and promote for my son. While I understand he might feel conflicted by his mosaic cultural heritage, I hope he will also be proud to be a part of the traditions and teachings of all the cultures that inform his identity. Whoever he chooses to be, I hope he feels he has a choice.

Chapter 16:

Music.Football.Fatherhood: Music Artist Management Meets Grassroots Football Management. Me, My Daughter and the Fight For Equality

Billy Grant

If You Know Yer History

'He's so annoying.'

Bella was having another moment having to deal with 'the boys' as she would so often refer to them as with a frustrated tone. It was the eve of Brentford's historic League Cup Semi-Final with Tottenham. Historic in the fact that it was the furthest Brentford had got in any cup competition. Ever.

'Frankie said we're going to lose 5-3. He doesn't even know anything about football. He says he supports Manchester City. What type of "fan" supports Manchester City if he doesn't even come from Manchester?' She may support an unfashionable team, but she gets it. Zero glory hunting and zero giving

your backing to the team who just happened to have won the Premier League the previous season.

The Spurs match was twelve years on from when five-month-old Bella attended her very first football match, Bradford away. Three generations of Grants were at Bradford's Valley Parade to watch Andy Scott's Brentford team pick up one more point to see them edge a step closer to the Division Two title. The fact that Bella was born into Brentford's 'golden era' meant that she was not privy to the full complement of serial disappointment that many Brentford fans have had to endure from years and years of underachievement. But she knew about them.

From that promotion season on, Brentford have only looked forward. Plans were put in place that would see The Bees fighting for a spot in the Premier League. But ten play-offs played and ten play-offs lost and six Wembley or Cardiff finals played and six Wembley or Cardiff finals lost, they were still trying to get there. That is Brentford's legacy in a nutshell. Bella only experienced one of those losses which was the 'no fans' play-off final defeat against Fulham in Summer 2020. This wasn't the first time she had experienced real football heartbreak though; England's loss to Croatia in the Russia World Cup hurt but this defeat, to Brentford's biggest rivals, was much worse.

There is an old terrace chant that goes:

'Oh, it's a fine old team to play for.
And it's a fine old team to see.
And if …. you know …. yer history.
Well, it's enough to make your heart go woooooooh.'

Back to the Spurs match. Taking jibes was not new to her: she had to endure the wrath of constant jibing from 'boys' whose radar Brentford did not even feature on for years.

'Brent who?'
'Brentwood?'
'Bradford?
'Brentfoot?'

And now, because the team's stock has risen considerably, finally acknowledgement.

'Oh, Brentford.'

But delivered with a touch of disdain. She was used to it. As her dad, I had coached her on how to ride the insults and come out the other end better.

But as the Spurs game approached, for once, she was hoping there would be no need for her to reply and that the team would do the talking on the pitch. In the end, Brentford didn't disgrace themselves and despite going 1-0 down fairly early in the match, they gave Spurs a run for their money and were one VAR-spotted kneecap away from an equaliser. The final result was 2-0 and it wasn't to be.

Bella was hugely disappointed with the result and even more frustrated by my matter-of-fact attitude to yet another Brentford defeat.

'It's all right for you. You're used to it. You've seen them lose in ten play-offs.' And there you have it.

'You gotta know where you're coming from. To know where you are going to.' A phrase my mother used to say to me a lot when I was young. She said it so much, it was engrained into my brain and became part of my DNA.

In football terms *'And if … you know … your history.'*

Bella certainly knew her history. It doesn't make losing any easier but there's comfort in knowing that there are others who understand what you're going through.

Early Childhood

Bella is the youngest of my two kids. They have both had different experiences growing up but ultimately, the values I used in parenting them have been based on how my parents brought me up. I was raised in Isleworth, West London, in the seventies, a short hop, skip and a jump from Heathrow Airport. I was born into a strict West Indian family. My father emigrated to the UK from Jamaica and my mother from British Guiana in the late fifties.

Like their Windrush predecessors, they boarded their respective ships to England, excited at the prospect of what the motherland had to offer. The British government had promised a warm welcome and they were quick to respond. The reality was much more abhorrent: rather than being welcomed with open arms, they found themselves walking into a cold, hostile environment of hate and victimisation. Jobs and accommodation were hard to come by for the new arrivals as England revealed a racist inner core not mentioned in the government's immigration marketing pamphlets. But that only fuelled my father who was always upbeat and positive, and he worked two jobs whilst studying to become an engineer. By the time I was born, he had bought two houses and had moved from Acton to leafy Isleworth and was about to embark on a career at the BBC. He rented out rooms to tenants who were struggling to find suitable accommodation under the 'No blacks, No Irish, No dogs' policy which many landlords were enforcing.

We lived in a semi-detached house and as well as my mum, dad and two brothers – Trevor and Reggie – there was also my cousin Keith, my dad's sister's son, who was sent over from Jamaica to be educated in the UK. There were only three black families on the street and I was the only black child in my school from what I can remember. Saying that, I don't remember being racially abused when I was at primary school but I do remember often feeling different. Being treated differently to my classmates at times but I didn't know why. Looking back, it was an early form of the systemic racism I learned to accept as I got older.

One example was an incident at primary school I remember very clearly. I was around seven at the time. My teacher was casting for the school play and told me she had given me a very important role with a special outfit. I even remember her showing me the outfit. I ran home to my mum that evening, very excited to tell her my news.

No, I wasn't given the lead or any major part in the play. I was to be the Golliwog.

My mum was mortified. I have no idea if she rang the headteacher or not – I suspect not – but I was kept off school until the play was over. I didn't really understand at the time why my mum was so angry, or why I had to miss the school play. As far as I was concerned, the golliwog was that cute little figure on the Robertson's jam jar normalised to the masses by TV advertising. I was too young to understand the double meaning of kids in the playground telling me *'See you at teatime'* which was the strapline for the Robertson's jam campaign.

We lived in an area which was 98% white but to keep me in check with my roots, my mum and dad used to constantly drum home positive black messages. I do remember one time saying to my mum *'I wish I was white'*. I was very young and must have been triggered by negative things that were going on around me. My mum immediately shut that thought down. *'Don't you ever say that again. Repeat after me: I'm black and I'm proud. Black is Beautiful.'*

To this day, I have never, ever had that thought again.

It was hard being a black kid in England in those days. No matter how many people tried to tell you it was not so, you *were* 'different'. Having said that, I was incredibly comfortable in my black skin and the idea of being proud British. Proud black. And being proud of my West Indian heritage was something that underpinned my upbringing and stood me in good stead. Those were values that I made sure I would pass on to my children.

Getting despondent with the increase in racism and perceived lack of opportunity for their children, my parents took the family and emigrated to Jamaica with my father ironically keen to 'go back where he came from'. A fun couple of years that ultimately didn't work out, we returned to Isleworth in time for me to prepare for secondary school.

And start my love affair with football.

Secondary School and a Fledgling Football Passion

I had no real interest in football before I left for Jamaica. My dad was a workaholic and he had no passion for any form of sport whatsoever so I had no one to influence me when it came to choosing a team to follow. I vaguely remember seeing Leeds lift the FA Cup on TV a few months before we left for the Caribbean but when I came back to the UK, every kid was bang into football. I needed a team to support.

'*So, what team do you support, then?*'

"*Er … Leeds.*"

… and that was that. I was a Leeds fan.

As a kid, playing football was a thing. And I loved it. My dad was hardcore, plying us with hours of extra schoolwork every single day. The education system in Jamaica was so advanced that when I came back to the UK my dad insisted I go into the year above, meaning I went straight into secondary school, a year younger than my classmates. Every day when I came home from school, I would then plough into two hours of 'dad-algebra' followed by an hour of piano practice. He would often tell me, '*As a black man, for you to get on in this country, you can't be just as good as your white colleague. You have to be twice as good.*' This was his way of ensuring I didn't slack. When my work was done, I would run off to the park to play football with the local kids until sundown. My football journey was progressing and I was sporadically getting to live matches. Cousin Keith took me to Fulham to see his best mate Ernie Howe play alongside George Best, Rodney Marsh and Bobby Moore, and my mum took me to QPR to see Leeds. Then one day, in 1979 something happened which would change my life. Forever. It was a Saturday lunchtime and we were in the middle of playing a match at the park when two older girls came up to us, saying: '*Who wants to go to Brentford, then? It won't cost ya. We'll go over the turnstiles.*' The two girls walked four or five of us younger lads down London Road to Brentford. When we got to the ground, one of the girls – Joanne was her name – had a word with the turnstile operator, Paddy. Next minute we were in and straight over the turnstiles as promised. The girls walked us to the stand behind the goal and I remember going up the stairs and looking out onto the pitch. The ground was enormous, a huge sprawling terrace full of people chanting and jostling. Loads of kids my age threw bags of homemade newspaper-confetti in the air as the teams came out of the tunnel. The buzz of the place was something else and I loved it.

I can't remember who Brentford played that day, or the score. They probably lost as they would lose a lot in those days, but it didn't matter. I was hooked and after that, I started going to every home game. Meanwhile, all the piano practice was paying off and my music had taken off somewhat. The good news was that I had been accepted to The Royal College of Music Junior Department to study piano, trombone and percussion. The bad news was that it was in Kensington on Saturday mornings, right opposite the Royal Albert Hall, which would make getting back in time for kick-off tricky.

Right from the start, I hated it. Well, actually, I loved the percussion but hated everything else. I just didn't fit in. I would often bunk off my trombone lesson and amble down to Kensington Market for a few hours to chat to Gaz Mayall, son of legendary Blues musician John Mayall, who had a stall in the basement selling rude-boy gear. We would chat for hours; Gaz was a very cool guy who seemed to know everything happening in the emerging ska scene which I had embraced. I discovered the Specials fairly early on and I lived and breathed their music and all the associated ska and two-tone bands. The Selecter, The Beat, Madness, even Bad Manners. It was not just the music; it was the message. The Specials in particular sent out a very strong anti-racist message which resonated with me. Growing up in a predominately white area was tough at times, particularly during the time of the rise of the far-right National Front. The NF were very active at Brentford matches and I found myself regularly being racially attacked by my own fans.

We moved from Isleworth to Acton and in school I was doing well. It was challenging in the playground at times but in class I was flying, so my mum and dad were happy. I was attending a prestigious music school that my mum would proudly tell her friends about, but in reality, I was going backwards from when I attended private lessons. I was getting more and more into British street music; I started a band and began organising gigs.

Saturday music school was seriously getting in the way of my football. Yes, I could just about get to home games but those elusive away games, that everyone said were on another level of excitement, were a no-no. Something had to give.

By the time I reached sixth form, I decided to end my time at The Royal College of Music. My mum was not happy. 'All those music lessons gone to waste,' she said. Little did I know at the time that I would use my knowledge to forge a career in the music industry years later.

The Thatcher Years

It was 1980 and Margaret Thatcher had just become Prime Minister. Within a year of her coming to power my parents had decided they'd had enough, again. England was going through turmoil and the country had just come out of the Winter of Discontent with strikes aplenty and high unemployment. My parents felt the ruling Tory party was racist and divisive. Enoch Powell's infamous 'Rivers of blood' speech struck a chilling chord. Suddenly they were being blamed for the fact that some people didn't like the colour of their skin. They felt the opportunities offered by Thatcher and her government would be limited for our family. My brother Trevor and I, two middle-class black kids, had been stopped and searched by the police more than once. Tensions were on a knife's edge and the black community had had enough. Brixton burst into riot. And there were copycat riots all over the country: Liverpool, Birmingham, Leeds. Even in Acton. And the following day the police turned up at our front door with a warrant to search the house for stolen goods. It comes to pass that our next-door neighbours also had the same experience; the police found nothing in either house. There were only two houses searched on the whole street and both were owned, not rented but owned, by black families. Coincidence or what?

When my dad came home and found out, he was seething and dragged me down to the police station to have it out with the police for a good hour. He didn't mince his words. That was the tipping point and he made the decision to emigrate to the States. But I worked extra hard to get into university – I wanted to stay in the UK as I was really beginning to enjoy life.

The music lessons had stopped but I was getting my musical fulfilment in other ways. My band was selling out gigs all over West London. I had a steady girlfriend and I was a fully signed-up member of the London Soul Boy scene, with pirate radio stations JFM, Invicta and Horizon, and later LWR and Kiss, forming the soundtrack to my weekend. I was now regularly going to Brentford away matches with my best mate Paul in between partying up and down the country. Ironically, I met Paul at my very first Brentford away game, minutes before I got chased by a large mob of Reading fans shouting 'Get the nig***'. Racism and violence at football was an ongoing problem but I was streetwise enough to handle it. I was on the verge of going to university, why the hell would I want to go to America? The time came and my family moved to Miami to start a new life in the next promised land. And I moved to Brighton to start life as a student.

From Brighton to Miami

Brighton. What a place to live. I had a great time; I was a proper geek, doing an Electronic Engineering Course but my extra-curricular life was anything but geekish. I had a weekly show on Radio Falmer: 'Billy Gee's Sunday Function', which catapulted me to DJing.

I first started playing at the Crypt, the campus night club, before graduating into town, playing at The Brighton Belle, The Escape, Hollywood Greats and Toppers around the same time as Norman Cook and Carl 'megamix' Cox were doing their early Brighton rounds. I even organised the legendary Sussex Soul Society boat party down the Thames that Carl Cox and I DJed at.

A brilliant three years in Brighton came to an end and I graduated as an engineer, which was what my father always wanted. But the fact is, it gave me no joy whatsoever. Music and football were what drove me. I had no idea what I was going to do with my qualification, so I decided to give the States a shot. Miami in the late eighties was a far cry from Miami in the 2000s. Miami beach was a dive, many of the hotels on South Beach were dishevelled and the nightlife scene was pretty poor.

I'd left the UK in the middle of a very cool, very vibrant warehouse music scene. I lived and breathed warehouse parties. 'Jacking' music such as Marshall Jefferson's 'Move Your Body' and Farley 'Jackmaster' Funk's 'Love Can't Turn Around' formed the soundtrack to my summer before leaving London. So, to go to Miami to find a music scene so backwards, hurt badly. My natural draw was always going to be the underground and I eventually found myself hooked into the coolest underground Miami scene. The indie scene emanating out of the nightclub Fire and Ice and the continually rotating party venue location Avenue A were two of my favourites. My nightlife soundtrack had shifted from Maze and Steve 'Silk' Hurley to The Cure, Psychedelic Furs and Big Audio Dynamite.

Watching football was also a huge challenge. Quite simply, America wasn't interested. There was no Internet in those days so I would have to phone home every week for the Brentford results. And I paid the local newspaper, the

MUSIC.FOOTBALL.FATHERHOOD

Middlesex Chronicle, to post the back page of their paper with the Brentford match report out to me every week. There was one bar, however, that showed football. Churchill's Hideaway was a rundown bar in the Haitian area of Miami run by a Stoke City fan called Dave. He had a huge satellite dish installed in his backyard and was able to illegally pick up matches being transmitted across the world. I didn't even like First Division football, it was so far removed from what I was used to watching but the prospect of driving twenty miles to watch a match between Arsenal and Coventry City in a dodgy pub in North Miami drinking beer at 9 a.m. was too much of a lure for me. It was like the warehouse party of sport and I was hooked. I found myself there every week.

I spent a year in America and really enjoyed it. Mainly because I had no real responsibilities. I worked as a waiter in one of the first ever TGI Fridays before moving down to a private members' club in Key Largo where I got my first real experience of an openly racist America.

It was a private gated club community for the rich and famous with its own airfield and private yachts rolling in hourly off the Atlantic Ocean. One of my colleagues from TGI Fridays worked there and hooked me up. They had vacancies in one of the main restaurants and she had put in a good word with the manager for me. So I called him, in my best English accent. The guy was incredibly welcoming and told me to come down to talk terms. A few days later when I walked into the restaurant, I could see his face drop. Surprise surprise, the waiter vacancy in the restaurant had been filled but he offered me a busboy job collecting empty dishes from the tables. I was a bit peeved but went for it anyway. I was given a staff accommodation apartment which meant I moved down to Key Largo. I won't lie, I had a great time working and living there, but I couldn't help notice that there were no black waiters. All the black people were working as dishwashers and cooks in the kitchen, all behind the scenes, and I was the only front-facing black person in the whole resort. Not only that, I also found that I was the only black person living in my accommodation block. The residences were split: the multi-level block was where waiters and busboys lived and the low-level block, nicknamed skid row, was where the dishwashers and cooks lived. I was the only black person living in the multi-level block whereas everyone, bar one person, in the low-level block was black. I was friends with everyone in the living quarters, but my black friends were afraid to come and meet me in my block. They weren't allowed. They often asked me how I got to stay in the 'white quarters'. I couldn't give an answer and felt quite bad.

221

After Key Largo, I moved up north to Boston under the premise that New England was going to be like England. Unfortunately, it wasn't. Football was still non-existent, but it was fun working two jobs, hanging out with the chess players of Harvard Square in between shifts, and heading down to Cape Cod beach on my day off with my buddies Derby Dave and Mark. I was loving going out every night in Boston; it wasn't London but after Miami, it was revolutionary. DV8, at the infamous Spit club, on a Tuesday night was the place to be with hip-hop and house music upstairs and new wave downstairs. The Americans were really feeling my London fashion – MA-1 flight jacket, dungarees, DMs, boy patches, safety pins up and down my sleeves. Straight out of the UK warehouse party scene – and I was beginning to feel at home there. But as much as I loved my time in Boston, it was time to head back to London. I was missing my music, my football and my friends.

Entering the Music Industry

London's nightlife scene had embraced rare groove and it was bang up my street. On top of that, hip-hop had fused with house music to give us hip-house. It was all going off. Meanwhile, I was back on the terraces at Brentford. The team were much stronger than before and were really starting to make some waves. I started my first job, as a programmer at BT, and from day one I realised I hated it and needed to get out. I spent my whole spare time either organising unofficial coach trips to away games for my football mates or DJ parties for my non-football mates. I loved the fact that my two worlds, music and football, were so separate. Other than with best friend Paul, my clubbing world and my football world were mutually exclusive.

Then one day, I had a rude awakening. Walking into an acid house party in a film studio in Wembley was Brian, one of the guys who came on my football coaches. Hold on, what's going on? This wasn't meant to happen. This was the moment when my two worlds collided; it was quite a seminal moment of my life. What's more, Brentford actually started becoming good and by the early nineties, I saw us reach an FA Cup Quarter-Final at Anfield, lose a couple of play-offs games, win the league title before getting immediately relegated and win Brentford's first competitive game in Europe against Ascoli in the Anglo Italian Cup. I was running almost biweekly away trips by this stage, much to the displeasure of the club. We went to matches by coach, by train, by plane, even by barge. 'By any means necessary', as Malcolm X once very famously said. I even ran the first ever football boat, 150 of us on a six-hour cruise to a match in Southend.

I secretly did a postgraduate marketing diploma in the evening whilst working at BT, and at the very first opportunity, I left the computing world for the world of brand sponsorship. By day I was organising husky dog racing championships for beer companies and art exhibitions for telecommunications companies. By night, I was fully immersed in London's clubbing scene. If I was short on cash any week, Gilles Peterson's 'Talkin' Loud' jazz dance at Dingwalls on a Sunday afternoon was my one must-go. Meanwhile, my main client, Labatt's, took me on to run their music sponsorship of the Hammersmith and Manchester Apollos and suddenly, I had one foot in the music industry door and, boy, did I make the most of it, burning the candle at both ends even more.

My time at Labatt's led me to my first proper job in the music industry. Telstar Records were advertising for an A&R manager for their compilations. It was the mid-nineties and Telstar were dominating the compilations market. They were known as 'The Millwall of the Music Industry'. 'No one likes us. We don't care' was their motto and the culture was one of 'heavy social' which suited me to a tee. The bosses encouraged us to go out loads, network and spend as much money as possible on our Telstar credit cards, fostering relations with anyone and everyone in the music industry. Which I did; I battered it. Every year the whole company flew abroad for an all-expenses-paid lavish three-day 'conference' where chaos and mayhem were the order of the day. I was the proverbial pig in shit; I absolutely loved my job. I would get in at 9.30 a.m. every day, stay in the office till 7 or 8 p.m. at night, head into town until 3 or 4 a.m. then get home, wake up and do it all again.

As well as producing compilations, which made the company a hell of a lot of money, I got my feet wet working in A&R with a wide variety of artists from PJ & Duncan aka Ant & Dec and Conner Reeves to Hunter from Gladiators and E17. I had built up a strong relationship with the urban community by commissioning mixes by various up-and-coming producers but because urban music wasn't really fashionable at the time, I found that the music wasn't taken seriously by the record label promotions team. To get my artists' records played, I would travel up and down the country, knocking on the door of radio stations. From pirate, to mainstream, daytime DJs and specialist, I got to know everyone from head of playlist to the receptionist. Some of the mixes were fab, but there is only so far you can go with a Darkman mix of PJ & Duncan or a Linslee Mix of Ben from Curiosity Killed the Cat.

I was reluctantly moved from doing compilations and given the role of Senior A&R manager for the Telstar artists. I was gutted; I loved doing the compilations and we had a lot of success. A&R was a proper jump into the deep end for me and it was a bit scary. I decided to set up an urban A&R and promotions department with Rob, who would become my future business partner. With no interest in urban music whatsoever from the rest of the company, Rob and I could pretty much do what we wanted and our hard work was to really pay off when this young seventeen-year-old kid walked into the building. He was tossing up between signing for BMG or Telstar via imprint label Wildstar. He was sent down to meet 'the Urban department' with the sole intention of us convincing him to join the label. An hour of talking later and the artist, a young Craig David, told his manager he wanted to sign with us. From that moment on it was a whirlwind. We spent a good six to eight months setting his project up. We hooked Craig up with the hottest producers, pressed up lots of vinyl records and sold them to specialist shops and DJs whilst promoting his music to radio stations, from Pirates to Radio 1.

We must have sold 50,000 promos before the official release of the first single 'Fill Me In'. The buzz at street level was enormous. Alongside working Craig and the other Telstar artists in the stable, I had just signed a girl band called Mis-Teeq. The three girls; Alesha Dixon, Sabrina Washington and Sue-Elise Nash, went on to become the biggest UK garage girl act. We had so many laughs making their album and the four of us – I say four as I was accused by my bosses of being the fourth member of Mis-Teeq – were very, very tight. My bona fide at the time was a producer called Tim Blacksmith. We were like batty and bench and we went everywhere together. Tim would work with all my artists including Fierce, Conner Reeves, Craig David, Mis-Teeq and E17 and I was the first UK A&R he had taken to Trondheim in Norway to meet a set of producers called Stargate who he had just started to represent. I went out to Norway a lot and we became really good friends. Soon they started working on my artists, including Mis-Teeq's biggest hit 'Scandalous' and an absolute monster for Fierce: 'Sweet Love'. A few years later, I signed them.

Football was good in those days too. I signed the England Unofficial Anthem for World Cup France '98 called 'Vindaloo' by Fat Les after a rather surreal meeting with actor Keith Allen and artist Damian Hurst at a flat in Notting Hill in which Keith told me that he had written the song after attending an away game at Bristol City. When I asked him who he supported and he revealed he supported Brentford's main rivals Fulham, we immediately hit it off – talking football for a good hour. The irony of a top five record being signed because of a mutual respect between two fans of opposing clubs will be lost on most. Fat Les were performing in Marseilles the day I took a coach of UK-born Jamaicans to Lens for 'The Reggae Boyz' (the Jamaican national football team) first ever World Cup finals match against Croatia. We had barrels of rum punch on the coach and a wicked hip-hop, R&B and reggae music soundtrack. The trip to Lens was a party from start to finish. Jamaica lost 3-1 but the pandemonium on the terraces when Robbie Earle equalised will live with me forever. After the match we headed back to an after-party I had arranged after hiring out a nightclub in the city of Lille. I was DJing to a tired but happy crowd before flying down to the riot zone of Marseilles in the morning to catch up with Keith Allen and watch England.

Back at home, Brentford had been relegated to the bottom tier of the football league and were looking to bounce straight back. Ron Noades – yes, he of 'the problem with black players is they can't take the cold' fame, had bought the club and decided to throw a load of money at it, buying some quality players and we were flying. Little did we know that season of big spending was to push the club to the verge of bankruptcy but at the time, we were delighted as we won the Third Division Title at the first hurdle.

A few year later, a Noades-less Brentford were thirteen minutes away from promotion to The First Division, which is now called The Championship. I invited Alesha Dixon to Griffin Park to stand on the Brentford terraces with my crew to witness what I thought was going to be a monumental moment. The day didn't quite go to plan as Brentford lost, again. Alesha was racially abused outside the ground by Reading fans, and her boyfriend at the time, Harvey, rightfully called me up to give me an earful on how I should protect Alesha more when she was out with me. Two weeks later, Alesha and I were amongst 400 guests at David Beckham's pre-Japan World Cup party. My friend Nina hooked it up for Mis-Teeq to perform at the party whilst also arranging for me to accompany them.

Brentford had lost the play-off final to Stoke the previous day and I was so gutted, I really didn't want to go to David's party. But I put on a brave face and in the end, I had a blast. My crew were all there from the garage scene: Spoony Omar, Robbie Craig. I got chatting to all sorts of celebrities who had no idea who I was. Cilla Black. Joan Collins. Elton John. Gary Lineker. I even stepped on David's injured foot as I went to say hello. Victoria wasn't happy. Probably even less happy when she saw I managed to sneak into the *Hello* magazine photoshoot, being hilariously credited in the article as 'and another guest'. My friends still rib me about that to this day.

A few weeks later, I went to Japan for the 2002 World Cup. England only had a handful of black supporters who would regularly travel to matches around this time. Many of my friends were scared by some England fans' reputation for hooliganism and racism and often questioned why I 'put my neck on the line'. Proud British and proud black, I would tell them. The fact is I never once got any grief personally. And the few incidents of racism I did come across, I would call people out on face-to-face with the perpetrator apologising profusely every single time. I knew things would get easier for black and Asian fans. It was just going to take a bit of time.

The Japan World Cup was a complete sea-change compared to previous competitions. I've now been to fourteen major tournaments: seven world cups, six European championships and one Women's World Cup and I can guarantee you, the Japan World Cup will never be beaten. The travelling crowd had a different air about them and the atmosphere amongst England fans was incredibly positive. What also helped was that the Japanese were the most welcoming, fun and enthusiastic hosts ever. I've never been to a tournament when you come out of the stadium and the fans are queuing up for autographs and photos of England fans. At night, hundreds of Japanese supporters were clamouring to get into bars full of their English coun-terparts to sing songs with them. There was lots of mutual respect and it created a fantastic atmosphere. I flew over with a load of Craig David test pressings and used them as collateral to get me into clubs. My mate Aki, who worked for Craig David's Japanese record label, showed me around Tokyo; it was amazing.

Immediately after that World Cup, life changed dramatically for me. I had been trying to negotiate with Telstar to get my own label. But things didn't really progress the way I wanted it to so Rob and I decided to leave. I remember telling the Mis-Teeq girls the news in the middle of a recording session in the USA and they were disappointed and a little angry. I felt really guilty. It was like abandoning your children as I felt responsible for them. But the decision was made and with a really heavy heart, I left Telstar to set up my own company, called 2Point9, with Rob.

Becoming My Own Boss and Becoming a Dad

Going independent was a brave move. We left Telstar with literally one month's wages and we didn't really know what we were going to do, apart from manage the productions of a young British-Asian producer called Rishi Rich.

Rishi was an interesting character I had built up a great relationship with whilst he was producing tracks for a number of my Telstar artists. After I left, he very specifically told me, 'You can manage my Western stuff. I'll take care of my Eastern stuff myself.' Basically, any time Rishi was short financially, he would go to one of the Asian record labels who would give him a fee to produce an album for them. We were very busy commissioning Rishi productions on the likes of Mary J Blige, Britney Spears and Craig David so we were fine with him handling that side of his business. Rishi Rich was flying in the R&B world but only a few months into managing him, something would happen that would alter the direction of my life. Forever.

Rishi invited me to one of his Asian events after he had finished recording another album. The launch was at the Asian Mela at the NEC and I was not expecting what I saw that weekend. Rishi was staying at the adjoining Hilton Hotel and was given five-star treatment; everyone was swooning over him like he was the sixth member of Take That. The Mela itself was absolutely packed – there must have been about 20,000 people in the place. Rishi performed some tracks from his new album with bhangra singer Juggy D and a few other artists. The place went ballistic. I left the Mela educated.

The following week, I had organised an anti-racism event at the Roof Gardens, Kensington for Kick It Out. Looking back on it, it was an excellent event which included a panel with Chris Kamara and Chris Powell. I'm still friends with them both. We had over 200 people in attendance and after the event, I threw a party to see the evening out.

During the night I remember Rishi coming up to me and saying, *'My label just told me that I sold 25,000 albums last week. Is that good?'*

'How much did they pay you?' I asked.

'£3,500.'

The albums were selling for a tenner. A quick bit of maths. That was some profit in a short space of time for the label.

'I better start managing your Eastern stuff too,' I said to him.

And that was the moment when it all *really* started. It was like a whirl-wind. Within months we had signed a stable of artists including bhangra singer Juggy D, R&B singer Jay Sean, Hindi songstress Veronica and hip-hop producer Mentor.

We built a website, made some music, sold some vinyl and licensed a track to Bollywood. The track blew up; we had gone international.

Jay Sean signed to Virgin Records and a Bollywood star appeared in one of his videos. We blew up even more. From there we were on *Top of the Pops*, had a popular Sony award-nominated radio show on Kiss FM and took producer Timbaland shopping in Southall for music. We were collaborating with Jamaican reggae artists, Puerto Rican reggaeton artists and Japanese hip-hop artists. We were being flown all over the world every week to perform to thousands and thousands of screaming people. Our artists were superstars in their own world. We did a gig at Olympia once and the security described the reaction as 'like Beatlemania'; the crowd were going absolutely bonkers.

I was literally walking our records into Radio 1, 1Xtra, Choice FM, Capital Radio and all the other stations where I had built up a terrific relationship from my Telstar days. Rishi Rich was getting more work than he could handle and 2Point9 was absolutely flying. *The Guardian* newspaper, who listed us at No 20 in their Ethnic Minority Power list, were quoted as saying *'[2Point9] have done for black and Asian music in the UK what Def Jam did for hip-hop in the US'.*

I had been seeing my girlfriend Aisling, a radio producer at BBC 1Xtra, for a few years now and we were spending a lot of time together. She had also been briefed on my all-consuming football activity and vowed not to change me. But I was struggling to find time to run a business, watch football up and down the country every week, spend quality time with my girlfriend and party till 3 a.m. most nights of the week. Something had to give.

It was the turn of the year 2005 and Brentford were now being managed by one of the most exciting and bonkers managers ever, Martin 'Mad Dog' Allen. And they were starting to soar. Brentford were about to play their fourth round FA Cup match at Hartlepool. Aisling was nine months pregnant with my son who was due any day. Was I ready for fatherhood? I put my hands up and say that kids were not on the cards for me around that time. I had too much going on and I wasn't willing, or able, to make too many sacrifices. Not yet, anyway. We did have very loose plans to have kids at some stage, we just didn't expect it to happen so quickly. Nevertheless, we were both over the moon when we found out. Needless to say, I didn't make it up to Hartlepool that day, but I did bring my TV to the hospital appointment, much to the duty nurse's disgust, to ensure that I could catch all the FA Cup action on Sky Sports news. The Bees were victorious and booked themselves a fifth round FA Cup tie away at Premier League Southampton. The match, their biggest game for years, was only seven days later. Panic set in: my son wasn't even born as yet. This could be tricky.

Three days later and Elias was born. It was a beautiful moment. We were both totally overcome by emotion. I was a dad. A proud dad to a beautiful son with a full head of hair and eyes wide open, inquisitively gazing at every nook and cranny of the world around him. From the moment he popped out, we could tell he was a special boy.

Meanwhile, there was mayhem at Griffin Park. Brentford unwittingly had put all its allocation for the Saints game on sale at once. Tickets sold out in minutes with many loyal supporters, including me, stuck without a ticket. I got a call; someone had secured me a gold-dust ticket. I was facing my first father dilemma. What was the protocol for disappearing off to see your team's biggest game in years two days after your newborn son was taken home? Dilemma resolved. Two days later, I was making my way down to Southampton. The result was irrelevant really; we actually came back from 2-0 down to force a replay, but what was relevant was how that afternoon impacted my relationship and what kind of father I was going to be in the future.

On the work front, 2Point9 was in its ascendency. I needed very little sleep, had incredibly high energy and worked with clients in both India and the USA so the night shift was perfect for me. I would be chatting to various labels and promoters in the early hours in between feeding Elias and changing his nappy. When I was in the UK, I was at home a lot. Well, it was a lot if you compare it to say a bank manager or an advertising agency director who would leave the house every day at 7 a.m. and not get back home till 7 p.m. The problem was, I was also travelling a lot. And it was the times when I was away that were difficult for Aisling.

Within two weeks of my son being born, I was off to Thailand for yet another Jay Sean tour. I was just about managing to juggle being a dad, a music mogul and a super loyal football fan. But what I didn't really know was how my wife was coping. The fact is, she was not finding it easy. And it was only years later that I was to find out how difficult she found it. And how much that trip to Southampton had helped to compound how she was feeling.

2Point9 was going from strength to strength and I was literally travelling all over the place. We would sometimes fly off to India just for a night before heading back.

I couldn't do it all.

It put a real strain on our relationship, but I came up with a solution to try and resolve things and redress the balance. I managed to convince international promoters to trade my business class seat for two economy seats. That way, Elias and Aisling could piggyback on a few tours. It was perfect. Elias and Aisling came with us everywhere for a few years: Miami, New Zealand, Australia, Beijing and Puerto Rico. Elias had travelled half the world before the age of two. I had the best of both worlds as I was getting to spend time with my family whilst working abroad. As a result, I formed a really close bond with my son whilst also taking some of the strain off Aisling.

Meanwhile, over the next couple of years, 2Point9 was undergoing huge a transition. The company had got so busy, it was starting to crack under the strain. We were victims of our own success. There were only three of us and we were finding it hard to divide our time. Some artists felt they could do better on their own and decided to leave the camp. It was back to the drawing board for 2Point9. Jay Sean, who had been dropped by Virgin, was delighted that he was now to become our number one focus and by late 2007, we were concentrating on recording his new album whilst he toured around the world. Luckily for me, Brentford were going through an appalling spell. Terry Butcher was managing the team straight down to non-league, playing terrible football. I still went but not nearly as much as I used to, which gave me more time to focus on building the company.

Twelve months later, we were smashing it again.

2Point9 released Jay Sean's album independently and shocked the whole music world as it reached Top 10 in the UK charts. We then licensed the album to Cash Money Records, one of the most successful hip-hop labels in the States. More shock.

Meanwhile, I was due a second child. But this time around, it was going to be very different.

The Birth of Bella and the Rebirth of 2Point9

Despite still being massively busy with Jay Sean, I had a much better work-life balance going into the birth of my second child. Jay Sean was still touring extensively but I was picking and choosing the tours I went on and delegating the remaining events to people who worked with me. My footballing life was more balanced as well. I was due to go to Berlin to see England play but cancelled that trip because it was too close to my daughter's due date. It was time to put priorities first.

A few weeks later, I witnessed the birth of my beautiful daughter, Bella. We were expecting a boy as boys run the length and breadth of my family, so we were completely gobsmacked and completely over the moon when a beautiful girl popped out.

Luckily there were no World Cups or European Championships coming up and I didn't have any international work trips for a while so I could really appreciate the first year of Bella growing up.

Things were very much different this time round. Knowing I was going to be around much more was majorly reassuring for Aisling. We had got married a couple of years after Elias was born, providing a much more stable family unit. We were working together better, and we also had the experience of bringing up Elias so everything was so much smoother, so much easier. It was all one big learning curve and the whole family, and particularly the kids, benefitted from it.

Twelve months after signing to Cash Money, Jay Sean's 'Down', which featured Lil Wayne, hit No. 1 in the US Billboard chart. That should have been the pinnacle of our careers to date. The headline: *'a small two-man indie label from West London remortgage their houses to fund a relatively unknown British-Asian artist's rise to the top of the US charts'*. We were ahead of the game. American labels weren't really breaking British artists at that time, not British Urban artists anyway. 2Point9 had smashed boundaries and we should have been excited and proud, but we weren't. As soon as the record blew up, we could see them moving in. The vultures. The vultures who were nowhere to be seen when we were pouring over £100k of our own money into the album. Within weeks it wasn't our project any more and everyone was gatecrashing the party. Major labels were eyeing up how they could claim more market share, random managers were muscling their way in for a slice of the cake and by the time Jay Sean walked on stage at Hammersmith Apollo to announce his No. 1 to a sold-out Lil Wayne gig, we knew it was all over. Rob and Simon, our distributor, and I walked out of the venue to find solace in a bar across the road and we just sat there and said nothing. For ages. An empty feeling ran through us and we turned to each other, 'Cheers.' It was the most soulless 'Cheers' you would ever see. The next few years were spent with lawyers battling against Jay Sean, Cash Money, Universal, everyone. It was a truly demoralising time and once again, we had to borrow money but this time to pay lawyers' fees. We came out winners in the end but the battle left me deflated. So much time and energy and passion had been put into getting to that stage. How many times had I put my artists before family? That was all going to change.

It was at that point my focus shifted from throwing all my energies into music artists, to working out how I could support my family whilst finding alternative forms of income to keep the ship afloat.

Meanwhile, the kids were growing up fast. Elias had always been full of beans. He was a great kid. Proper live wire. Incredibly busy. You couldn't take your eye off him for a minute. When Bella was born, we were really nervous that we would have to go through the same pattern of endless sleep-less nights and constant supervision, but we didn't. From day one she was content, calm and incredibly self-contained. She used to sleep for hours on end, so much so, we would often check on her to make sure she was OK. If Elias and Bella were born the other way around, it would have been a real shock to the system. But I have to say, raising Bella was an absolute breeze.

School was starting to become trickier for Elias as he continued to find social situations more difficult. The next few years were challenging for Aisling and me as we tried very hard to manage our time between Elias and Bella, who was often overlooked, following in the shadow of her very clever, but incredibly dominant, older brother.

She adored him but as she got older, she would also fight back. She wasn't taking any nonsense any more and would give as good as she got. She just got on with it and in fact, having two very different kids with very different sets of needs really levelled us up, making us even more open and tolerant. I started to take Elias to football matches from the age of three. Grimsby, Notts County, Preston, Birmingham, Wolverhampton, Gillingham, Middlesbrough: we went everywhere. We even went to Leipzig and Dülmen in Germany for pre-season friendlies.

I knew Elias did not really like football, but I never forced him to go. I would always ask him if he fancied going to a match and he would always say yes. He enjoyed the social element, going to the pub and playing on his Nintendo DS, rides on the train and general hanging out. Football was one place where Elias felt incredibly comfortable. He could temporarily put his school struggles behind him because, at football, he was accepted for who he was. All that mattered to the Brentford fans I hung out with was that he went to Brentford every week. Taking Elias to games was good for him; he had a routine that he loved and a place he felt comfortable and safe.

As Bella got older, she became a playmate for her big brother as we travelled up and down the country. She very quickly got into the matchday vibe with the pre-match hang out at Brentford's The Globe pub the place to be. I was now also co-running Brentford's main fan media outlet Beesotted and this was our base. The kids would have their own table set aside so they could play their games, leaving me to socialise with my friends or record another podcast video or video blog. For me, it was all about them just enjoying themselves in a football environment, having a burger, or a pizza, or some sweets, playing on their consoles or in the garden. For away trips we would make a day of it, like the time we travelled to Ipswich and went bowling before the match. For us, football gave them an opportunity to get out of the house, see the country and hang out as a family, with other people and with other children. By the time she was six, Bella was going to a dozen or so games a season. She was still quiet but as she got older, her personality started to come out. She started to get more athletic, she loved the outdoors and she loved sports. She first started kicking a ball around at a Little Kickers session which involved lots of boys running around going mad whereas our little serious girl just wanted to get the ball, run with it and kick it, without all the mayhem going around. When Bella started to show more than a passing enthusiasm for the game, my heart warmed. As she got older, she continued her football, signing up for an after-school football club. She was doing really well and even won a couple of awards. But one day she came home from school and said, *'I don't want to do football any more.'* The boys were 'being silly' and kept on telling her that she couldn't play 'because she was a girl'. She decided she only wanted to play football again if it was for an all-girls' team. She set out her stall and I had to find her a girls' team to play with.

Meanwhile, Elias was struggling with the tricky year six transition. He didn't do change well and stopped going to school for a whole twelve months. As my wife had just returned to work, I made the decision to cut back on my music duties to stay at home with him at this time. The label was still bubbling away but I needed a new outlet, something I could do from home, and I spent the next few years building up a portfolio producing audio, video and written content for various media companies including Sky Sports and Channel 5.

The following year, Elias would go off to boarding school in Shropshire, coming back home two or three times a term. Bella picked up Elias' football mantle and started to go to more and more Brentford matches with one of her schoolfriends. I signed them both up for England Supporters Club member-ships so we could also go and watch the England national team. She was watching more and more football off her own bat, often coming home from school and looking at endless YouTube clips of matches from the weekend just gone. Going to live matches is so important for a young child with a keen interest in the game; seeing how the players react and hearing the fans before, during and after the match. This was all part of the education. Even though it wasn't being forced down them, they were picking up on what it was like to be a true football fan; the culture, the lingo and the ups and downs. Bella loved it, it was right up her street and she made a real effort to get further invested. The more Bella saw of the game, the more she questioned. She wouldn't take anything for granted, it had to make sense in her head.

One cold December, we were sitting in the stands in Preston. Bella was sitting next to Aisling and she turned to her and said, *'Mummy. Why are there no girls in the team? Only men?'*

'You better ask Daddy?' answered Aisling.

So she turned to me and asked the same question to which I fudged an answer.

'Er. Because men and women aren't allowed to play together. It's the laws of the game.'

'That's stupid,' she said indignantly then turned around and continued watching the game. My wife, being an ardent advocate for women's rights, has always been passionate about supporting Bella every step of the way in her

life journey as a young woman. And as her dad, I made it very clear from a very early age that Bella was not to subscribe to gender stereotypes. She hated dolls, she hated pink and she loved exciting activities like skateboarding and football. Taking a leaf out of my mum and dad's West Indian parenting book, I would often tell her that she could do anything she wanted to if she put her mind to it. Bearing in mind her previous experiences, I would often tell her not to let others put her down, or more explicitly, bring her down. But I didn't really need to teach Bella this, she seemed to pick this up on her own. She would always question any perceived inequality, so she didn't need a lecture from me or my wife, more of a nudge and words of encouragement to give her confidence to continue thinking the same independent way.

As for taking up playing football, it was slow. There was no girls' team at her school and although Bella pushed hard, it wasn't deemed enough of a priority for someone to pick up the ball, literally, and run with it. The boys' team was up and running and had been for years, but the girls' team was an afterthought. Bella would often get frustrated as the same old excuses were churned out. 'Girls don't like football' or 'girls can't play football' or 'there isn't enough interest for a team' or 'we haven't got the staff'. Basically, it wasn't a priority. Fair play to Bella, she took things into her own hands and rounded up her mates to start a lunchtime girls-only football club. They made up a load of fliers which they handed out in the school playground and got enough interest to get the idea off the ground. The head teacher was so impressed, he found a staff member to set up regular after-school sessions and enter the team in a league. Prior to her getting her school team up and running, I had finally found an out-of-school girls' team for Bella to train with. I had been struggling to find anything for a while but when I found a session in East London, which is a fair hike from my house, I was more than delighted to travel. What's more, it was at 9 a.m. on Saturday morning, so sacred Saturday afternoons on the terraces were safe.

Having a season ticket, Bella was now even more invested than ever in watching Brentford, so any extracurricular activity had to work around Saturday afternoons. I took Bella and a friend down to the session to check it out. Lot of kids, many of them new to football and all enjoying themselves. Perfect. I never considered her playing competitively at weekends for a team, football was always meant to be fun for Bella and I just wanted her to be in an environment where she felt comfortable. Two weeks in, the coach threw a spanner in the works as he wanted both girls to trial for a new team they were setting up. Most parents would rush at the idea, but I really wasn't sure, I just wanted her to enjoy football without the pressures of playing competitively just yet. I wasn't sure if she would get in the team as I felt it was very early, she had only just started her football journey and I wanted to protect her from the feeling of failure. What happened if her friend got in and she didn't? That would cause a massive dent in her self-esteem and she really didn't need that. Not now. But I was being gently cajoled, so I took them both along.

To my surprise they both got in. Panic set in as it dawned on me that I had set myself up for a life of taxiing my daughter to and from East London and Essex for the foreseeable future. I tried to convince the girls to trial with a more local club. No chance. The feeling Bella got from being accepted by this club was overwhelming and she didn't want that taken away. She had passed the test, she had been accepted, on merit, for something that she really wanted to do. She was happy that she was competing in a more accommodating environment, one where she could be measured on her actions and ability and not on what the social norms were.

She was living in a world where women were constantly being told that they didn't 'belong' to football and football didn't 'belong' to them. She had seen it everywhere, from the playground where the boys wouldn't allow the girls to join in their game, in a school where there was little priority placed on creating an atmosphere which would encourage girls to play football or on TV, where Bella would often comment on the lack of female faces talking about football. She would ask why there weren't more female presenters, and I could never give a coherent answer.

She would also ask why there were no female managers in the men's game but there were male managers in the women's game. She was posing all the right questions. And I wasn't able to give an answer except *'Dunno. It's pretty stupid'* but then reinforce the message that she could change all that if she really wanted to.

She knew everything about Jose Mourinho, Jurgen Klopp, Dean Smith, Thomas Frank, Frank Lampard and Wayne Rooney. She knew all about their managerial strengths and weaknesses because it was all over the TV. But what about Casey Stoney, manager of Manchester United Women, or Emma Hayes, manager of Chelsea Women, or Jill Ellis who guided the USA Women's team to two World Cups? How good were they as managers? And if Frank Lampard and Wayne Rooney could walk straight into a top-level football league job, why couldn't they?

She was always challenging the status quo of football. Would the USA Women's team beat England Men's team? Would they beat Nigeria's Men's team? Would they beat Manchester United? Or Norwich? Or even Brentford?

My West Indian parents had drilled into me that I could do whatever I wanted. *'As a black boy, you will always find people will try and hold you back. Don't let that ever stop you. Keep your head up. You can do whatever you want when you put your mind to it.'*

I didn't get it at first but as I grew older, it was so true. I learned what I needed to do to get on and sometimes that meant 'playing the game'. The less of a threat I was, the better chance I had of getting on. Bella was well aware of the constant prejudice and injustice I had to go through when I was younger. As a family we would sit and watch programmes about Black Britain and racism in the seventies and eighties then discuss it afterwards – programmes like the BBC series 'Small Axe' and the seminal eighties movie 'Babylon'.

I would always be one of only a very few black faces in a crowd of tens of thousands at each and every one of the anti-racism and anti-apartheid demonstrations that I attended over the years. I was frustrated as to why more black people did not come out and demonstrate for the black cause. But times have changed. The Black Lives Matter movement ignited something not seen in my day. Tens of thousands of people taking to the streets to voice their disapproval against the same racism and prejudice as thirty years back. And, unlike in my day, there were many black faces in the crowd. Of course, it was not only black people marching but the fact that there were so many black people making a stand made some folk feel very uncomfortable.

And Bella was right in there. She didn't see why she should have to put up with any nonsense and she wasn't prepared to compromise like we had to back then. About race. About gender. About anything really. Why should she?

Being mixed race, she was beginning to understand her Irish heritage and her West Indian heritage and how it was impacting on her life. At the same time, she was also getting her head around women's issues; the inequality in society and the negative perceptions. I wasn't able to protect her from that for much longer. But what I could do was to give her the tools, and the confidence, to deal with it head on. And I could ensure that my wife and I were role models for her and we always treated each other and others as equals. Having suffered racial injustice over the years, I have made sure Bella is well schooled on what is right and what is wrong. The Black Lives Matter cause is well and truly on her radar. If a player doesn't take the knee before a match, she'll clock it. She is fully aware of various recent situations of racial abuse at Brentford, and in football in general, and she's not happy with it at all.

Getting into the football team was brilliant for her, she absolutely loved it. Waking up at some ungodly hour to drive into deepest Essex every Sunday and hang out on touchlines in places like Billericay, Chelmsford and Basildon soon became the norm and I loved it. As much as it was a new experience for the girls, who were getting their first taste of coming together and growing as a team, it was also a new experience for most of the parents who were bonding as they watched. As a dad, I always saw my role as the taxi driver, the spectator and the person who Bella could vent to, and discuss things with, after the match. I never saw myself as a sideline coach like some parents of the opposition teams seemed to and as for touchline anger, that wasn't for me. Enthusiasm and encouragement were the way forward.

A few seasons on, the club decided to switch to a boys' league to give the girls a more challenging experience. It had been a tough few years for Bella as she was moved from pillar to post, switching teams pretty much every half-season. The whole concept of 'growing with your team' had been lost a bit as the club – who, to be fair, were very well organised and incredibly ambitious – went through a massive expansion, increasing from one U11 team to three in just one season. There was an uncanny parallel with the rapid expansion of 2Point9 and Bella, like some of her teammates, felt rejected, unloved and that she wasn't good enough, and it was hard to pick her up from that body blow. No matter how much I switched into mentor mode, the constant changing of teams was compounded by the challenge of having to play against boys. Lots of change in a short space of time and the girls just weren't ready for it. They say working with girls is very different to working with boys, particularly in football, where confidence is key. Boys can be naturally confident and cocky, even if they are not very good whereas girls may be technically excellent but often need support with gaining confidence. This is 100% because of society's perception of what girls should and shouldn't be doing and that was something, as a dad, I had to help Bella deal with.

Week after week they were coming up against fast, self-assured, sometimes arrogant boys, many of whom had played together for three or four years. They were not necessarily better players but they were more organised and better drilled. Bella had gone from both winning and losing close enthralling matches to losing every week by large margins and it was soul-destroying. Her faith in her abilities had taken a right shoeing and she was beginning to lose the love for playing. To try and keep her motivated, I took the focus away from the match itself to her personal performance; bigging up her skills, her speed, her resilience, her reading of the game and her eye for a pass. I told her not to dwell on the fact that the team had let in nine goals but instead focus on the other ten goals that she prevented the opposition scoring. Or to remember her series of one-on-ones with the striker which stopped him getting through on goal at least half a dozen times. That helped somewhat. But what I couldn't prepare her for was when some boy angrily dropped her in the mud after she dummied him before taking the ball around him. That hurt more than the 10-1 thumpings.

She was constantly battling in the playground, having to prove that the girls could occupy the same playing space as the boys. One time she organised a game of girls v boys at lunchtime at school. Ten minutes in, the girls were whooping the boys 8-1. The boys were getting really annoyed. So annoyed, they stopped the game and demanded a restart because … er … they were being beaten by girls. Another time, a boy started crying simply because he had been nutmegged by a girl. Bella would come home and tell me these stories and they would make me chuckle inwardly. She was never braggadocious about it, more matter-of-fact and questioning why.

Four years after she stopped playing football at the after-school club, Bella had finally proven to her male peers that she was worthy of stepping on the same football pitch as them. Plus she had the additional experience of watching professional matches in person both in the UK and abroad. So, whenever any boy in his Arsenal top tried to make fun of her and belittle her footballing commitment, footballing knowledge or the team she supported, she was able to cut him down in a millisecond.

Football Coaching

March 2020 saw the pandemic call a halt to football. I decided to use my spare Saturdays to get myself on the coaching ladder and signed up for an FA Coaching course. I had been asked earlier in the year to work with an established club to help set up a new U12s team, but I had a number of dilemmas. When I signed my daughter up for football, I honestly had no interest in getting involved in coaching. How would I juggle my love for travelling to watch games week in, week out and coaching a football team? I was also incredibly nervous at the prospect of coaching my daughter in an area which had become our hobby and shared passion. I spent the next few months chatting with them to try and find a way we could make it work. But once the pandemic hit, it changed everything; I felt it was time to try something new.

Bella decided to leave her East London team the following summer and started training with not one, but two, local clubs. One of those was the club I had just joined as a coach. By the end of the holiday, the team was up and running.

Coaching – I was loving it and pleased I was able to find another channel for my enthusiasm for football. I managed to maintain my relationship with my daughter by putting a few house rules in place which kept a distance between us both at practice and on match days. I have no interest in becoming the next Klopp or Pep but what excites me is the opportunity to get more girls to grow to love the game, both watching and playing. I also made sure I learned from Bella's previous experiences and did my best to create a positive ecosystem in which the team could operate within.

Women's World Cup

As well as having watched Brentford, or Chelsea Women and England men, Bella and I also go to watch non-league Dulwich Hamlet together every now then, both the men's and women's matches. Anti-racist, anti-sexist and anti-homophobic, Hamlet is a fantastic community club with a great atmosphere and a fantastic ethos where I feel 100% safe and comfortable taking my daughter.

We normally make a date to go to the Women's FA Cup final every season. One year she even took some of her teammates and they met both the Manchester City and West Ham finalists and got a photograph with Karen Bardsley and the FA Cup trophy after the match.

I do notice the difference when she watches the women's teams play as she definitely identifies with the players more.

In the summer of 2019, Bella was lucky enough to attend a number of Lionesses matches at the Women's World Cup in France. We had a fabulous time, a proper football trip which saw us head backwards and forwards from France six different times.

The football was great but for me what was more important was Bella attending a tournament in which she had some sort of vested interest and she felt some ownership. Gangs of girls and women on awaydays and female athletes on the pitch from all over the world. Inspirational. The tournament had a massive impact on my daughter; these players have given her a purpose. A feeling of 'I can do it'.

Yes, she's only twelve. And alongside her aspirations of playing the game professionally, she has already pinpointed a number of non-playing jobs within the game she quite likes the sound of, including manager and physio.

And I love that. I was never given that type of choice when I was young; I was always going to be an engineer.

So as long as she does her Maths, English and Science at school, she can aspire to do whatever else she wants.

Lessons Learned

I was definitely late to the party with fatherhood, holding on to my last moments of semi-bachelor life with both hands. I remember my music industry buddy Tim Blacksmith saying to me back in 2002, *'If you were to drop dead now, Billz, you would have had a good innings'* and he wasn't wrong. I've had a great life, I've seen loads, I've experienced loads and I wouldn't change it for the world.

One thing about me: when I get into something, I throw myself in head first and give it my all. There's no holding back. Hence my reticence to sometimes get involved in things.

I loved my work. It was all-consuming. And I gave a lot of time and energy to my artists. And in the end, it took a huge turn of events to make me realise I had to do things differently.

Being a dad gave me a completely different outlook on life. I was nervous at first, worried that it was going to be really tough and scared that it would change me massively, but I'm still the same positive-minded, happy-go-lucky person, with the same values. The reality is, when your child is born, you just get on with it and make it work. You also become more focused as many things stop becoming important to you. Material things.

If I have any regrets, I would have loved for both my kids to have witnessed the madness of the peak of my 2Point9 days. I would have also loved for my dad, who died just before the millennium, to have seen my music career evolve and acknowledge, although I didn't quite make it as an engineer, what I ended up doing wasn't all that bad.

I could have very easily gone on to work for a mainstream record label, which would have offered my family security, and I would probably have been very successful. Being self-employed can be so draining as you never really switch off and have the constant worry about where the next penny is going to come from. But if I hadn't struck out on my own, I would never have enjoyed the life that I have had. Not only has it been fun, but I have also had the flexibility to try whatever I wanted, whenever I wanted. More importantly, I wouldn't have been able to spend as much time seeing my family grow up as I have done.

One big lesson I learned is that it is so much easier if you can work together as a family. Yes, we all strive to maintain some level of independence but to make it really work as a family, you all need to compromise. I am incredibly lucky to have a brilliant wife who supported me all along the way, even when it looked like things were going horribly wrong. And that support was reciprocated as I found ways of making things work when she decided she had to return to the workplace after having kids.

Another important lesson is to be true to yourself. So many people alter the way they are and end up changing what makes them happy. Yes, you have to adapt in life but ultimately, you still have to be you, so it's all about getting the balance. And learn to trust people but always be wary that your relationship with them may not last forever. Cherish those friendships while you have them.

I'll put up my hand and say I've made mistakes. Some terrible mistakes, both as a dad and as a person. But we all make mistakes and it's acknowledging them, learning from them and moving forward that is important. It's something that is sometimes hard to do, but you feel so much better when you do, and modelling that to your children is key.

Passing it On

I have tried to pass on my values and outlook to my children, always encouraging them to try and be confident, and proud of who they are whilst giving them the tools to help them to succeed in whatever they want to do no matter what society tries to tell them. I would like to think that they won't let people put them down and they will never be afraid to try something new.

I had a fantastic upbringing with my parents teaching me the virtues of hard work and not letting standards slip – something that I have passed on to my children. However, I went through my early life doing what I was expected to do as opposed to what suited me as a person – Science, Engineering, Computing. There were all choices forced upon me in an age where academic ability was respected more than creativity. Yes, education is important. But to balance it up, I am equally as militant in ensuring that my children have as full a social life as possible, particularly Bella with her sport, and that they both end up working in a field that they enjoy and suits them as this is something, as a young adult, that I had to discover for myself.

I'm so, so pleased that both my kids do not subscribe to gender stereotypes. Bella, in particular, does not see 'girls' roles' and 'boys' roles' but just roles and is sick to the back teeth of constantly hearing me tell her to substitute the phrase 'I can't' for 'It's difficult' when I hear her say that she can't do something.

Respect for others is key. I have taken time out to make sure that they know their history, understanding not only my journey but what black people in the UK have had to go through. That, I believe, will go a long way in defining not only how they will treat other people but also, how they will accept being treated themselves.

And I want my children to have plenty of opportunities. Opportunities that I didn't have. And travel. I want my kids to meet as many people as possible and see as many places as they can so they will be worldly, open-minded and diverse in their thinking.

Hopes for the Future

Where are we at now? Well, 2Point9 is still going strong. Our back catalogue is doing well on streaming platforms and every now and then someone samples our records, which is great.

I've had a productive last few years creating content for sports TV and online, and I am currently looking at expanding my operation overseas.

On the football front I'm still podcasting and blogging. I still see Paul at matches and we have even bought a season ticket to sit together at Brentford's new stadium. Meanwhile, my team are currently going strong at the top of the Championship and are hot tips for promotion. Whether they will actually defy history and take it one step further and get promoted to the Premier League, we will have to wait and see.

Elias is back from Shropshire and is going to school in East London whereas Bella and I are off to the European Championships in the summer, with tickets all the way to the final. We've both got our fingers crossed that they will actually let fans into the stadiums for matches, something that we both miss so badly.

And on the coaching front, I am really looking forward to the season restarting, getting back on the pitch and getting the girls playing football again.

In the longer term, as with every parent, my one main hope for my children is that they remain healthy. I will guide and support them as much as I can, but then eventually, they will have to go it on their own. And at the end of the day, all I can hope for is that they are happy and that they fulfil their dreams.

And I know that sounds like the final few lines from a Hollywood film script, but it's true.

And I really can't ask for any more than that.

Chapter 17:

Living and Growing:
Childbirth Trauma and PTSD

Elliott Rae

I was blessed to have experienced very little trauma during my childhood and early adulthood. I say 'very little' because there was that one hot summer day in a peaceful scenic park, when I was nineteen years old, when I had a gun put to my head after a 'misunderstanding' with some guys I used to go to school with.

Impressionable, excited and slightly naïve boys often get caught up with the wrong people, eager to impress and fit in. I was one of those impressionable, excited and slightly naïve boys. Overly trusting and with very little awareness of consequence, I was the mutual connection between two groups who didn't much like each other. And I almost paid the ultimate price for it.

That season changed my life and I still think about it to this day. Not so much the actual incident, but the aftermath. The experience of shock, the replaying of events in my mind over and over again, the isolation, the stress, the support my cousin Jordan gave me, the huge dent in my pride, the deliberation about how to respond and ultimately, acceptance. There's something about going through such an extreme life-threatening incident that either makes you fight or take flight. I chose to fight that day, but later I fought through self-exploration and self-reflection. This allowed me to grow from a person who was somewhat floating through life, to a more focused and determined individual. That season has helped me to know myself more, to understand the fragility of life. Ironically, we sometimes learn the best life lessons from our most painful experiences and, with the privilege of time, I can look back at that period with gratitude. Unwittingly, even though I have never fully processed those events, it helped me prepare for the next traumatic experience that I was to go through.

My upbringing was well balanced. I grew up in West London in an area between Wembley and Ealing that had just the right mix of everything. This means I can generally find something in common with most people. The Working and Middle Classes seemed to coexist. As did people from Black, White and Asian backgrounds. Looking back, I really do appreciate the decisions my parents made. They came to London from the Caribbean in the sixties and built a life for me and my sister, sacrificing their own self-interests along the way so we could enjoy some Reebok Classics and Saturday School tuition.

My solid home foundation meant that the expectation of academic success and hard work was paired with the trust and freedom that led me to attend many parties and raves as a young teenager. Growing up, I was absolved of most responsibility, protected by the naivety of youth. My father was, and is, an honest and hard-working man. Coming from the sunny Caribbean Island of Grenada to the UK in the sixties, he and my mother had high expectations for me and my sister. Hard work was non-negotiable. He was keen that I took advantage of the opportunities he didn't have growing up. I remain eternally grateful for my parents' sacrifices and I am lucky to have a positive reference of family which has set the blueprint for my own parenting style.

The sharp turn my life took on that summer's day was the first time I would really begin to understand how it feels to get stuck in your own head and question whether you are cut out for dealing with life's adversities. When events take an unexpected turn and we relinquish control, we can feel like passengers in our own lives – like watching a film on the sofa, only that we are the lead character heading for a not-so-happy ending. I remember at the time I was listening to 'The Life' by Styles P on repeat as the shock stitched into my psyche. It was my soundtrack to the season and a way to drown out the noise of my head processing the events. Even now, music is my go-to for encouragement and support, a way to make space in my head and a welcome distraction from the curveballs of a life lived.

***

My twenties were eventful – full of travelling, music and business ventures. I spent a few years working with young people in North West London, using music production to engage on wider topics such as self-esteem and gang violence. Those were some of the most rewarding years of my life.

Soneni and I met when we were both in our mid-twenties. She is one of the most talented and kind-hearted people that I have ever met. We grew together through our shared love of music. We even went on to form a band together, playing afro-soulful music as 'Soneni and The Soul'. As you've probably guessed from the name, Soneni was the lead singer and songwriter while I took care of production and played the bass guitar. I knew pretty much straight away that I was going to marry her. By the age of thirty-one, a year after our wedding, I was ready to be a dad. I was the male version of broody. We had a plan to go on as many holidays as possible in one year before we started trying for a baby. Zimbabwe, Ibiza and Madrid all preceded our trip to Lisbon which marked our final holiday together as a twosome. I remember feeling incredibly excited to get back home and start building our family. I was ready.

We were blessed to conceive easily and the pregnancy was smooth sailing for the most part. The scans put my heart in my mouth, but everything was ticking along, so we focused our efforts on getting our flat ready and researching every possible baby product that we could find. We also took hypnobirthing classes each week. Everything was seemingly going fine, until we received a letter following a test Soneni had after telling the midwife that she had been feeling discomfort. The letter was very matter-of-fact with little acknowledgement of the emotional distress and confusion the news may have on already anxious parents-to-be. It said something along the lines of 'you have an infection which could affect the baby's health and you'll need intravenous antibiotics during labour'. The infection was called Group B Streptococcus, or GBS for short. We had never heard of it. The delivery of the letter, and accompanying pamphlet, was so nonchalant you would think it was a note to tell us about a new restaurant that was opening nearby. This definitely added to our anxiety, being told something so serious in a short letter in the post. So, as most expectant parents do, we went into research overdrive and immediately booked a midwife appointment to help relieve our fears.

GBS is a bacteria carried by 20-25% of women and usually shows no symptoms or side effects. However, the bacteria can be passed on to the baby around birth and can have devastating effects. One in sixteen babies infected with GBS will die. GBS can also cause meningitis and half of the babies who survive GBS meningitis will be left with a long-term disability, like deafness or cerebral palsy. If you are lucky enough to have identified GBS during pregnancy, the mother will be given intravenous antibiotics during labour. These antibiotics reduce the chance of a newborn baby falling ill with GBS by 85-90%, but even with these measures in place, in the UK, two babies every day develop GBS and one baby per week will die from GBS. GBS is not routinely tested for but you can pay a small fee to be tested privately.

As most parents will know, those two weeks leading up to the due date is a time of intense anticipation. We prayed and looked to the birth with positivity and excitement – after all, they had identified the infection and were confident that the antibiotics would mean everything would be OK. I felt I was ready to be a dad and, as the due date passed, the realisation that I was going to have my own little family any day now was exciting.

***

My wife's labour started in the early hours of Saturday morning. Contractions began at around 5 a.m. and by 7 a.m. we made our way to the hospital where we met my mother-in-law. When Soneni was 10 cm dilated we were taken from a waiting room to our birthing room, just as the books had predicted. It was lovely, an oasis of calm with a birthing pool and the kind of relaxing music you would hear in a spa echoing on the sound system. I remember it being spacious and quite homely with a friendly midwife to boot. We got chatting to the midwife as she administered the intravenous antibiotics. All was going well. An hour or so later the midwife noticed that my wife's blood pressure and temperature were much higher than was to be expected. Soon after, we had another scare as our baby's heart rate dropped. I have watched many an episode of *Casualty*, but I was still surprised to see how quickly the doctors all rushed in, seemingly coming from nowhere, talking in distinguished medical talk, running tests and agreeing the best way forward. I was slightly alarmed but still felt a sense of calmness. I had heard from many people that a birthing plan is just that, a plan.

Hours went by and we both drew on the hypnobirthing breathing techniques we had practised to keep present and keep calm. I found myself awed over and over again by the woman in front of me. My wife was amazing, and her strength and courage truly came out in the labour ward as I marvelled at her amazing ability to grow a baby and prepare to give birth.

In the early hours of Sunday morning, after twenty-three hours of hard labour and a couple more heart rate scares, our little girl was ready to make an appearance. She was slow coming out so the doctors started to get a bit worried. Eventually they used a ventouse to bring her out.

When our daughter appeared, they laid her on my wife's chest. I waited for my baby girl to cry out, but the room fell silent. She didn't make a sound. With a lurch I realised that there was something seriously wrong. Our little girl was grey in colour and didn't seem to be breathing properly. It's hard to put into words how I felt in this moment, and I would be lying if I said I remember all the details about what was going on in the room. For a few seconds, the world paused.

I was standing behind my wife in a state of helplessness and shock, looking on at my little girl, not sure if she was alive. Suddenly it felt like the start button was pressed again and the world began speeding up. The doctors acted quickly, taking our baby to a side table where they used a tube to suck the fluid from her throat to clear the airwaves. She made a faint sound before they put her in an incubator and announced they were taking her to intensive care. I looked back at Soneni; she was losing a lot of blood so there was another set of doctors gathering around her. I moved to the middle of the room, surrounded by people all busy working, talking and discussing what to do next. But I couldn't hear them, the noise all merged into one wall of sound. I felt like I was watching a movie. I felt like I was watching it all like a fly on the wall, looking down and seeing the events unfold. I couldn't believe this was actually happening, it felt like the moment must belong to somebody else.

'Mr Rae, do you want to stay in the room with your wife or go with your baby to the Intensive Care Unit?' the doctor asked. Still in a daze, I decided to go with our little girl. She had just come into the world and she needed me. So I kissed my wife and told her I'd be back soon.

I raced after two doctors pushing my baby in the incubator through the long white hospital corridors. I was breathing heavily and my head was spinning. I'm sure we passed people in the halls, but they just seemed like shadows in the night. I had an overwhelming sense of helplessness, I felt like a child again. Directionless and in need of someone to take over, I tried to call my mum, but there was no reception in that part of the hospital.

'You need to be strong for your daughter, you are no use like this and you need to be there for her.' These were the words from the doctor who stared me dead in the eyes as she greeted me at the Intensive Care Unit. Those words brought me back. I was no longer watching events taking place like a

CCTV recorder, I was present again and quickly trying to process what had just happened. This was real and my daughter needed me to control myself. There was no time for self-pity in this moment. So I got myself together and kicked into business mode. What had happened? Despite the antibiotics my wife was given during labour, our little girl had contracted the GBS infection. After the letter we received, I had done lots of research about the infection so I knew just how serious it was and what the various different outcomes could be. I looked on as the doctors placed needles and wires in her. Her eyes were shut, she made no noise, our baby seemed oblivious to what was going on – maybe she didn't know she was born yet. I was comforted by the fact that she didn't seem to be in pain, but also haunted by the fact that she didn't seem alive enough to feel the pain either.

A couple of hours passed and the Neonatal Intensive Care Unit (NICU) was getting ready to welcome all the parents in for the day. NICUs give parents the opportunity to have a private consultation with the doctors once a day, so each morning the parents sit in a waiting room and await their turn. That waiting room was a gateway to a world I didn't even know existed, and I couldn't believe the strength of the people I met there. Some parents had babies who had been in the NICU for weeks. The parents were on top of procedures and were there to ensure their baby was getting the treatment they needed. There are loads of babies in a NICU at any one time, and they are there for a variety of different reasons. The majority are premature, but others have serious life-threatening illnesses. I met a couple who had been in the NICU for weeks, their little boy had a heart condition and they were waiting to be transferred to Great Ormond Street. I couldn't believe how they were able to function; they were so strong.

There was something special about that waiting room. A sort of solidarity between complete strangers, all brought together under unexpected circumstances, but with a common purpose. I had a couple of pep talks from some of the other parents, as they echoed the words of the doctor: 'You need to be strong for your family.'

***

I spent Sunday going back and forth between the NICU and my wife's room. Hours passed and in the late evening, Soneni was well enough to visit our daughter. Weak and washed out from the extreme blood loss, she was in a wheelchair, so I helped push her through the hospital and into the NICU. Hospitals can be confusing places, but by this point I knew the route well, even taking shortcuts to make the journey quicker. We were allowed to take our daughter out of the incubator for the first time and I put her on my chest. She opened her eyes – seemingly recognising, for the first time, that she had been born. I will never forget that moment as she tried to reach up to touch my face. Finally, we were all together as a family and it was the best feeling in the world. We took turns holding her and marvelling at her beautiful features, her perfectly formed fingers and toes. Mostly we just gazed at her in wonder. Soon it was time for us to leave the NICU, so we put our little girl back in the incubator. Her tiny hands flailed upwards and it looked just as if she was reaching out to me, begging me to stay. My heart felt like it was being physically squeezed. How could I leave my daughter by herself overnight? I knew, of course, that she would be well cared for, but leaving her alone in a plastic box hooked up to monitors on that very first night of her life was one of the hardest things I have ever had to do in my life. I was heartbroken.

Men and partners weren't allowed to stay in the maternity ward, so I drove home that night. You would think that having been awake for nearly forty-eight hours I would be tired, but the adrenaline was seeing me through. I drove home and put the key into the door. The house was cold. This felt all wrong – I never imagined I would be going home alone that night. I could feel an encroaching sense of loneliness, shock and fear, but I suppressed those feelings. Remembering what the doctor had told me – I had to be strong for my family. I was the man, and I was a father now. My overriding feelings were of urgency and responsibility; I was fully in fight mode.

I spent the next three days going back and forth from home to hospital. Arriving as soon as visitors were allowed in and leaving as late as possible, literally staying until the midwives asked me to leave. But this was tiring and we needed to be together. We were so lucky that on the Wednesday morning a private room in the maternity ward became available. This meant that I could stay overnight, so I packed a few things and we made that room our new home. By this time our little girl was able to stay with us on the ward but she would still need to visit the NICU four times per day for her medication. We had our own room but it was anything but private. Every three hours, and often in between, a doctor or nurse would come bursting through the door to check my wife's blood pressure or summon our daughter for her next round of medication. This happened twenty-four hours a day, so we only ever got about two hours' sleep at any one time.

The three of us lived in that room for another week while family came to visit, bringing food, clean underwear and words of encouragement. I kept sane by listening to music. At that time there was a historic rap battle going on between Chip and Bugzy Malone. This was the beef between a veteran Grime MC and a newcomer; they both set the internet alight by dropping rapid diss tracks. Chip, one of my all-time favourite artists, had just dropped '96 Bars of Revenge' and it was fire. The soundtrack to my panic was soothed by these beats that punctuated my long days and sleepless nights.

We got regular updates from the paediatricians who told us how our little girl was reacting to the medication. The GBS infection was stubborn – one day we would get some good news and then the next it felt like we were back to square one again. I don't remember feeling anything. I think it was my mind's way of protecting me from breaking down, to push it down and away. I was on autopilot and just doing, making sure my family were OK. I didn't have time to cry or think anything but positive thoughts. This was about survival and I had to be strong for my family. I just thought about my wife and my baby girl and putting one foot in front of the other.

On day nine we finally received the news we were hoping for. The infection was significantly decreasing and the doctors were happy that it wouldn't return. We were over the moon but it didn't last long. Out little girl developed a large bump at the back of her head. The mood changed and for the first time the medical staff themselves seemed genuinely worried for us. That afternoon the midwives all gathered to come and clean our room and make us tea. They offered to bring us lunch rather than us go and collect it for ourselves. A new, more senior paediatrician had a meeting with us and explained the situation. We were booked in for an emergency MRI scan in the morning and our worst fear was that the bump on our baby's head could be a tumour.

After keeping all the emotions in, this was the bursting point. We were so tired. I realised that although I had tried to be strong, I couldn't control everything. So I handed control over to God and just hoped for the best. We cried and prayed for hours that night. I cried so much that I wasn't sure where all these tears were coming from, it was like an endless river of emotion pouring out and finally being let loose. After being strong all week, I had no more strength to give. I felt like I was living in a nightmare.

Nagmeh, a midwife we had got to know quite well, joined us in our room and we all prayed together. I'm sure her colleagues must have been wondering where she was, as she was with us for what felt like an hour at least. Our faith became an incredible prop in these moments of fear and confusion.

The next morning, we took our daughter for the MRI scan and we waited for the results back in our room. We prayed again and tried to be positive, trying to not think about all the potential outcomes and what that could mean for the rest of our lives. An hour or so later, the doctor burst through the door and ran into our room. She embraced us both with a massive hug. We had built some strong relationships with some of the NHS staff; they were on the journey with us, so any good news for us was also good news for them. The bump on our little girl's head was just bone structure and nothing to worry about. A wave of relief hit us as we were told that we could finally go home as a family.

***

The NHS often receive a lot of criticism, but I would like to give them a shout out in this instance. The care we received was world class and we are forever grateful for the love and care they showed us. They have one of the most difficult jobs in the world. So please, be kind.

The whole experience brought my wife and me closer together. When you go to the depths of your soul with another human being, you share an experience that only you both can fully understand. We spent the next few months talking a lot, about the events and our feelings. My wife was diagnosed with Postnatal Anxiety from the trauma. This manifested in anxiety about leaving the house and extreme worry about our daughter falling ill again. My wife received counselling for her anxiety as was entirely right. In contrast, no one asked about my own mental health.

I got on with life and tried my best to emotionally move on from the birth experience, although I knew that it was haunting me. Without an outlet, my mind was struggling to process what had happened, and why. I knew the medical reasons as to why, but I was struggling to accept why it had happened to us. To help, I began writing. I started a blog about being a new dad and it very quickly grew to the platform that is now MusicFootballFatherhood. I didn't realise at the time, but just as I needed a space to talk about my experiences as a dad, so did so many other men. I discovered that there is strength and comfort in community. The contributing team grew quickly, and I am proud that MusicFootballFatherhood is now an essential space for fathers to connect, share and grow.

I know now that I never really addressed my feelings around the traumatic birth experience and it all came to a head when my daughter had a severe allergic reaction at eight months old. Just as we seemed to be getting the hang of this parenting stuff, and into some sort of routine and rhythm, we were hit with another bombshell. This brought back all the feelings from the birth and triggered what was eventually diagnosed as Post Traumatic Stress Disorder (PTSD).

I developed insomnia and I couldn't sleep at night, even though I was extremely tired and unproductive in the daytime. I couldn't concentrate at work and I was having flashbacks that were taking me back and evoking feelings of fear and worry. I kept reliving the events and thinking about how much worse it could have been. I've never been much of a worrier, but I couldn't stop thinking about what could have happened. As any father can relate to, your family is your world and the thought of losing them is inconceivable – but I couldn't shake those thoughts from my mind. I would randomly feel overwhelmed with emotion and I was disinterested in the things I would usually find pleasure in. PTSD can be crippling and have a profound effect on your ability to effectively go about your usual day-to-day activities. I found myself struggling at work and at home. I was a shell of myself, and this lasted for a couple of months.

At the time I didn't speak to anyone about how I was feeling, apart from my wife. I hid it all from my friends and colleagues and put a brave face on as much as I could. I didn't want to be judged or seen as weak, or dwelling on something that I should have been over. There was a sense of guilt in it all as, on the face of things, I had the perfect life.

Years later and I have only just started to take the steps to getting professional help. It's become a priority because we will soon be trying for a second child and I'm anxious about the whole process, especially the birth.

A traumatic experience is an incident that causes physical, emotional, spiritual, or psychological harm. Usually memories are filed in a certain part of our brain, the hippocampus. But if we experience a traumatic event, the mind can go into fight or flight mode and the part of the brain that is associated with fear is switched on. This part of our brain is called the amygdala; this is the primitive part of our brain. The traumatic memory can get stuck in the primitive part of the brain, rather than being safely filed away. This can result in the looping of the memory and trigger the feelings of the experience over and over again.

There are two types of treatments that can be used to treat childbirth trauma, helping to process and recover from these specific events. These are trauma-focused cognitive behavioural therapy (CBT) and eye movement desensitisation and reprocessing (EMDR). Trauma-focused CBT is used to focus on thoughts, beliefs and attitudes and how they affect feelings and ultimately, behaviour. The aim is to identify, and change, the negative thinking patterns which can lead to negative emotions and behaviours. EMDR involves making rapid eye movements while recalling a traumatic event. The aim here is to stop difficult memories from causing distress by helping the brain to reprocess them properly.

***

Trauma in childbirth is often something that we think affects only the mother. And of course, women go through all the physical pain, but the emotional and psychological stress can, and does, impact both parents. New mothers and fathers are more likely to experience Postnatal Depression or poor mental health if the birth is a traumatic one.

This is the first time I have written about my birth trauma in such detail and it has helped me to feel more at ease with my own vulnerability, but I must admit that it's not easy. I know that some people will read this and think that it's not the right thing to do; they question how much of a 'man' I am. And I suspect this is a big part of the reason as to why lots of men don't ever open up. But for me, the positives will always outweigh the negative responses from the small minority. I know I'm not alone when I say that hiding and suppressing feelings can eat away at you, so I'm truly grateful for my own growth and the opportunities I've had to share my experiences.

As men, we don't talk enough about how the things we have been through have impacted us. And if we don't talk enough about how we feel, then we don't even know how we feel because we can't be honest with ourselves. Through my experiences, I have learned that talking is the best thing to do. I have learned that I need to be OK with expressing myself and see it as a strength rather than a weakness. I have also learned that we shouldn't be afraid to seek professional help. Looking back, it would have helped to have seen a doctor or therapist after we got back from the hospital. I think, slowly, this conversation is changing and perceptions are shifting as conversations open around gender roles. Recently there has been a new law introduced to screen the partner of a mother who has experienced Postnatal Depression. This is a great step in the right direction. But it strikes me that more could be done faster if men only learned to speak out. To recognise when they need help and to ask for a raft when or if they are drowning.

My birth trauma experience, and the years that have followed, have given me a renewed sense of appreciation for life, and my passion for the things I love has deepened. I am now much more aware of the fragility of human life and I think that has made me value my time on earth even more. This has made my life a more wholesome experience as I've learned that it's OK to feel all the feels, and talk about them.

My daughter is now a lively and energetic five-year-old who has completely transformed my life. I love her so much and I grow prouder of her each day. She's so clever, inquisitive and kind. Our little girl has inherited her parents' passion for music and you'll often find us dancing and singing at home in the living room; she even teaches us a few moves! I knew that becoming a father would be life-changing but I could never have predicted the impact it would have on my emotional, spiritual and physical being. Becoming a father opened up a whole part of me that I never even knew existed. And through my journey of sharing my experiences and connecting with other dads, I've been opened up to a whole new world.

Chapter 18:

Faith and Fatherhood:
How Finding Faith Shaped My Identity, Parenting and Life

Cal-I Jonel

Who Am I?

I'm Cal-I ... and I love my name (*exhale*). I used to dislike it with a passion. It wasn't your regular name: Steven, James, Michael. It was *so* different...
Cal-I.

Yes, with a hyphen, and the 'I' *has* to be a capital, according to my parents! Now, of course, I appreciate its uniqueness, but growing up, it made me feel so different to everybody else; I didn't want to be different when I was a child. This would become my story growing up in East London as a working class, third-generation Caribbean-British male.

My parents, both Jamaican, were God-conscious and 'roots-y'. I was raised with wholesome values and a real heart for showing kindness to others. My parents were loving, caring and nurturing. I had a pretty decent moral compass – knowing right from wrong – and besides breaking the odd plant pot or glass dish, I kept myself out of trouble and away from the rod, for the most part!

I came from humble beginnings. For the first eight years of my life I shared a room with my two older sisters in a two-bed flat with our parents on Retreat Place estate in Hackney. We played outside our apartment block until Mum called us in for our corned beef with rice or Saturday soup. The finer things in life were a privilege and a luxury (McDonald's was a rare treat, if ever!). My siblings and I knew no different so we were cool. Life wasn't easy but we were provided for. Moving higher up the social stratum wasn't even a thought; we really didn't know what we were missing.

I grew up in a traditional household of sorts. Mum, a gifted tailor and dressmaker, kept the ship moving day to day; she clothed, fed and watered us whilst keeping us in line. Dad was a calm and solid source of strength who was called upon to handle the *big jobs* (including the big discipline if I or my siblings ever transgressed too far!). Dad would often come home late from work to find us already in bed. He was an active member within the local Hackney community and I recall countless visits to the local community centre on Arcola street where he worked. It would always be filled with members of the Caribbean community and the sound of loud discussions over a game of dominoes, quiet gatherings in a meeting suite and food cooking in the kitchen for an event happening the very same night. It was a cultural hub and was the backdrop to my weekends and school holidays for the first ten years of my childhood.

Life was good, and I was a real Hackney boy. Hackney was my hometown and I still feel the same way to this day. Then one day, we upped and moved to Essex. I changed school and then changed school again and before I knew it, Ilford town centre would become the soundtrack to my step. My family finally moved to a rented three-bedroom house in Ilford. This is where the rest of my youth played out.

Despite the upheaval from life as I knew it in Hackney, home was always a safe space for me. Though the Muirhead household had its ups and downs, it was filled with love, care and bundles of laughter.

A Fractured Sense of Self

Despite my sense of security at home, my sense of personal identity was somewhat fractured. It's only in hindsight I realise that the move from Hackney to Essex was a significant shift in culture and class that I couldn't have articulated at the tender age of ten. I was formed and shaped in the eighties and nineties – a time when preconceived and often misguided notions of what it meant to be 'black', male and Caribbean were rampant and the black-British experience was largely misunderstood by many institutions. I had a sense of African and Caribbean heritage (more so Caribbean), but this was never reflected at the schools I attended in Essex. My 'Caribbean-ness' didn't fit my daily context, my friendship groups or cultural experiences. I had a diverse group of friends but I was acutely aware that I was amongst the minority culturally and socially. By this point, my dad was working more than one job to make ends meet. When friends would ask, 'What does your dad do?' I'd simply curate a version of my dad's work that sounded impressive. I wasn't used to this question. The culture was different here. Most of my friends had home-owner parents and could afford the school trips abroad. I didn't attend a single one, understandably. My parents would often use the line, 'You can't travel, because you are asthmatic.' I now know that was a euphemism for, 'We don't have the money.'

This period in my life was strange; I was now exposed to opportunities I'd not seen before. I was surrounded by more people who did not look like me or relate to my socio-economic standing. Even some of my closest black friends were fairly middle class.

After I began attending secondary school, I witnessed several young black males within my peer group struggle to navigate their way through social circles and the school system for a number of reasons. Largely, they struggled to integrate and follow the status quo, which was something I became well versed in doing. Consequently, I suppressed any notion of cultural heritage in exchange for a more neutral and pluralistic version of popular youth culture that could work seamlessly within my friendship groups.

With this, came the desire to fit in and be *liked*. I was never a 'roadman' but my glimpse into the experiences of family and close family friends helped me to become a little streetwise. Neither was I the typical 'boffin', but I could identify with a few *neeks* and *geeks* because I enjoyed school and tried hard to be a 'good' student. I wasn't the top athlete, but I could hold my own with a couple of lads on the basketball court and running track. I was, however, very creative and did connect very well with the artistic clique. I rapidly became known for my singing, acting and comedy impersonations of teachers in the school, even by staff members, who would stop me in the corridor for a quick laugh at my latest teacher impersonation. Despite this, I was still somewhat of an 'all things, to all men' type of guy; a chameleon of sorts. I didn't really know who I was.

I did well at the end of my GCSEs and was excited to progress to the next phase of my educational journey, though after a heated discussion with my dad, I was strongly encouraged to study Computing and Business Studies and any other subject that would lead to a job. I wasn't happy about it so I secretly chose Drama and Theatre Studies and struggled through my other subjects.

At sixteen I landed my first job at a local Londis grocery store and interestingly, have stayed in employment ever since. This job paid me £1 an hour. My dad agreed it would teach me the value of hard work, which it did. Though, I remember the moments of embarrassment I felt seeing my friends working at Tesco and JD Sports whilst I mopped floors and cleaned up dead mice in the stockroom for fun.

I worked my second job as a cleaner, earning a little more money but waking up at 4 a.m. for a 6 a.m. to 8 a.m. shift before college. I think I was asleep half the time during my Computing and Business Studies classes, but regular impersonations of teachers kept my tutors laughing, me well liked and them off of my back. I'd love to say it all worked out with my A levels, but it didn't. I passed Drama and Theatre Studies with flying colours and massively underachieved in my other subjects. I didn't tell my parents the day I went to pick up my results. To this day, we have never discussed my grades. I was deeply embarrassed. Whilst there was a desire to see my siblings and me do well in school, the priority was to see us clothed, fed and safe. Subsequently, this meant I got away with coasting and failing my A level studies without anyone batting an eyelid; it's easier to hide when amongst a group of six brothers and sisters. Some might even call it Middle Child Syndrome! At this point in my life, I'm seventeen, with no real idea of what I want to do with my life and my self-esteem is in tatters. I was starting to see the glass ceiling.

With no stable sense of core identity, what emerged was the personality of a young black male who was talented, popular and well liked but also insecure and afraid of leadership. I'd spent so many years trying to please other people that I hadn't developed my own personal convictions about anything, or any sense of vision for my own life. In fact, I struggled to see myself as a leader of any sort growing up despite wanting to do something significant with my life; it felt too far removed from my reality. I didn't see enough leaders who looked like me and I was fundamentally afraid of the future by the time I transitioned to my early twenties. I didn't foresee a future where I would become a successful man let alone a husband and father.

Looking back, I realise how 'on the fence' I was as a teen. I'd always made a conscious effort to fit in and be *different* from the seemingly disaffected young black males in my peer group; this came with a price. I had spent so many of my teen years trying to please and avoid offending everyone else (friends, teachers and family members alike) that I had suppressed my desire to take risks. I stayed in a box, censored myself and lived a very 'safe' existence.

Church: The Training Ground

Amidst the not so positive, my silver lining was regularly attending my local church. I began attending a Pentecostal church at the age of twelve; my siblings and I were sent to Sunday school to offer my parents some light relief following a late night out. What was great about church was the strong sense of community and opportunity to learn about and develop a relationship with God. It soon became my *church family* and I decided to become a Christian when I was thirteen. Church was a priceless training ground for me and presented opportunities for me to fill some of the identity gaps that had left me with low self-esteem for so long. I was invited to lead and hold positions of responsibility, which fostered a stronger sense of personal identity, enabling me to develop greater self-esteem. Most importantly, this was a context where I did see more examples of black male and female leadership and a sense of African and Caribbean culture, however this was firmly rooted within a primarily church-based context. Unfortunately for me, this context didn't necessarily help me to understand how to navigate the world as a young black male with cultural confidence. Whilst I gained a significant amount of confidence from a place of spirituality, which I'm tremendously grateful for, what I was also yearning for was a dose of cultural identity and heritage to balance the scales and provide me with a more well-rounded sense of who I was. Nonetheless, being a part of a church community fulfilled my human need for significance as a teen and young adult.

The Leader Within

I grew to understand *hope* and *faith* more profoundly as my relationship with God deepened. It wasn't until I was in my late teens that I began paying more attention to the life of Jesus and how his style of leadership was fundamentally through his acts of service; it was at this point that I began to understand the true spirit of leadership. This discovery, coupled with my growing interest in the literary works of the late Myles Munroe was a game-changer. In 2006, I had an awakening! I'd been reading a selection of Myles Munroe books about leadership and masculinity (namely, *Understanding the Purpose and Power of Men* and *The Spirit of Leadership*) which awoke a confidence and boldness in me I had not experienced in my twenty-three years on earth. I understood that leadership was inherently linked to my identity in God the creator. The idea of leadership no longer terrified me because I understood that I was intrinsically born with leadership qualities. It was my birthmark, my inheritance, an innate part of who I was and am. For the first time in my life I believed I was a leader. It was my right, my responsibility and my duty. My faith became a fundamental ingredient in helping me to rise above the gravel of low self-esteem, self-doubt and negative self-perception I'd been buried beneath for so long. I understood who I was by understanding who had created me. My life took on a whole new sense of purpose. It was now about, as Munroe would often write, *living full and dying empty*; leaving no stone unturned; pouring out everything in service to the earth before we reach our grave. This helped me to understand my life through purpose. For the first time ever I was able to see my life beyond myself and my immediate surroundings.

Faith Activated

I began to make changes. I left my job in supermarket retail to pursue a career in teaching; I asked my best friend for her hand in marriage and purchased my first property, all at the age of twenty-four, with very little savings at the time. We most certainly exercised faith to achieve this!

Fast forward to four years later, when we were expecting our first child, I honestly didn't feel fazed: not because I had it all figured out, but because *I was born to do this*. This responsibility was a *calling* more than it was a role, title or personal decision. Amidst any fear or trepidation, I had a perfect peace (in God) that surpassed all human understanding. I was born for leadership, and fatherhood for me, was the ultimate leadership calling I could have ever realised. It was time to pour into and serve my children.

The popular Bible verse from **James 2:26**[1] states that, *'For as the body without the spirit is dead, so faith without works is dead also.'* This verse is a constant reminder to me that faith in Christ should result in good work. For so many years I had no reference point, little hope and a heart full of fear.

---

1 Scripture taken from the New King James Version®. Copyright © 1982 by Thomas Nelson. Used by permission. All rights reserved.

Having faith in God provided me with a new blueprint for my life. My role as a husband and father came from a heart which had been transformed (through faith) by God.

Family

My wife and I now parent two children: my daughter Ebony-Grace, aged eight and my son Elijah, aged six. They are eighteen months apart so the first twelve months was pretty intense but *so* worth it. They've grown together wonderfully and I'm constantly reminded how much my faith is on direct display each and every day through my actions. This is the faith that I profess has changed my life, which I demonstrate every day to my children.

For instance, the Bible declares in **Mark 10:8-9**[2]: *'and the two shall become one flesh"; so then they are no longer two, but one flesh. Therefore what God has joined together, let not man separate.'*

This to me establishes my marriage as a calling. When I declared my vows to my wife, it wasn't simply out of my love for her, but my commitment to the institution of marriage under God. I fundamentally believe that this is the foundation in which I am empowered to raise my children in the best way possible. Waking up and saying, 'yes' is a decision I make each and every day irrespective of how I am feeling. It comes from a place of faith in the principles of God.

It's now a daily challenge for my wife and me to help our children understand that everything they do should come from a place of faith. At home we spend time in devotion where we will converse, sing songs of praise and discuss Bible scriptures after dinner. We don't always manage to do it! However, it's most certainly become a feature within our household and our children are always keen to take the lead and pray for us. Elijah likes to pray for us and share an encouraging word whilst Ebony-Grace happily shares a Bible verse and leads us in song. We have truly had some of our most profound and teachable moments when we have allowed the children to take the lead during our family devotion. This is how it should be. We truly feel we are giving our children a stable sense of who they are based on their faith and their cultural heritage; a far more stable foundation than the social norms that shaped me as a child. I didn't have the faith-based traditions in my home growing up. In fact, there were times when my commitments at church and

2 Scripture taken from the New King James Version®. Copyright © 1982 by Thomas Nelson. Used by permission. All rights reserved.

the demands from my family clashed. But I acknowledge how fundamental my faith has been in helping me to understand who I was when I was at my lowest point of self-esteem.

Fundamentally, faith has enabled me to understand that my wife and children are my first ministry. The first group of people that I serve, nurture and cultivate. That said, we strive to keep our relationship with God at the centre of everything we do and every decision we make as husband and wife, parents and human beings.

Faith, Fatherhood and Career

Over the years, faith has continued to play a key role in the decisions I make for the benefit of my family. When I decided to leave a twelve-year career in teaching and middle leadership along with a decent five-figure salary, it invited some scepticism and bemusement. Culturally, this is not what *men* do. Financially, this is not what parents can *afford to* do. Don't get me wrong, it wasn't an easy decision to make, and took me four years to wrap my head around the idea of leaving my Monday to Friday grind and stable income.

It was clear that I'd reached a stage in my life of relatively decent success as a professional. I was a successful teacher and middle manager. I was a family man, with an amazing wife and two wonderful children. Nonetheless, I didn't feel as though I was enjoying it. There were times when I was enduring each day with the stresses and struggles of a super busy life with multiple responsibilities and no time to stop and be a present father and husband. I'd become unwell, suffering from stress, ongoing back problems and headaches and felt as though I was living for the next half-term break! I was missing the moments with my children, and I wasn't happy with the way things were. My conviction wouldn't allow me to live like this for much longer.

To some, I seemingly had it all, but to me, I was aware I'd become comfortable, safe and complacent, again. This wasn't the version of fatherhood I wanted to give to my children. I'd seen my mum and dad work so hard over the years to provide for us all, and I'd witnessed our family mealtimes become smaller in number as gathering around the table to break bread and converse was no longer a priority. I didn't want this to become a reality for my family. Despite this, I was tragically living a version of fatherhood I thought I'd worked so hard to avoid. I wanted to nurture my children by remaining as present as I could and it was clear that I could only do this if I sacrificed money to gain my time back.

Leaving teaching was a difficult choice. I had to cling to my faith in order to do so; **Proverbs 3:5-6**[3] teaches us to: 'Trust in the LORD with all your heart, And lean not on your own understanding; In all your ways acknowledge Him, And He shall direct your paths.' This verse challenges me daily and most certainly gave me impetus when I finally made the move out of the education sector to a life of freelance and part-time study. In 2018, I left my job as an experienced and well-paid practitioner and took the plunge to go back and study part-time at an acting school. I'd always wanted to pursue a career as a performer and this was my opportunity. No parents to dissuade me; it was my choice. I wanted my children to witness me pursuing my passion in their lifetime. Did I feel insecure – yes! Especially on my first day at drama school as the oldest student in the room. Nonetheless, I was grateful to be doing what I genuinely loved for the first time in my life. I trained as an actor for a year before signing with an agent and landing a role in the West End and making my professional West End debut in 2020, six weeks before the Covid-19 pandemic hit. But, that's a story for another chapter...

To date, I've spent more time with my children than I could ever have imagined. Taking a step back from the hustle and bustle has given me the opportunity to really *see* my children and who they truly are. Discovering their love for performing arts and creativity and fully appreciating their love for imaginative play, formed the inspiration behind the performing arts provision my wife and I run (Love Create). It is a service that provides literacy through arts workshops for children aged five to eleven. This is our faith in action: trusting wholeheartedly that God has placed these two children specifically in our care because no one else could raise them in the way that we could. We are their first teachers, mentors and guardians.

Faith, Fatherhood and School

Choosing any school for our children was always going to be a challenging decision. Our desire was to place them in an environment that would stimulate godly values and principles away from home. We finally decided to send them to a Christian school. Even still, perhaps one of the boldest moves regarding their schooling has been our decision to flexi-school. We currently have the time, skill set, in-house resources and the desire to have a greater stake in the education our children receive. Not to replace, much rather, to complement

---

3 Scripture taken from the New King James Version®. Copyright © 1982 by Thomas Nelson. Used by permission. All rights reserved.

the work their school does for the greater good of our children. This venture is new and exciting territory for us.

Once a week my wife and I homeschool our children with the aim of playing an even more significant role in nurturing their gifts and talents. This has also given us more time and freedom to grow in unity and fellowship as a family. All of the aforementioned comes from a place of faith, believing that we are called to play an even greater role in our children's lives than we are often able to due to the pressures and constraints of traditional work patterns and pressures of life.

As far as possible, my desire is that my children will avoid the self-esteem issues I carried around as a young man. I want to help them to understand the very 360-degree nature of their identity, undergirded by faith. Parenting through faith is showing our children how our sense of identity is not defined by a socially constructed title or role. Their identity is all of the things, people and experiences that make up who they are, ultimately validated by our faith and sourced by God the creator. I'm challenged daily to keep faith at the core of all we do; interconnected with every aspect of who we are. Not excluded from, not at war with but totally informing our sense of ethnicity, esteem, cultural heritage, character and purpose. It all comes from a place of faith and relationship with God – that's how we teach our children to make sense of the world around them.

I grew up in a time when my understanding of cultural heritage and social mobility was limited to my immediate surroundings. Though I grew up in a loving home with nurture and care, I could not see a life beyond my immediate social circumstances. Faith changed this reality for me and it is this blueprint I desire to pass on to my children.

Some may argue that faith isn't needed to achieve these things, however, faith has helped my family to develop the power of habit and discipline, a constant striving to be better than the day before. Faith has encouraged us to keep working at life, to continue investing in our marriage so that we can continue to convey a healthy model to our children. Faith says, when our patience wears thin, to stop and empathise; when we are hurt, forgive and move forward; when we are wrong, it is our duty to say sorry. Faith reminds us to teach our children that when they go to school, they are there to make a positive contribution and difference in their community; to be *the salt and the light* (**Matthew 5:13**). Faith reminds us to encourage our children to lead and not to follow, to stand up for what they believe in and to balance love and humility with wisdom and boldness. And, though things do not always go the way we want them to go, faith encourages us to push forward when faced with life's great tests and trials. And this is what we teach our children.

Faith, Parenthood and Legacy

Ultimately, parenthood is bigger than us. It's our *duty* to nurture the leaders of tomorrow. Leaders who are secure, wise, loving and resilient human beings with integrity. By God's grace our children are the legacy we will leave behind when we are gone. So, our challenge today is to train up our children in the way of the Lord so that when they grow older, they will not depart from it (**Proverbs 22:6**).

Chapter 19:

Exploring and Embracing the Unconventional: Co-parenting and Raising Happy Kids as a Divorced Dad

Toby Hazlewood

My name is Toby Hazlewood and of the many roles I hold in life, the one that defines me most significantly and provides the greatest rewards is being a DAD. I was relatively young when I first became a father – just 23 when my first daughter was born in the year 2000. Fatherhood has dominated much of my adult life and everything else that I do fits in around that, has been influenced by it or is done in a bid to enable me to be the best dad that I can be.

I was born in Cambridge and until leaving for University in Nottingham at the age of eighteen, grew up in East Anglia. I consider myself extremely lucky to have grown up in a close, loving and supportive family. My parents were each other's first loves and together with my younger sister I grew up in a happy home, living next door to my paternal grandparents. I reflect on a childhood that was fundamentally happy and settled, and I suppose that this served to shape my intentions about the sort of family I'd aspire to create in later life. I guess it's strange then that things took a very different path.

Roll forwards a few years and I had finished university and started my first job in the IT industry. With the new millennium fast approaching I felt excited and optimistic about life.

My girlfriend and I had only been together for about three months when our daughter was conceived. We'd met through my sister who was studying on the same course as she was. It wasn't the ideal start to a relationship in retrospect, and if she hadn't fallen pregnant, I don't know whether we would have stayed together. That said, I'm certain we would have remained good friends. Nonetheless, armed with the spirit of indomitability and a determination to make things work, we set up home together in Manchester (where she was from – far away from where I'd grown up). We did as all expectant parents do and prepared ourselves for the arrival of our child, buying every product and gadget that seemed essential for sustaining a baby and bracing ourselves in anticipation of our lives changing for good.

As parenthood approached, life felt like something of a blur. I was barely a year into my career in IT consultancy and having initially enjoyed the feeling of having abundant money after years as a student, I now worried about the pressure of having to support a family of three. I guess it was difficult for family and friends to get used to the idea too and it initially put an unwelcome strain on some of those relationships.

To further compound difficulties, in the wake of the dot-com boom I was made redundant from my first job during the pregnancy, which brought about incredible stress and upset for us both. Thankfully, I found a new job almost immediately, such was the job market in those days. I often reflect that the redundancy payment actually set us up for the next few years – something for which I'm immensely grateful.

While the pregnancy was a stressful period for all involved, most of all for my then-girlfriend, by the time the baby was due everyone had largely resolved their differences and we all eagerly awaited the new arrival.

Our daughter was born just after the turn of the millennium and we both did the best we could to bring up a happy, confident and loved child. It was a struggle at times but immensely rewarding too.

The rigours of being a parent to a newborn were challenging, but we seemed to take them in our stride. I found myself more able than my partner to cope with the sleepless nights, and immediately found a strength of bond with my daughter that I could never have anticipated. After many years of parenting, I can say with rose-tinted certainty that the years of looking after a newborn were the easiest to deal with. I don't know if that's a popular viewpoint!

We moved forwards buying a house, renovating it, then buying another. In 2003 we got married, and our second daughter was born later that year.

By now parenting was a significant part of our lives. Two kids under the age of five meant that we had our hands full. By now we were living on a quiet road with a lot of young families, which meant that our situation seemed very much the norm. In fact, at some point one of the parents on our street figured that there'd been a child born on the road every month for the last eighteen months. It was enough for our local TV news channel to feature our story as a public-interest piece.

There were always playgroups to go to, and opportunities for parents to gather for coffee and play dates. It helped keep the kids entertained and it also gave opportunities for various dads' or mums' nights out too, which helped maintain balance for us. On reflection, I now see how important and helpful that was, particularly at points later on when it was lacking and we missed the support.

Life continued in the same vein for a couple of years, but with such a 'grown-up' existence, both my wife and I probably started to feel like we'd grown up a bit too quickly and too early on. We were both in our mid- to late twenties but had a life that seemed more befitting to those in their thirties – indeed many of our friends and neighbours were a little older than us.

At the end of summer 2005 we reached the reluctant but mutual conclusion that our marriage was over. There were no catastrophic events as such, and neither of us blamed the other. We both acknowledged we'd just got together too young, had kids at an early age and our relationship had burnt out after six years together. We'd punctuated our time together with many momentous events which had distracted us from the fact that we simply weren't happy together or in ourselves. To part while we were still relatively young (I was thirty when we eventually sold and moved out of our home) seemed the responsible choice to give us both the chance of a happy life.

At the forefront of our minds was a desire to limit the effects of our parting on our daughters. We were jointly resolved that we wanted to each play an active role in raising them even though we were no longer together. Our relationship with each other was over as a couple but our relationship as parents to our girls would remain for all time, whether we chose to honour that or not. To do so seemed instinctive and logical to us both.

When we first parted, the girls were aged six and two, so it seemed sensible that they'd initially live for the majority of the time with their mum, due to being so young. I was keen to maintain an active and regular role in their lives as well, and resolved to do whatever it took to maintain my place in their world. I initially moved back down south, this time to Wiltshire to be near my sister (who would provide the emotional support that was much needed to heal from the divorce), but I used to drive back to Manchester to collect the girls for three weekends in four so I could spend time with them, as much as was humanly possible. Driving an average of 2000 miles each month seemed a small price to pay to see them regularly.

Leaving work early on a Friday, I had my iPod for company and regularly cycled through the 1000 or so songs on it. I bought a cheap set of screens and a DVD player for the car, so that when the kids were with me, I could keep them entertained through the long journeys and occasional traffic jams. It was by no means quality time, seeing them for hours of our precious weekends together in the rear-view mirror of my car, but it was still good to be around them and maintain regular contact. They were still very young and would sleep for much of the journey to my house – I used to love carrying them in from the car, asleep on a Friday night, and our weekends would start in earnest on Saturday mornings.

This rhythm continued for about eighteen months.

It's worth noting at this stage that my ex and I had parted as amicably as was possible but we still had differences, resentments and anger towards each other. I think that's inevitable in the breakdown of any relationship. Crucially though, we were each resolved to separate this from any discussions and arrangements regarding our daughters, and followed this principle from the very beginning of our lives apart. I can understand for many divorcing couples that this will be harder to accomplish, but I'd still contend that all should aspire to a similar set-up If a third party or mediator is required to make it work, then so be it.

It probably also helped that our families were all encouraging of us putting the kids' needs to the fore – I don't doubt that they were each keen to ensure that they could continue to play a part in the kids' lives too. I suspect that this side of things often gets neglected in custody arrangements around divorce, certainly falling some way down the priority order. It's a shame, as I feel our kids have benefited from the ongoing relationships they've enjoyed with grandparents, aunts, uncles and cousins on both sides of the family. That's another thing for which I feel blessed.

Fundamentally, as we parted and in the years that followed, we saw it that our kids had done nothing to deserve the parting of their parents and we felt it was our mutual duty to put their needs first. For this reason, we confined discussions about them and their lives from any other conversations, for example, those regarding money.

We never resorted to courts to agree financial terms of our settlement – it seemed common sense that I would provide financial support to my ex to bring equilibrium to our lives, and to reflect that she was supporting the kids for the majority of the time. She in turn enabled as much visitation and custody as I wanted, recognising that my involvement was for the benefit of the girls.

Equity and equality were fundamental to how we lived and to how we've continued to approach parenting – that, and the principle of guiding all decisions by what is in the best interests of our girls.

When we first parted, we had gone to lengths to agree a unified and consistent message regarding our reasons for parting, which we shared with the kids to help them understand the forthcoming change to their world. I doubt, in truth, that the message really sank in, certainly for our youngest daughter, but it outlined principles that have remained true to this day.

We wanted to emphasise that life would change in a number of key ways but in many others would remain just the same:

- We would no longer all be living together in the same home at the same time.
- The kids were still loved equally by us both and had no reason to feel like anything *had* changed or *would* change in that regard in the future.
- While they would initially be apart from one or other of us for a few days at a time, they could always speak to the other parent as and when they wanted to.
- They would still see all their grandparents, aunts, uncles and cousins on both sides of the family.
- They could always talk with either of us about what was happening, how they were feeling and so on and we'd do what we could to answer their questions honestly.

I felt a little helpless as a parent in trying to deliver such messages to kids who were so young. My instinct as a father was to feel like a failure. I'd felt since their birth that my biggest responsibility was to protect them from harm and from feelings of hurt and sadness, yet we were throwing them into uncertainty and chaos.

In spite of how I felt, I was resolute that I'd stick by the message we'd given them and determined that I wouldn't lose my place in their childhood. I'm proud to say that we've both remained consistent in delivering against those promises to this day (our daughters are both now legal adults, one at university and the other likely to head off in the near future too).

After I first moved away, adjusting was really hard. I'd always been an active and hands-on father, I did the night-time feeds and had always relished the challenges of parenting babies and toddlers. In truth, I suspect I coped better with young kids than I have more recently as they've progressed through school and the teenage years!

To be separated from them for so much time, even though I saw them often, was incredibly painful. It wasn't helped by the inevitable harrowing phone calls in the early days after parting, when my eldest daughter would call me in tears. She couldn't come to terms with why things had changed, and didn't understand why we couldn't all still live together. She missed me, of course, but I think she also missed the structure that had been lost in her life. I wondered how her younger sister processed it too. She's grown up without any living memory of us all being together as a family unit before divorce and I guess it's always been the norm for her. Nonetheless, it's hard to contemplate whether she was suffering or not at the time, or even aware of what was going on.

I always did what I could to answer the kids' questions honestly and to minimise the impacts of our parting upon them, and their mum did the same. We assured them that we both loved them the same and that we were both there for them however and whenever they needed us.

We went to lengths to demonstrate through our actions that we were both still their parents and jointly attended events at school – plays, assemblies and so on. This was difficult in the early days due to me living further away, but it has remained a feature of our joint parenting throughout. When my eldest daughter turned eighteen, we all got together to celebrate her birthday – such celebrations have always been treated as a joint family event.

We made sure there were never raised voices or visible signs of discord or anger between us. It was difficult at times and, while our parting was amicable, there was still emotional pain that we each needed to process. We were careful to ensure that our girls were shielded from any of this and have never used them as go-betweens, to convey messages or to act as intermediaries between us in any way.

All that time spent driving during those first few months gave me a lot of opportunities to think and reflect. The period reaffirmed just how much I wanted to be an active father to the girls, and the lengths I'd go to in order to maintain that contact.

Around eighteen months after parting, I was tired of the endless driving and had developed bad knee and back pain from the hours spent behind the wheel. The cost of the miles and of keeping my car on the road were becoming problematic too, and I'd amassed nine points on my driving licence from careless speeding offences. The girls had become used to it but it was clear that the travel was a challenge for them too, as much as it brought us together.

It was at this point that my ex first proposed the idea of changing our arrangement and moving to equal co-parenting.

The premise was that I'd find a new home and job back in Manchester where my ex had remained and where the girls were now at school. We'd then each take on 50% of the custody of our daughters with them moving between us and living in each home for alternate weeks. In line with us each sustaining and supporting the kids equally, we also agreed that I'd no longer make a payment of financial support to her. She'd by now established a good career for herself and our incomes were broadly equal. Had this not been the case, perhaps there would have been a case for a monthly payment of support between us, but this wasn't deemed necessary. We also agreed that any extraordinary payments (such as for school trips, sports clubs and the like) would be split and funded by us equally. The finances were just one aspect of it, of course, but these were the terms of the agreement as discussed.

Having agreed to the idea, I started looking for a new job and somewhere to live close to the girls' school. In what seemed like a blessing from fate, I found a house and secured a better-paid job with relative ease. In the interview, I recall being open with my prospective employer about my commitments as a part-time single parent who'd require a bit of flexibility in the weeks when I had my kids, and this was well received and thankfully honoured by them once I began work.

That openness about my circumstances has been something that I've continued to extend to prospective employers to this day, and I haven't felt like it's held me back in building a successful and interesting career. For many years I've worked as a freelance project manager and writer, changing clients often and occasionally working overseas or in other cities – this has all been balanced alongside my requirement to be home for alternate weeks when my daughters were with me.

I'm fortunate that I've never had any difficulty in securing flexible working conditions and I'm not quite sure why this is, particularly in contrast to research showing that some dads have problems securing such concessions. I can only put it down to the fact that I've always stated such requirements as an essential and at the outset of applying for and interviewing for new jobs. I've never sought to down-play that I have my kids with me for alternate weeks and have always been honest that this will impact on my ability to travel for work or to work for long hours during those weeks. On the flip-side, I've always been flexible and willing to travel as much as has been required and have made sure my work diary is managed to arrange meetings as much as possible in weeks I don't spend with my kids.

As a freelancer, I have dealt with recruiters and agents often. I've seen little point in being anything other than open and honest about my commitments, which has perhaps cost me some roles at the point of screening or applying for them. I'd counter, though, that this is more sensible an approach than finding the dream job or client and then having to disappoint them or withdraw as my request for flexibility is denied.

Being open and upfront with prospective clients and employers at the interview has ensured I've been able to secure the roles I've wanted, with the necessary flexibility to fulfil my parenting role too.

We first transitioned to the equal co-parenting model in October 2007, and it has remained the basis of our parenting since. I remember the early days as being incredibly arduous in many ways. It was lovely to be back around the girls for more time but the logistics of getting them to the childminder (herself an essential part of our divorced family set-up) before and after work, working full-time and then keeping the household running around all that, were stretching to say the least. I realise that this is something that many others do much more elegantly and with less support or resources than I do, and I'm full of admiration for them. It got easier over time and we settled into a routine with it, the girls adapting admirably to living alternate weeks between their mum's home and at mine.

I think there were various principles that made it work so well from the outset and, while the situations have evolved over time, the same basic features remained at the core of it.

1) The kids have always had regular and equal input from both parents. Assuming that a relationship hasn't ended due to reasons of abuse between the adults or towards the kids, or for some other horrendous reason that should preclude one or other parent from being allowed to remain involved, I can't think why this wouldn't

be something that all kids should benefit from. I'm firmly of the opinion that my daughters have benefited from having an active mother and father in their lives and I think that their bonds with each of us are stronger than they might have been had we actually remained together. Their time with me has always been all about them, and I have compartmentalised other aspects of life into the times when the kids aren't with me.

2) As parents, we have both had our share of the highs and lows. We've each benefited from free time to work through the pain of parting and then to build our careers, establish new lives and eventually to find new partners. We've always tried to ensure that neither of us became the fun-time parent, and neither one of us bore the brunt of the hard work of raising them. In many separated families, it seems to me that one parent can end up feeling exhausted through being the primary carer, with limited time to live their own life. The other parent gets less contact with the kids than they'd like and is often forced to pay restrictive financial support that makes them miserable too. Nobody wins!

3) The logistical sides of the arrangement have always been kept as simple as possible. We have never wanted the kids to feel temporary or transient through living between two homes. To that end, we've tried to minimise the amount of 'stuff' they've had to move between homes (which inevitably increased as they got older). As much as has been economically viable, we've had duplicate sets of clothes at each home, some toys (and later, gadgetry) and pictures of all sides of their extended family at both homes so that they could feel relaxed and settled in each place without moving in and out each week with all their essential possessions in tow.

4) Flexibility and structure have always been equally important in making the arrangement work. Structure and repeatability for the kids has meant they have a sense of consistency – they're in each home for one week at a time, not chopping and changing on the whims of their parents. The week-on, week-off structure has always been largely fixed in calendars for months and even years ahead. That said, we've always tried to be flexible, for example to accommodate summer vacations (if one of us wanted to take the girls on holiday for two consecutive weeks) or at Christmas (which we've broadly alternated between us).

These principles have formed the enduring basis of the arrangement. Observing and honouring them has, I suspect, been one of the biggest reasons for the set-up enduring as it has for many years now.

Equal co-parenting remains an unconventional outcome for separated families but it has been the basis for our kids' entire childhood through to their teenage years and early adulthood. While we have faced our share of challenges (as happens in all families), these are easily outweighed by the numerous benefits that we've experienced as kids and adults alike.

It feels like the ideal set-up, and while it's been made easy through us being amicable as parents and focused on the kids' needs first and foremost, it hasn't demanded much in the way of direct contact between us. Many cite this as a potential barrier, but I really don't see it as such. If we didn't get along as well as we do, I suspect we'd still make it work for the benefit of our kids.

When we first parted, aside from being concerned about the potential harm to my relationship with the girls, I found it hard to contemplate that I might ever have a life of my own again. The thought of being able to enjoy a career of any significance seemed challenging. I couldn't picture anything other than a life alone, and the idea of dating as a single dad seemed quite impossible.

As the years pass though, it seems to me that the innate resilience of human beings kicks in – we recover, we move forwards and life evolves. Co-parenting became the norm and we all adapted to it as the means by which we managed our separated family life. The girls flourished, and all was good.

As time went on, both my ex and I entered into new relationships. In my case, five years after formally divorcing I met the woman who I would go on to marry. She too was a divorcee and had two kids from her first marriage. We married in 2015 and have a blended family of six when we're all together. My ex-wife has remarried too.

Crucially, as we entered into new relationships, we were both careful to preserve and protect our co-parenting arrangement as sacred. I positioned this as a prerequisite to be accepted by any future partner, and my second wife has only ever known me as a part-time single parent who is committed to living with his daughters for alternate weeks.

My new wife and I decided that it was important not to cause too much disruption for our kids, who were all well established in their respective schools. Instead of inviting my wife and her children to move in with me and the girls, or taking my girls to live with her and her kids, I rented a home near the girls' school for use when I spent time with them, and then moved into a house with my wife which was to be our permanent home together near her wider family. My ex did a similar thing, renting a home to spend time with the girls in, and moving into a separate home with her new partner.

As such, my ex and I ended up in the situation where we each had a home that was used solely for the weeks when the girls were with us and which sat empty for half the time. This seemed inherently wasteful and represented an excessive expense for each of us to maintain.

Our daughters were now teenagers and occasionally expressed annoyance at having to pack up their possessions every week to move between houses. Both places were equipped to make them comfortable for our daughters, but a growing list of essentials (including gadgetry, chargers, clothes and cosmetics) all needed to be shifted on a weekly basis to meet their needs. An arrangement known as Bird's-Nest co-parenting promised to be a natural way of overcoming this and providing greater stability.

Bird's Nesting (as it's also known) is an arrangement whereby the kids of divorced families remain in a single home and the adults move in and out as custodial parent of the week. It's an established means of co-parenting that probably originated as a means of allowing divorced couples to transition out of a family home while allowing the kids to remain in a familiar environment. We were drawn to nesting many years after first divorcing as it seemed an ideal means of giving the kids a stable, single home and rightly placing the burden on us the parents to move between homes rather than the kids having to do so. It also seemed to offer a direct means of addressing the minor problems and dissatisfactions that were starting to arise for us all.

I was initially sceptical of nesting as a concept. The financial savings from maintaining a single home were appealing; both my ex and I would be able to dispose of the homes that were unused for half the time and instead share in the upkeep of a single property that would be primarily the girls' home. But I still felt uneasy about how it would work in practice.

How would I feel about the close proximity and visibility into the life of my ex (and vice versa) afforded by the shared space?

How would the arrangement be perceived by family, friends and most importantly, the kids?

Even though my ex and I were never likely to be in the same home at once, would it not feel uncomfortable to be sharing a living space, albeit conceptually?

Our new partners, along with many others that I spoke to, were supportive of the idea and emphasised that we needed only to give it a go to see if it could work. I'm glad that we did.

Finding a suitable property took time but we gave up our rental properties that had been used for co-parenting and secured a three-bedroom apartment to serve as our nest.

The parents' bedroom was self-contained with an en-suite bathroom and storage for us each to leave possessions at the nest. We wanted to keep the place as free of our own personalisation and possessions as possible – our focus was on making it feel above all like the kids' home. Nonetheless, it was useful to have a bit of storage space each to store bedding, exercise gear and so on. We didn't want to have to move excessive possessions weekly either!

On a Monday morning I would strip the bedding and leave the place clean and tidy for my ex. She would arrive on a Monday evening and use the apartment as resident parent until the following Monday when we would switch back again. The kids remained in place throughout. The arrangement took some getting used to just as it had when we were first co-parenting, but gradually we all settled into it.

We shared the financial upkeep, splitting the rent, bills and so on. We both bought cleaning products (used with occasional, begrudging assistance from the girls) and treated the place primarily as the kids' home. I would bring groceries with me for the week when I arrived and would be responsible for catering and managing the home. She'd be responsible in her weeks. Nesting didn't demand excessive contact between us, particularly as by now the girls didn't need to be handed over between us. Regardless, we regularly spoke anyway to discuss matters affecting the girls as we have always done. Communication is key in parenting, and especially so in co-parenting after divorce.

As a result of the nesting arrangement, the girls were able to enjoy greater structure and stability in not having to move back and forth from one home to the other. For the first time since the divorce, the kids had a single place to call home. Making that statement makes me feel slightly sad, but in fairness they'd always had places that were safe, comfortable and loving, so I guess the minor difference between them and their friends was at least bearable, if not ideal? I hope so.

In the nest they were surrounded by their possessions and felt less transient and temporary about where they lived from one week to the next. It also felt like a comfortable place for us as parents to live when we were with the girls.

The financial savings helped, and I for one enjoyed the feeling of putting the kids' needs to the fore in allowing them greater stability.

Putting the kids' needs first has been our guiding principle since divorcing, but successful nesting demanded a few additional considerations too.

Most fundamental was to demonstrate trust and respect for the other parent. I would always remain mindful that it was her home when she was in residence and I wouldn't just pop by unannounced or let myself in to make a cup of tea; the same was always true in reverse too.

It took time for the kids to adapt to the two different sets of rules enforced by their mum and me – our rules came and went with each of us as the live-in parent in residence. We have always been united in expectations of behaviour, manners and diligence at school, but inevitably we run our homes differently. For example, I have always wanted to eat dinner together around the table with my kids each evening, whereas their mum has always been more relaxed about them eating in front of the TV. I find life easier with structure and am a stickler for tidying up as I go, doing the dishes after each meal, packing school bags and packed lunches the night before, whereas their mum has always found life easier and more harmonious when the girls were given more autonomy to organise themselves. I like to be prepared where she's more comfortable going with the flow.

Both systems work, and the kids have always been good about adapting and accepting both ways (although I'm sure they've preferred her ways!) At the very least, we've given them experience of both ways and I'm sure they'll find the way that suits them best when they go on to have families, if they ever choose to do so.

I suspect that the girls found it easier to adjust to these changing structures and sets of rules when they were physically moving between homes. In nesting, the rules changed with the arriving parent, which I suspect would have been hard for younger kids to adapt to.

Not long after we established the nest, I tried to establish some 'House Rules' on a homemade poster but this served only to attract ridicule and graffiti; another lesson learned! With a bit of patience and flexibility, however, we all adapted well.

My new wife remained in the permanent family home when I was living in the nest, just as she had when we were co-parenting from separate homes. At weekends when I was at the nest, we would often make use of it as a blended family, all six of us staying there if we had something we wanted to do together. The nest was used as a second family home when it was my week in residence, and my ex-wife did the same when it was hers. This represented a further benefit arising from the arrangement.

A final challenge throughout nesting was in dealing with occasional doubters and critics.

Nesting is an unconventional means of family living post-divorce, as was equal co-parenting before that. Comments and criticism were occasionally expressed regarding our motives and speculating over the consequences for the kids and our new spouses resulting from the arrangement. Some might have felt that the move would endanger our new marriages through the inevitable (if notional) proximity with our exes, but that overlooked that the entire arrangement is centred on putting the kids' needs first. Our kids were also old enough to recognise that the arrangement didn't indicate a desire for us as their parents to get back together as a couple.

Our aim was always to give our kids the best childhood possible rather than one that was inferior or second best as a result of us divorcing when they were young. I have always believed in my heart that this is the best motive we could possibly have had for such choices in how we lived, and I've never doubted the merits of what we did for our kids. There will always be people who disagree and feel it's their right to express criticism – it's a fact of life, unfortunately.

I've summarised below a number of guidelines that require consideration for nesting. Many of these were learned in our experience of living with the arrangement.

Guidelines for Successful Nesting

1. **Treat your ex with trust and respect and assume they will do the same.** When they're in residence at the nest, it's their home and should be treated as such.
2. **Nesting doesn't necessarily increase the interactions with your ex.** In your conversations with them, focus on being polite, business-like and cooperative. Communications should be focused upon the mutual purpose of raising your kids jointly (and probably need to cover little else).
3. **Strive for an equitable split of the costs of maintaining the nest.** These may be apportioned in line with other divorce finances. It can help to consider the upkeep of the nest as funding a stable and constant home for your kids.
4. **Nesting does not need to be prohibitively expensive.** In our case it offered a financial saving, and it can be a means of ensuring a

more equitable split of costs and responsibilities as well as ensuring you all get to share in the rewards.

5. **Nesting won't be suitable for every divorced family.** However, some of its principles, along with those of co-parenting can be employed in virtually every divorced or separated family and will likely offer significant benefits for children and parents alike.

Nesting may seem a difficult or unfeasible option for many divorced families. I believe that most of its principles and those of co-parenting offer enormous potential benefit over conventional structures, to children and parents alike. It's not a silver-bullet solution to all the challenges associated with raising happy kids after divorce, but I believe our experiences have demonstrated the merit of unconventional solutions to common problems.

Both our girls are bright, polite, academically accomplished and emotionally well-adjusted. I'm biased, of course, but I'm exceptionally proud of both of them. Their lives haven't been free of the emotionally challenging times and upsets that beset everyone, but nor have they been any worse off as a result of the arrangement. Fundamentally, though, I don't believe they've suffered unduly from having a childhood that has been made worse or harder than any of their peers from non-separated families. For this reason, I'm equally proud that my ex and I have set aside our differences and while raising them jointly, have put the needs of the girls first.

In the fifteen years since parting, I've learned that the demands of being a parent, divorced or otherwise are constantly evolving. An arrangement that works in the years immediately after divorce will likely be different to what works when the divorcee enters into a new relationship. A set-up that meets the needs of toddlers and infants will need to change if it's to cater for the needs of teenagers and young adults. There is no one-size-fits-all and just as you think you've figured it all out, the demands placed upon you change again.

This is true for *all* parents.

We've sought to change our co-parenting arrangement throughout the years, and co-parenting evolved into nesting. If and when that is no longer desirable or preferable to us all, then it will change again. Once both daughters have left home, we will no longer need a formal structure for co-parenting. Even then, I believe that lines of communication will remain firmly open between me and my ex on matters concerning our daughters as our relationship as their parents will remain for life.

It's important to emphasise that both parents of children deserve to be happy, and to live their lives as best they can as individuals, not just as a parental team. A happy parent will raise a happy child, after all.

Looking back on our original decision to split up, it was an important moment where we recognised that our dissatisfactions as a couple would likely have made us a less-effective parenting team had we remained together. Instead, as a separated couple we have each been able to live a life that is fulfilling individually, and as parents of the kids we created. I know I haven't got everything right by a long way, but I've always done my best by my kids and always put them at the heart of all that I've done.

That is the achievement of which I'm most proud in life.

My greatest fears at the outset of us parting as a family were that my daughters would be harmed as a result of divorce and that I'd lose my place in their lives. I'm relieved to report that neither of these fears has manifested.

I feel lucky to have been so actively involved in their upbringing and I enjoy a closer relationship with them than I might have had in a conventional family setting. I certainly don't advocate divorce but equally I don't see that it has to end a father's relationship with his kids. A study by the Judicial Council of California echoes this sentiment. Their twenty-year investigation of 173 divorced families showed that the majority of kids of divorce felt that their relationship with their fathers had remained stable or improved over the years following divorce – I find this heartening and hope that other fathers on the verge of divorce or separation might also feel reassured.

Divorce is certainly hard for all involved. The effects of parting for the kids (and for the parents) will be determined significantly by the quality and frequency of communication between them and by putting the kids' needs first in all decisions about how they live life after divorce. Arrangements like co-parenting and even bird nesting are merely tools that bring this ethos to life and which offer a framework for life after divorce. In themselves they won't bring about the positive effects unless the parents are willing to put in the work. Nothing is easy, of course, but that's true in all aspects of life, isn't it?

But for divorcing dads who are willing to put in the work, I believe with certainty that there is always hope.

Chapter 20:

The Rebirth:
How Becoming a Dad Helped Me Pursue My Passion

James Roach

I was born in 1981, and like most youngsters I was heavily influenced by the musical artists that I listened to. They were mostly from the US, where everything seemed cooler and more rebellious at the time. Gangster rap was the go-to, of course – artists like Dr Dre, Snoop Dogg and Bone Thugs-N-Harmony were my idols. By the late nineties and early noughties, producers like Pharrell and Timbaland (who produced some of the biggest hits for Missy Elliott, Justin Timberlake and the late Aaliyah), were who I wanted to be when I grew up.

Music really got its claws into me in my teen years. It affected everything from the clothes I wore and the movies I watched, to the friendship groups I had. Music helped me identify, and I loved that I could pick and listen to something that could resonate with me, no matter what mood I was in. The fact that a song could be so powerful in altering your state of mind, or opening your eyes to the world around you, was fascinating to me.

A lot of the music I listened to in my early teen years was pretty dark, and I remember listening to one of my favourite albums ('E. 1999 Eternal' by Bone Thugs-N-Harmony), which plays out like a rap horror movie, throughout the duration of my family holiday to Disneyland Florida when I was around fourteen. Quite the juxtaposition really, running around chatting to Mickey Mouse, while listening to tales of murder, Ouija boards and robberies told over haunting hip-hop beats. Funnily enough, it's still one of my favourite albums to this day, although I have since found much more optimistic pieces of music for a pick-me-up on those cold, rainy commutes to work.

Although my family wasn't particularly musical, my brother taught me to DJ. He had been DJing for years, mostly jungle and drum and bass, so those were the records I started to learn with.

By around '97/98, I was bitten by the UK garage bug and started hounding my parents for my first set of decks. My journey began as a DJ at small parties on the local circuit and eventually residencies at small bars in the local area. A life full of riches and all the trappings of fame awaited me, I thought, just as soon as I'd perfected my craft. In order to do that, I needed some kind of training, so going off to university to study Music Technology seemed the logical thing to do.

To their credit, my parents were great in supporting my dreams. They didn't bat an eyelid and parted with their hard-earned cash for my tuition fees and rent pretty easily. Not once did they question my course, or dictate what I should do, and I have to thank them for that. It can't have been easy for them to hold their tongues at times.

University came and went, and I managed to produce for some local Midlands rappers in Wolverhampton who were getting some shine at the time, in magazines like HHC (Hip-Hop Connection), for those who remember that. Essentially though, I came out of university with some great life experiences (I could now cook frozen pizzas for myself), but not much in the way of furthering my music-making career.

It was down to me alone to continue the push towards fame and success. I did this by working part-time and living with my dad, again, with no push-back. My life at this time is summed up perfectly in a song by Kid British: 'Part Time Job/Shirt & Tie'. Never has a song had it so on point for me. I guess the scenario I found myself in was pretty universal for the struggling wannabe musician.

After working in one of the worst estates in North West London at a housing association repairs company for a few years, I eventually landed a studio engineering/general skivvy job at a private music college in the trendy Shoreditch area of London. This was the beginning, I thought.

That started a great two years of my life that I thoroughly enjoyed, even though the days were long (twelve-hour shifts were the norm), and the money was dire (£12k). With a salary like that, I was taking home £900 per month and still travelling into London and buying lunch etc. However, whilst there I learned everything about music production that university didn't teach me, and I built on my CV by actually teaching and managing people – skills that could help me in the real world. At this time, the future looked bright. I was surrounded by like-minded people who all shared the same passion, and I was building on my own skill set. It would only be onwards and upwards from here, surely?

Well, not quite. With a change of role at the college that saw me moved to an office instead of a studio-based environment, things declined fast and I left soon after. Although my next career move would see me earn more than double, and keep me employed for the next eight years, it wasn't in music, and that dream of making a living in the music industry was slowly starting to fade.

My Relationship

One thing that remained consistent throughout all of the above, was my relationship with my now wife. We've been together since I was seventeen years old, so she has seen every single transition. She's heard all the bad beats I've made, attended the DJ competitions, listened to me play the same loop over and over again. She gets it, even if it was a major annoyance at times. It makes me laugh to think of the times when she'd be downstairs talking to my dad whilst I DJed or played the same repetitive drum loop at max volume for hours on end. That's love right there.

Of course, as time went by, music-making and DJing started to become more of a hobby and less of a potential career path. I'd come to the realisation that if I was ever going to make it in the music industry it would be through hard work and graft, but that I also had to have a decent job in order to make the moves my now wife and I needed to further ourselves in life. After moving in with my wife into her flat, she'd still be happy for me to return to my dad's (where my studio was set up in my abandoned bedroom) every now and then to work on my craft. That was until we eventually moved into our first joint house together and I joyfully commandeered the spare bedroom as my studio. What a day to be alive that was – my own dedicated music room, the stuff dreams are made of.

I would make music in most of my spare time, and everything was right with the world. I didn't have anyone else to look after so it was relatively guilt-free.

But as time went on, things did start to slow down as I fell out of love with music-making. I came close to selling all my gear, as I just couldn't find the passion for it any more. I was done, or so I thought.

The Birth

The year 2016 saw the arrival of our beautiful baby boy, Teddy, and you don't need me to tell you what a game changer that is.

Before Teddy arrived, I wasn't too concerned about how it may affect my passion for music, as I'd already started to fall out of love with it anyway.

With my new-found responsibilities and early mornings, just about everything else went out the window for the first year and a half, apart from my Thai boxing which I still needed to keep me sane. Smashing pads and getting hit in the face by people much younger than you is a great stress reliever. But other than that, coming home and dedicating more time to any activity that wasn't watching TV was a stretch too far.

The Rebirth

It was around this key time of Teddy's birth that things were implemented that eventually paved the way for me to have a bit of a renaissance with music again.

My wife had been great with making sure we all got into a routine when Teddy was born. This was vital to us all maintaining a balanced and clear head throughout what were undeniably some of the toughest and most sleep-deprived times of our lives. Times when even the simplest of tasks could be a struggle.

The key thing that she was so adamant on was sleep training. I'm not judging anyone else when it comes to how you train your children to sleep, or whether you decide not to at all. But this one thing was key to making the rest of our lives balanced and allowing us the time and space to feel like our old selves again. Sure, it takes some time and persistence to get it into place, but the first time you get your little one down for a full twelve hours without interruption will be the day you kiss the sky and rejoice (I'm not even religious).

There are lots of different books available that have processes for sleep training – parents need to figure out which method suits them best, but we found one that worked for us, and we had Teddy out of our room and into his own bed within three months and sleeping through the night, from 6 p.m. to 6 a.m., in six months.

With this in place, it meant that my wife and I started to have our evenings to ourselves again. This was time to relax, catch up, and, of course, dabble in my music again.

My Boy, My Inspiration

As Teddy began to develop a personality, it was only natural that he was introduced to new music. Seeing his reaction as he digested all these sounds for the first time made me excited and gave me a new-found level of enthusiasm. I made a playlist for him that we still play in my car today, and it was clear that he had a thing for house music, something that I had dabbled in, but not really paid too much attention to trying to make before. But I loved his reaction to it, and so I set about making some music that he would enjoy.

At the same time, a colleague at work and I were discussing our passions outside of work, and we both made a pact to go the extra mile with something we had always wanted to do. Hers was to source more freelance design work, and mine was to put out a song.

With a renewed focus and passion, I started studying house music a little harder, listening to the sounds that were used, seeing what I liked and what resonated with me. I applied some project-management-style deadlines to things (learned from my new role as a Project Manager at work) and in 2018 I released my first song under my new moniker, MIDLO. Although the track wasn't a huge success, it was a breakthrough for me. I loved the process; I had hit my target deadline and I had done it. I finally put something out, like I said I would.

That one song spiralled into more, and by the end of 2018 I had my songs featured on the BBC (Introducing in Beds, Herts and Bucks), remixed for a German production duo, and had one of my songs featured on the official Spotify UK House Music playlist alongside Calvin Harris & Dua Lipa, Leftwing, and Gorgon City. I was so chuffed with what I had achieved in such a short space of time, and it feels surreal to think that I was averaging 30,000 listeners per month for a lot of 2018.

The quick success I managed to gain has spurred me to keep going, and what I first felt a little embarrassed about (rekindling my music passion at thirty-seven), I now own and wear with pride. Who cares what people think?

Who cares if some people don't like my music? I like it, and I enjoy it, so as long as that continues, then I'll keep on going.

I've gone through ups and downs when it comes to pursuing my music, and although I am resigned to the fact that I will never reach the dizzy heights of what I aspired to when I was younger, I'm at peace with that. I'm doing it for the fun of it now. And I'm able to get instant feedback and gratification with the Internet and social media being how it is, something that was not as prevalent back when I started.

Finding my passion for music again has also helped me disconnect from the real pressures that come with working and helping raise a family. Sometimes we all need an outlet, somewhere we can totally switch off and think about nothing but the task at hand. I get this from music (and Thai boxing), and I can definitely vouch for both of those passions being key to me being more present and involved with both my wife and son. It's not about being selfish at all – everyone needs to hold onto things that make them who they are. If you don't, all sorts of unsavoury things can start to happen, with feelings of resentfulness and the degradation of your mental well-being and happiness, and of those around you. One thing I know from being with my wife for so long is that we both need to be firing on all cylinders, the majority of the time, to maintain a good healthy home on a day-to-day basis.

But as I've said, I wouldn't be in the position I am in life if it wasn't for all the support I've had along the way. Whether that be from my parents, when I was younger, in letting me pursue my dreams, no matter how wild they sounded. Or, of course, my wife, who was a rock when Teddy was born. Were it not for her hard work laying the foundation for how we all now live as a family unit, I wouldn't have the time to be pursuing my passions.

So with that all said and done, starting a family doesn't have to mean the end of pursuing your passions or pastimes. There may be a slight lull as you get your shit together, but with the right support and determination, you can get to a point in your life where there can be a balance that works for everyone.

About the Authors

About the Authors

Alec Grant

Alec is a forty-eight-year-old dad with two young boys. He is a co-founder in a tech start-up business and works on various social impact projects to encourage and help provide opportunities to under-represented communities. He is an advocate of the #tech4good movement that aims to use technology to solve society's most challenging problems. Over the past eight years, he has raised his two boys following the passing away of their mother. This chapter is for those dads going through something similar, to let them know that they are not alone.

medium.com/narratives4men
Twitter: @narratives4men

Andy Kapadia

Andy is a university administrator who has two children who keep him both entertained and exhausted. His spare time is taken up with playing the guitar, being an independent podcaster and watching his beloved Leicester City!

Twitter @aggyfox4

Arion Lawrence

Arion is a married father who was born and bred in London. He is in an interracial relationship and continues to live in London with his wife and their son. Arion is a primary school teacher and a regular contributor to several websites and platforms. He is also a writer for his own platform where he regularly discusses politics, race, culture, education and mental health. Arion enjoys training regularly and travelling and is a long-time follower of boxing.

iamalaw.medium.com
Twitter: @iamarionlaw

Billy Grant

Born in West London to strict West Indian parents, a love for music saw Billy deeply entrenched in London's music and street fashion scenes. Working with artists from Craig David to Alesha Dixon, he went on to set up his own independent label, travelling the world and scoring a US Billboard No 1. Meanwhile, football was a huge passion and Billy still found time to co-run Brentford's main fan site and podcast and sit on the board of the Football Supporters' Association. As it became harder to balance family life and constant globetrotting, he diversified his career – creating football content for companies such as Sky Sports and Channel 5.

beesotted.com
Instagram and Twitter: @billythebee99

Cal-I Jonel

Cal-I Jonel is a qualified teacher and creative artist from East London. He worked as a curriculum and pastoral leader in schools across London for ten years before leaving the teaching profession in 2018 to retrain at Identity School of Acting and Maktub theatre company. He made his professional and West End debut at the Prince of Wales theatre in 2020. Cal-I is also a singer-songwriter and playwright with independent single and EP releases (To Whom It May Concern, 2016) and a stage play under seed commission. He is father to two wonderful children, Ebony-Grace and Elijah and husband to an amazing woman, Zara.

cal-ijonel.com
Twitter: @jonel1

Danny Herbert

Danny Herbert lives near Walthamstow Wetlands with his wife Cleo and their two children Charlie and Lola. He has been a civil servant for over twenty-five years, although he still dreams of being a film director. Danny runs a group for dads of children with additional needs in Waltham Forest. He is also a poet and has had poems published in various anthologies and has a poem on National Archive submitted as part of Black History Month. Danny tweets poetry every day as @HerbieHerb and was the official Micropoet for the Words Over Waltham Forest Literary Festival in 2012.

Twitter: @HerbieHerb

Elliott Rae

Elliott is the founder of MusicFootballFatherhood, a powerful speaker and an experienced Diversity & Inclusion (D&I) leader with specific expertise in gender and race. As one of the leading voices in the UK for fatherhood and masculinity in the workplace, Elliott regularly works with organisations and staff networks to help support working fathers and parents, and work towards gender equality, through #EngagingDads workshops and talks.

Elliott has held senior D&I leadership roles, most recently as Head of D&I delivery at HM Treasury. The United Nations recently recognised Elliott's work and he is now the proud recipient of the UN Women UK's #HeForShe 'Changemaker of the Year' award for his work on gender equality. Elliott has written for various mainstream publications and even had his work shared online by none other than Dwayne Johnson AKA 'The Rock'!

ElliottRae.com
Instagram & Twitter: @iamelliottrae

Ian

Ian is a full-time father of two, business owner and founder of Freelance Print Staff. He's also an MFF contributor, paddleboarder, runner and enjoys anything else that's sporty. He's happiest by the sea, creating his own path in life and finding out about himself and what can be achieved. If Ian is doing something to move forward in life, then he's smiling.

Instagram: @iandoel
Twitter: @iandoel1

James Cooke

James is a writer and editor. More importantly, he is a husband and father of two. Living with his family in Kent, in his spare time, James enjoys reading, running, and watching pro wrestling.

Instagram & Twitter: @theJamesCooke

James Roach

A happily married father of one (boy), James is a Creative Manager by day, devoted father, loving husband, and passionate music producer by night. Born in North London, James has four siblings, of which he is the youngest. Having a mixed heritage (Bajan, English, Irish and German) has given James a unique perspective on life and equality, and on just what it means to belong, and to be comfortable with who you are.

His goal in life is to make sure he does the best by his family unit and to concentrate on being the best he can be both at work and at home, as well always learning and remaining passionate about new experiences that life brings.

Instagram: @midlo_music

Jamie Cowen

Jamie Cowen is forty-three and a father of two. He lives with his family in Tottenham, North London and runs a small literary agency. When he's not reading books, Jamie plays amateur football and the guitar, but rarely at the same time.

Twitter: @bigjcowen

Mark Williams

Mark Williams is a keynote speaker, author and international campaigner while setting up International Fathers' Mental Health Day. Working with Dr Jane Hanley, he has published journals on birth trauma and fathers' perinatal mental health. Mark has spoken on television and radio stations raising awareness and published a report in 2020 on the importance of fathers' mental health. Mark was awarded Inspirational Father of the year in 2012 and even invited to meet the Royal Family on World Mental Health Day in 2016. He was awarded the Points of Light award by the Prime Minister in 2019.

markwilliamsfmh.co.uk
Twitter: @markwilliamsfmh #HowAreYouDad

Michael Johnson-Ellis

Michael Johnson-Ellis is Dad to Talulah and Duke, stepdad to Katie, and husband to Wes. After having children Michael changed his career from a stressful city job, to being a surrogacy advocate, supporting those who are struggling to conceive. Michael now blogs and documents his life as a parent via TwoDadsUK® on Facebook and Instagram. Michael and Wes are both founders of TwoDadsUK®, The Modern Family Show 2021 and the surrogacy not-for-profit organisation My Surrogacy Journey®. Michael also writes for IVFbabble, the world's largest online fertility magazine.

TwoDadsUK.com & mysurrogacyjourney.com
Instagram: @TwoDads.u.k

Peter Kawalek

Peter Kawalek was born one of six children to Maureen and Tadeusz in Manchester. The family lived in Whalley Range. His wife is from Withington in the same city. Their home now is in the High Peak where their two daughters have grown up. He is a university professor, a career that has taken him all over the world, with associations to institutions in the UK, Ireland and Spain.

Twitter: @kawalek

Philip Robinson

Philip was born in Barbados and migrated to pursue further education and a career in information technology. These presented opportunities to engage with cultures across Europe and the United Kingdom in large and small organisations, professionally and socially. Besides working in technology, Philip is a musician, author and Christian worship leader, inspired to write stories and songs that celebrate family, community and humanity. He and his wife Nicole, also from Barbados, are parents to Nadrianne and Myles.

Twitter: @phildmusic
Instagram/Facebook: @kingdomsofcelebration

R.P. Falconer

R.P. Falconer grew up on the infamous Church Road estate in Harlesden and managed to navigate its many pitfalls and find his way. He went on to obtain a degree, and is now married with two children. With his mother's love for books, his passion to write was fuelled. He is the author of the novel *Lilif*, two short story collections *Compendium 3* and *Compendium 4*, one short story *The Springs*, with the first of his trilogy *The Sweat* on the verge of release.

rpfalconer.com
Social: @rpfalconer across all platforms

Saffa Kallon

Saffa is an accountant by trade and a father of two. In his spare time he enjoys watching, commenting and writing about football. Saffa also enjoys reading autobiographies, his favourites being Maya Angelou's collection of books, *Fela Kuti* and *Malcolm X*. Saffa is very much into yoga, meditation and mindfulness. He used to write and perform poetry a lot before he became a dad and still writes a bit from time to time. Currently he is a golf enthusiast, and one of the main reasons he enjoys the challenge of golf (and yoga) is because you are always learning; there is no ceiling.

Instagram: @saffsy76

Sam Draper

Sam Draper lives in London and is a father of two children. He's an ex-journalist who turned secondary school English teacher for seventeen years before taking parental leave and becoming a stay-at-home dad. A couple of glasses of red wine later, and he created The London Bookman, a magical book subscription that meant he could wander around bookshops with a pram. He supports Liverpool FC, has a lovely green VW Camper, resembles a hobbit, and has an unhealthy obsession with books.

thelondonbookman.com
Twitter: @alondonbookman

Toby Hazlewood

Toby Hazlewood is a dad, husband, writer and music fan living in the North West of England. Through his writing he explores and shares his thoughts, wins and losses in the hope of helping and inspiring others, tackling topics around personal development and growth, and how to live successfully and happily after divorce as a parent and an individual.

tobyhazlewood.com
Twitter: @TobyHazlewood

William Nicholson

William is passionate about social change and making a difference to the health and well-being of people and communities through networks, collaboration and relationship building. He believes strongly in facilitative approaches that empower by delivering through others and are founded on deep, trusted relationships. William works as a social facilitator, connector and catalyst with expertise in developing cross-boundary health and well-being initiatives and creating networks and social movements. His work involves working with community, private and public sector organisations including the NHS and local authorities, from start-up initiatives to established organisations and networks. He is also a qualified squash coach!

Twitter: @wnicholson7
LinkedIn: www.linkedin.com/in/william-alexander-nicholson

Support & Help

This book includes some deeply moving and personal stories. We know that it is likely that at least one of these stories will resonate personally with you.

If you need some more information and/or professional support, here are the details of some of our community partners and other amazing organisations that can help.

Autism

Carers UK

Every day 6,000 people become carers, looking after family or friends who are older, disabled or seriously ill. As the UK's only national membership charity for carers, we're here for you.

www.carersuk.org

National Autistic Society

The National Autistic Society is the UK's leading charity for autistic people. They run dedicated helplines and offer online advice and guidance for autistic people and their families facing major challenges in their lives.

www.autism.org.uk

Blogs and Podcasts

Black Mums Upfront

Black Mums Upfront is a sisterhood, podcast and micro community that strengthens and supports Black women from the diaspora to parent from a place from empowerment. We advocate and campaign for change to improve positive outcomes for Black parents.

www.blackmumsupfront.com

The Guilty Feminist

The Guilty Feminist, hosted and created by comedian Deborah Frances-White is about 'our noble goals as 21st century feminists and our hypocrisies and insecurities which undermine those goals'. It has had 85 million downloads in five years and has increasingly found an activist agenda and grown into its mission statement that 'you don't have to be perfect to be a force for meaningful change'. Deborah has also written a Sunday Times Bestselling Book of the same name.

www.deborahfrances-white.com

John Adams of Dadbloguk/DadPodUK

Dadbloguk is a pioneering and well-established dad blog. The author is John Adams, a stay/work from home dad with two daughters. He has been commentating on fatherhood issues since 2012, highlighting the challenges and successes fathers have to deal with and celebrate. Adams also produces the DadPodUK podcast.

www.dadbloguk.com

Diary of the Dad

Written by father of three, Tom Briggs, Diary of the Dad is a multi-award-winning blog. Still going strong after a decade, it covers a range of parenting topics. Despite describing himself as a 'pensioner in blogging terms' Tom retains the same enthusiasm that inspired his first post back in 2010.

www.diaryofthedad.co.uk

Bullying

Kidscape

Kidscape is a bullying prevention charity that provides practical support to children, families and schools throughout England and Wales. Our services are available to children, parents and carers and adults who help keep children safe.

www.kidscape.org.uk

Early Years Education

Laura Henry-Allain MBE

Laura Henry-Allain MBE is an expert international award-winning Early Education specialist. Laura is the creator of the characters of the renowned *JoJo & Gran Gran*, which is currently on CBeebies, she is also the series associate producer. She is the Vice-President of The British Association for Early Childhood Education, an educational consultant for the BBC and an ambassador for the Jermain Defoe Foundation.

www.LauraHenryConsultancy.com

Equality, Diversity and Inclusion

Avenir Consulting

Avenir is a team of highly experienced inclusion specialists, facilitators and accredited coaches. We offer advisory services, leadership development, workshops and coaching for organisations to support executive teams, managers and employees to successfully boost their performance via an inclusive and diverse workplace and increase profitability and growth.

www.avenirconsultingservices.com

Beyond Equality

Beyond Equality is rethinking masculinities, enabling men and boys to do better by women, girls and non-binary people, and by each other. We facilitate exploration of the positive roles men and boys can play in their communities, beyond stereotypes and peer pressure. We co-create safe, equitable and inclusive cultures with partners.

www.BeyondEquality.org

Daisy Chain

Daisy Chain is an online platform that matches and connects parents to flexible employers.

www.daisy-chain.com

Fawcett Society
The Fawcett Society is the UK's leading membership charity campaigning for gender equality and women's rights at work, at home and in public life. Our vision is a society in which women and girls in all their diversity are equal and truly free to fulfil their potential creating a stronger, happier, better future for us all.

www.fawcettsociety.org.uk

Global Equality Collective
The Global Equality Collective (GEC) was founded on the belief that achieving equality will ensure a better, fairer, more prosperous society for all. Our three-plus years of research took us all the way back to before birth, where a spectrum of imbalance lays out a map for our lives. Our work covers homes, education and business and takes various forms. Our constant aim is to interrupt these maps of imbalance, challenge norms, #SmashingStereotypes and fight for equality for all people.

www.thegec.org

Hayley Bennett
Delivering authentic equity, diversity and inclusion that connects with people and creates sustainable impact. Working with community and grassroots organisations through to large multinational corporations.

www.HTVB.co.uk

Krystal Alliance Ltd
Krystal Alliance is a team of multi-experienced friends committed to encouraging, supporting and inspiring greater equity in the workplace across all sectors.

www.krystalalliance.co.uk

Men and Boys Coalition

The Men and Boys Coalition is a mutually supportive network of responsible charities, academics, journalists and leaders committed to taking action on gender-specific issues affecting men and boys.

We enable the UK men and boys' sector to work together; promote a positive conversation about men and masculinity and put men and boys' well-being on the public agenda.

www.menandboyscoalition.org.uk

Pregnant Then Screwed

Pregnant Then Screwed is a grassroots campaign group and charity which supports pregnant women and mothers who face pregnancy or maternity discrimination. We lobby the Government for legislative changes that will improve the lives of families and will end the motherhood penalty which is the main cause of the gender pay gap.

www.pregnantthenscrewed.com

Sonshine Magazine

Sonshine is a magazine about raising boys for a more equal world. We take a positive look at parenting for gender equality, focusing on how we talk to (and about) boys. We publish four issues a year, each taking a different theme to help parents raise kind, brave, empathetic and thoughtful children.

www.sonshinemagazine.com

UN Women UK

UN Women is the only global organisation working to make gender equality a reality in every way: from grassroots programmes with the most vulnerable women and girls, to changing attitudes, and helping governments design gender-equal policy. UN Women UK's mission is to give every woman and girl the right to safety, voice and a choice.

www.unwomenuk.org

WeAreTheCity

WeAreTheCity was founded in 2008 to help women progress and excel in their careers. Through our various initiatives, our events, conferences and awards, we have helped thousands of women enhance their careers and provided over 10,000 women with the opportunities to upskill and network.

www.wearethecity.com

Family Relationships

FASTN

FASTN believes that everyone should have the same opportunities to form a stable family life and works in partnership to promote healthy, dependable relationships that support children, young people and family – in all its forms – to thrive.

www.fastn.org

Safe Ground

Safe Ground works to promote relationship skills as tools for empowering people to change. We use drama, dialogue and debate, along with a lot of group dynamics and processes and we expect a lot from our participants. We support often large groups to enhance empathy and encourage expression, developing self-awareness and promoting social justice.

www.safeground.org.uk

Football

Football Black List

While more than 25% of professional players in the UK are black, there is a worrying lack of representation in decision-making positions across all areas away from the pitch. To help address this and pay tribute to those in influential positions, the Football Black List shines a light on those who are inspiring the next generation to consider other roles in the sport.

www.footballblacklist.com

Lewes Football Club
Lewes FC is the first gender equal club in the world. We are 100% fan-owned, not-for-profit, and people-powered. We use football as a vehicle for social change. Anyone can become an owner and help us change the world through the beautiful game.

www.LewesFC.com

Pompey in the Community
Pompey in the Community is an award-winning charity which harnesses the motivational power of Portsmouth Football Club. A club run by its community, for its community. To promote education, healthy living and sporting participation and achievement among vulnerable and disadvantaged people of all ages.

www.pompeyitc.co.uk

QPR in the Community Trust
Creating opportunities, inspiring change and helping people fulfil their potential. The Trust works in partnership with communities to develop an inclusive range of sporting, educational, cultural and social opportunities, improving the quality of life for individuals and neighbourhoods. The Trust covers ninety participants across seven boroughs with people aged between three to ninety years old.

www.qpr.co.uk/community

Group B Strep

Group B Strep Support
Group B Strep Support is the UK charity dedicated to preventing group B Strep infections in newborn babies and supporting affected families. We provide free, confidential information about group B Strep, campaign for better prevention, and support families affected by group B Strep.

www.gbss.org.uk

Inclusive Publishers

Alanna Max

We create naturally inclusive picture books for children from all backgrounds that reflect the world they live in.

www.alannamax.com

Leadership Development

David McQueen

David McQueen is an executive coach and speaker. David works with companies to help them with leadership development and culture change.

www.davidmcqueen.co.uk

Mental Health and Well-being

Mind

Mind is the leading mental health charity in England and Wales and believes that no one should have to face a mental health problem alone. They are there for anybody experiencing a mental health problem, in their community, on the end of the phone or online. Whether somebody is stressed, depressed or in crisis, Mind are there to listen, offer support and advice, and fight their corner.

www.mind.org.uk

Minds@Work

Our purpose is to inspire and equip people to enhance mental well-being in the workplace. Our vision is to make work life-enhancing. We stage free events and programmes with the aim of inspiring, equipping and fuelling innovation through sharing and collaboration. We welcome all working people because we believe everyone has a role to play in creating a mentally healthy working environment.

www.mindsatworkmovement.com

State of Mind Sport
State of Mind was established to improve the mental fitness and working life of athletes, fans and communities. Our mental health and sport professionals deliver comprehensive education sessions throughout the UK in sports clubs, businesses, schools, colleges and community groups aimed at raising awareness of mental fitness within sport and life.

www.stateofmindsport.org

Dr Andrew Mayers
Dr Andrew Mayers is a psychologist, based at Bournemouth University, specialising in mental health, particularly in the perinatal period (for mothers and fathers). He is a campaigner and educator, seeking to improve services and get better support. He serves on several national advisory groups, including groups that influence NHS policy changes.

www.andrewmayers.uk

Motherdom
Motherdom is the UK's first media platform dedicated to maternal mental health and well-being. Founding Editor Anna Ceesay went through low mood and anxiety in her second pregnancy, and was alarmed at the lack of mums' and dads' mental health stories in the mainstream press. So Motherdom was born!

www.motherdom.co.uk

Miscarriage and Baby Loss

Sands UK
Sands is a UK-based charity that supports anyone affected by the death of a baby in pregnancy or after birth through email, phone and online platforms. We also work with professionals to improve bereavement care and promote research to reduce the amount of babies dying each year.

www.sands.org.uk

Miscarriage Association

The Miscarriage Association provides support and information to anyone affected by miscarriage, ectopic or molar pregnancy: women, men and non-binary people. We're here to help you through.

www.miscarriageassociation.org.uk

Parenting Authors

Sarah Ockwell-Smith

Author of twelve parenting books, ranging from pregnancy through to eighteen years. Including the bestselling *The Gentle Sleep Book* (how to improve baby, toddler and pre-schooler sleep without sleep training), *The Gentle Discipline Book* (how to improve behaviour without punishment) and *Between* (how to survive the puberty years!).

www.sarahockwell-smith.com

Sue Atkins

Sue Atkins is an internationally recognised parenting expert, broadcaster, speaker and author of the Amazon best-selling books *Parenting Made Easy – How to Raise Happy Children* and *Raising Happy Children for Dummies* as well as author of the highly acclaimed Parenting Made Easy resources. She regularly appears on the award-winning flagship ITV shows *This Morning* and *Good Morning Britain* and on Sky News. Sue is also the parenting expert for many BBC radio stations around the UK.

www.thesueatkins.com

Dr Anna Machin

Dr Anna Machin is an evolutionary anthropologist, writer and broadcaster who researches and writes about the science and anthropology of fatherhood. She is passionate about supporting and empowering dads to be everything they want to be. Author of *The Life of Dad: The Making of the Modern Father*.

annamachin.com

Parenting Community Groups

Dad La Soul

Dad La Soul is a revolutionary, grassroots movement that uses art, music, tech and play to battle the social isolation and loneliness felt by millions of dads across the UK, every day. Since 2016 we've been pioneering dad-friendly events/publishing.

www.dadlasoul.com

Leeds Dads

Leeds Dads is a support group to help dads engage with their pre-school kids. More than just an opportunity to socialise, we run activities, signpost to expert family support, and help fathers to become more confident and build strong, lasting relationships with their children.

www.leedsdads.org

Parenting Experts

Educating Matters

For twenty years Educating Matters have been supporting parents and carers with the challenges of educating children, parenting and integrating work and family. They provide talks in the corporate and public sector, schools, remote Positive Parenting courses for individuals and one-to-one consultations. Their guidance is described as being 'life-changing'.

www.educatingmatters.co.uk

Support for Children and Young People

Juvenis

Juvenis offers bespoke support and training enabling young people who are experiencing difficulties at school, at home or in the community to turn around their lives and (re)engage with employment, education, training or personal development. Our Vision is a future where all young Londoners have more than one chance to fulfil their potential. Our Mission is to support young Londoners by enabling them to improve their life chances and contribute positively to their communities.

www.juvenis.org.uk

Lads Need Dads

Award-winning, Essex-based Lads Need Dads, is the only UK long-term early intervention mentoring project that works with boys age eleven to fifteen with absent fathers. Male volunteer mentors equip, engage and inspire boys through personal development group work, outdoor adventures, practical life-skill training, community volunteering and ambassador opportunities.

www.ladsneeddads.org

Power Thoughts by Natalie Costa

Natalie Costa is an award-winning coach, speaker, author and founder of Power Thoughts, a coaching service designed to empower children and give them 'power' over their own thoughts! Through her private practice and workshops, she has helped thousands of children worldwide feel calmer, happier and more empowered!

www.powerthoughts.co.uk

The Man Den

The Man Den is a small community group which facilitates intergenerational mentoring through play by bringing together positive male role models and young boys to play board games. Our group is open to all boys and men aged eight to a hundred-plus.

www.themandenuk.com

Support for New Parents

Best Beginnings
Best Beginnings helps parents give their children the best start in life. We support parents through pregnancy and the early years to build their knowledge and confidence to help their children thrive. Our free, award-winning parenting app Baby Buddy is used by more than 300,000 people across the UK.

www.bestbeginnings.org.uk

Dad Matters UK
We are a parent/infant mental health project, based in Greater Manchester, Gloucestershire and Warrington (for now) and we support dads with under twos to understand development and bonding, acknowledge mental health issues in themselves and partners and to access services. Our social media is open access to anyone, anywhere!

dadmatters.org.uk

Future Men
Through frontline delivery of practice-led services, we work with boys and men to help them become dynamic and healthy future men. Our Fathers Development Programmes are delivered through one-to-one sessions and group support, engaging with men in their caring roles to support and encourage them to be actively involved in their children's and families' lives. We also deliver structured school programmes and youth hubs to individual one-to-one sessions and outreach work in the community. We provide the vital support and advocacy that can change boys' and men's lives for the better.

www.futuremen.org

Fatherhood Institute

The Fatherhood Institute lobbies for policy and practice changes that will support and enable fathers' greater contributions to the direct care of their children from the children's earliest years. The Institute 'trains the trainers' to deliver a range of innovative programmes to couples and fathers. The Institute's research summaries are world-renowned and the organisation participates in important research projects to improve family and health researchers' capacities to engage fathers.

www.fatherhoodinstitute.org

Parent Ping

Parent Ping is a daily survey app that helps you learn how other parents are dealing with life – all in just two minutes a day!

www.parentping.co.uk

Support for Parent Entrepeneurs

ISBE – Institute for Small Business and Entrepreneurship

The Institute for Small Business and Entrepreneurship (ISBE) is a network for people and organisations involved in small business and entrepreneurship research, policy, practice, education, support and advice. Our vision is to connect our membership and their communities to pursue excellence in small business and entrepreneurship.

www.isbe.org.uk

Support for Parent-Teachers

The MTPT Project

The MTPT Project is the UK's only network for parent-teachers, believing that parenting and teaching are hugely enriching and compatible roles. Focusing on the parental leave period, we inspire, empower and connect teachers choosing to complete professional development around their new babies and support teachers as they transition back to work.

www.mtpt.org.uk

Support for Working Parents

Equal Parenting Project
The Equal Parenting Project is an academic project led by Dr Sarah Forbes and Dr Holly Birkett. The project works tirelessly to drive gender equality in the workplace through rigorous research aimed at addressing the barriers that prevent equal parenting. The project also provides research-informed recommendations for organisations and policymakers.

www.birmingham.ac.uk/equal-parenting

Working Families
Our mission is to remove the barriers that people with caring responsibilities face in the workplace. We drive positive change by supporting and advocating for working parents and carers, collaborating with employers to build flexible and family-friendly cultures, and influencing government policy. We provide free employment law and benefits advice to working parents and carers. Our website has had over 1 million unique views.

www.workingfamilies.org.uk

Working Dads
At Working Dads we share best practice, advice, case studies and news on different ways of working, including flexible working, part-time and self-employment, and we carry job vacancies for positions that offer options beyond the 9-5 model of work.

www.workingdads.co.uk

Inspiring Dads
Inspiring Dads is a coaching business set up by Ian Dinwiddy to help stressed dads balance work and fatherhood, building meaningful connections with their partners and children, and focusing their energy to create purpose, calmness, and direction in their lives.

www.inspiringdads.co.uk

Widowhood

WAY Widowed and Young

WAY is the only national charity in the UK for men and women aged fifty or under when their partner died. It's a peer-to-peer support group operating with a network of volunteers who've been bereaved at a young age themselves, so they understand exactly what other members are going through.

www.widowedandyoung.org.uk

Acknowledgments

All praise and glory to God; I truly believe I have been used as a vessel, by you, to bring this whole project together.

Thank you to my wife Soneni. You have been a rock through the process of putting this book together and it would not have happened without you. I love you. To my daughter, Eleni, it is hard to put into words just how amazingly beautiful and talented you are. You are my STAR!

To my mum, dad and sister – thank you for being an amazing support system. My cousin Jordan, I owe you a lot; you helped shape me. To my long-time friends Jermaine, Duaine and Jonathan – you done know!

A massive shout to ALL the MFF team; I would like to mention all of you that were not featured in the book – Dubul Dee, Machel, Ana and Tom – thank you for believing in the movement and playing your undeniable part. To our social media manager, Matt: your hard work and contribution is invaluable.

To all at Wellspring Church, thank you for all the support you have given my family.

Thank you so much to all the people who have worked to make this book happen. Jamie Cowen, my agent – I appreciate you. Our editor Kirsty Ridge, you have been a joy to work with. Dumi Nkomo for the amazing photography and editing; Stacey and Saskia for all the invaluable guidance and support; James and Melanie at Easypress; Simon Rae; Shahila Perumalpillai; Paul Herbert; Leyla at Clays; and Brandon Layzell for the amazing cover design.

To all the journalists and media folk who have supported us along the way, thank you for amplifying our stories.

Thank you to all our community partners – let's make a real change together! To the nineteen other dads in this book who have trusted me with some of your deepest moments, thank you so much. You are amazing. We are friends for life.

Elliott Rae

Share your Story: #WeAreDad

We want this book to spark a change in how we talk about fatherhood experiences throughout society. Whether that be within families, between friends, in the media, through government policy or in the workplace.

As men and fathers, we all have our own journeys. The stories in this book of loss, love, grief, trauma, identity, race, culture, relationships and acceptance are commonplace. But too often, they are silenced. By us sharing these experiences, we help others to understand that they are not alone.

The process of sharing and listening is cathartic; it heightens the understanding of what it means to be a dad and that can only make us more compassionate and loving people. This will improve the lives of men, women, children and families while creating a more supportive society.

We want this book to be the start of a movement. The twenty dads in this book are only the beginning. We want you to share your story.

The #WeAreDad campaign

Our #WeAreDad campaign is amplifying the voices of dads and telling their stories. To get involved, simply post on social media:

- Share a picture of you with the book,
- Tell us why the book is important to you,
- Use the hashtag #WeAreDad and tag us in your post.

We will then share your stories with our community!

@MFFonline_

@MFFonline

Crowdfunding

This book has been made possible by our generous community who have supported our campaign to bring this book to life.

This is a self-published book (can you believe the publishing industry did not think there was an audience for this book!).

In our initial crowdfunding campaign, we raised an amazing amount in a short space of time. To everyone that has donated to our crowdfunder, from the bottom of our hearts, thank you so much.

We promised to give a special shout-out to all the people who donated over £100. Thank you to Jacqui Bull, Dermot Heron, Sharon Peake, Kerrine Bryan, Jeanette Gamble, Cleo Eastabrook, Heena Shah, Aislean Nicholson, Michael and Sandra Rae, Elizabeth McKeown, Dominic Ray, Sheena Kanabar, Sarah Forbes, Israel Amponsah, David Dennis, Vanessa Vallely, Anna McQuinn, Leah Williams Veazey and Raza Halim. Your generosity has been essential in helping us produce this body of work.

How you can continue to support us

We will be reinvesting money from book sales back into producing more copies of *DAD*. But we still need support to ensure we can continue to produce and promote a high-quality product so it gets to the people who need it most. We believe that this book is an important part of changing the conversation around fatherhood, mental health, masculinity and gender equality.

If you would like to make a donation to help us produce more books, please visit: www.crowdfunder.co.uk/WeAreDad